Enriching Heredity

ENRICHING HEREDITY

The Impact of the Environment on the Anatomy of the Brain

Marian Cleeves Diamond

THE FREE PRESS
A Division of Macmillan, Inc.
NEW YORK

Collier Macmillan Publishers
LONDON

The Free Press
A Division of Macmillan, Inc.
866 Third Avenue, New York, N.Y. 10022

Collier Macmillan Canada, Inc.

Printed in the United States of America

printing number

1 2 3 4 5 6 7 8 9 10

Library of Congress Cataloging-in-Publication Data

Diamond, Marian Cleeves.
  Enriching heredity.

  Bibliography: p.
  Includes index.
  1. Brain—Anatomy. 2. Brain—Adaptation. 3. Neuro-
plasticity. 4. Brain—Evolution. 5. Mammals—
Physiology. I. Title.
QM455.D49 1988   599′ .048   88-7151
ISBN 0-02-907431-2

The author gratefully acknowledges permission to reprint the following material:

M. R. Rosenzweig, E. L. Bennett, and M. C. Diamond. Chemical and anatomical plasticity of brain: replications and extensions, 1970. Figures 7A and 7B. In *Macromolecules and Behavior,* 2nd ed. J. Gaito, ed. New York: Appleton-Century-Crofts, 1970.

M. C. Diamond. Sex differences in the rat forebrain. Figure 1. *Brain Res. Rev.* 12: 235–240 (1987).

M. C. Diamond. Rat forebrain morphology: Right-left; male-female; young-old; enriched-impoverished. Figures 1 and 2. In *Cerebral Lateralization in Nonhuman Species.* S. D. Glick, ed. Orlando, FL: Academic Press, 1985.

S. Sandhu, P. Cook, and M. C. Diamond. Rat cerebral cortical estrogen receptors: Male-female; right-left. Figures 2 and 3. *Exp. Neurol.* 92, 186, 196 (1986).

M. C. Diamond. Age, sex, and environmental influences. Figure 9.2. In *Cerebral Dominance, the Biological Foundations.* N. Geschwind and A. Gallaburda, eds. Cambridge: Harvard University Press, 1984.

M. C. Diamond, R. E. Johnson, A. M. Protti, C. Ott, and L. Kajisa. Plasticity in the 904-day-old rat cerebral cortex. Figures 1, 2, and 3, and Table 1. *Exp. Neurol.* 87: 309–317 (1985).

M. C. Diamond, R. E. Johnson, and M. W. Gold. Changes in neuron number and size and glia number in the young, adult, and aging rat medial occipital cortex. Tables 3 and 4. *Behav. Biol.* 20: 409–418 (1977).

M. R. Rosenzweig, E. L. Bennett, and M. C. Diamond. Brain changes in response to experience. Figure 1. *Scient. Amer.* 22–29 (Feb. 1972).

E. L. Bennett, M. R. Rosenzweig, and M. C. Diamond. Time courses of effects of differential experience on brain measures and behavior of rats. Table I. In *Molecular Approaches to Learning and Memory.* W. L. Byrne, ed. Orlando, FL: Academic Press, 1970.

M. C. Diamond, D. Krech, and M. R. Rosenzweig. The effects of an enriched environment on the histology of the rat cerebral cortex. *J. Comp. Neur.* 123: 111–120 (1964). Tables 1, 3, 8, and 9. Figures 2 and 3. By permission of Alan R. Riss, Inc.

M. C. Diamond, F. Law, H. Rhodes, B. Lindner, M. R. Rosenzweig, D. Krech, and E. L. Bennett. Increases in cortical depth and glia numbers in rats subjected to enriched environment. Table 2. *J. Comp. Neurol.* 128: 117–126 (1966). By permission of Alan R. Riss, Inc.

M. C. Diamond, M. R. Rosenzweig, E. L. Bennett, B. Lindner, and L. Lyon. Effects of environmental enrichment and impoverishment on rat cerebral cortex. Figures 1A-B and 2A-B. *J. Neurobio.* 3:47–64 (1972).

M. C. Diamond, R. E. Johnson, and C. Ingham. Brain plasticity induced by environment and pregnancy. Figures 2, 3, and 4. *Inter. J. Neurosci.* 2:171–178 (1971).

M. C. Diamond. Anatomical brain changes induced by environment. Figure 9. In *Knowing, Thinking, and Believing.* L. Petrinovich and J. L. McGaugh, eds. New York: Plenum Press, 1976.

M. C. Diamond. Aging and environmental influences on the rat forebrain. In *The Biological Substrates of Alzheimer's Disease.* A. B. Scheibel and A. F. Wechsler, eds. Figure 2. UCLA Forum in Medical Sciences, 27: 55–64. Orlando, FL: Academic Press, 1986.

M. C. Diamond, A. B. Scheibel, G. M. Murphy, Jr., and T. Harvey. On the brain of a scientist: Albert Einstein. Figure 1. *Exp. Neurol.* 88: 198–204 (1985).

M. C. Diamond, R. D. Rainbolt, R. Guzman, E. R. Greer, and S. Teitelbaum. Regional cerebral cortical deficits in the immune deficient nude mouse: a preliminary study. Figures 4 and 5. *Exp. Neurol.* 92: 311–322 (1986).

M. C. Diamond, E. R. Green, A. York, D. Lewis, T. Barton, and J. Lin. Rat cortical morphology following crowded-enriched living conditions. Figures 1 and 2. *Exp. Neurol.* 96: 241–247 (1987).

M. C. Diamond, M. R. Rosenzweig, and D. Krech. Relationships between body weight and skull development in rats raised in enriched and impoverished conditions. Figure 1. *J. Exper. Zool.* 160: 29–36 (1965). By permission of Alan R. Riss, Inc.

Dedicated with Love to
my mother, Rose, and my father, Montague,
and to Dick and Arne
for reasons they would understand

CONTENTS

PREFACE

The neural basis of behavior is a subject that has fascinated me for over four decades. As a young girl, I used to look at people and wonder what was actually going on behind their eyes. How was it possible for people to think, and what was responsible for the process? A considerable number of us who study neurobiology took our first steps in the field of psychology, where we hoped to answer questions dealing with the fundamental processes responsible for mammalian behavior. Though many present-day investigators continue to concentrate their efforts on behavioral processes, others study the structural and chemical components of the brain in an attempt to understand its functions. We are now aware that ions and molecules form brain cells and the connections among them, which in turn produce the mind and behavior. Utilizing this basic knowledge, thousands of scientists today are working at many diverse levels—behavioral, structural, chemical, molecular-biological—to unravel the mysteries of human behavior.

This book draws on 27 years of research from my laboratory dealing with environmental influences primarily on the anatomy of the mammalian forebrain, primarily that of the rat. One major aim of the book is to bring together at one time this body of information gathered in a semistepwise fashion over the years. It can now serve as a foundation on which to build a global picture, on the one hand, or a more refined one, on the other. These anatomical findings can also provide other investigators with information about the plasticity of brain regions at different ages and can be used as guidelines for more sensitive types of measures by chemists or molecular biologists. Some of the material has not been published previously; we are introducing it now to strengthen the larger story. As the data were gathered into a single body, patterns of a developmental sequence became evident that were not clear in separate, scattered publications. Over the years, results were coming in at a rapid rate, and now I have had the opportunity to synthesize and correlate their meaning with greater insight. Facts that were discovered 20 years ago have now been integrated with our more recent data.

This book is intended for anyone who wishes to learn about the effects of different types of environmental influences on mammalian forebrain structures: both interested lay people and neuroscientists in all categories, from neuroanatomists, neurochemists, and neurologists to psychiatrists and social and behavioral scientists. Gynecologists and obstetricians, in particular, may gain valued insight into the effects of sex steroid hormones on cortical structures. Finally, this book can supplement a course dealing with neuroanatomy and behavioral biology or serve as a reference source.

The majority of the anatomical studies mentioned here have been completed in my laboratory with all of us working together: technicians, undergraduate and graduate students, postdoctoral fellows, and colleagues. These people have always been included as authors on the publications, and their names are found in connection with their research studies in the list of references for this book. As a rule, they are also mentioned within the text in conjunction with their work. The behavioral studies related to the early anatomical work were conducted by Professors David Krech and Mark Rosenzweig and Dr. Edward Bennett in the Department of Psychology at Berkeley. However, since the late 1960s, both the behavioral and anatomical studies have been confined to our Department of Physiology-Anatomy. I have not included all of the reported investigations dealing with environment and the brain. Emphasis here is on brain anatomy and the environment, and the results are primarily those from my laboratory, because these data have been collected to tell a particular story. However, when appropriate, some methods and results of experiments from other laboratories dealing with forebrain anatomy, chemistry, and behavior are woven into the text.

ACKNOWLEDGMENTS

Five minutes after Laura Wolff, senior editor of The Free Press in New York, walked into my office in Berkeley, I knew I wanted to work with her to produce this book. Not only is she clear thinking and wise but she is compassionate as well. Thank you, Laura, for a priceless collaboration and friendship. My copy editor, Richard Mickey, provided careful editing beyond compare. I am certain that part of his brain concerned with editing is enlarged into the upper one percent category of intelligent human beings. To Eileen DeWald, managing editor of The Free Press, I also am deeply indebted. What a team of excellence! Thank you one and all.

1

CAN WE CHANGE
OUR BRAINS?

The nature-nurture controversy in regard to human behavior is an ageless one, extending from the times of Plato and Aristotle. The controversy has continued over the centuries because of a lack of relevant data to support the belief that the environment interacts with inherited characteristics on the one hand, or that heredity is all-powerful to the exclusion of the environment, on the other. The differences which exist among individuals as well as those between groups have been cited by proponents of both views. Until recently it was primarily sociologists, psychologists, and educators who emphasized the importance of the environment—specifically, the social and political inequities affecting the aged, women, the poor, and members of minority groups, to name but a few—in influencing behavior. Others believed that human behavior was the result of the divine will or biological predestination rather than environmental factors. Now, however, with the impressive advances in the science of genetics, many biologists are justifiably inclined to stress the importance of heredity. But with the studies presented in this book, we have evidence to support the view that the environment plays a role in shaping brain structure. These are the first controlled laboratory studies to demonstrate that various types of experiential environmental conditions can alter the anatomy of the outer layers of the mammalian brain, which in turn affects the learning ability of the organism.

This does not mean, though, that others had not previously predicted that such changes could occur. As early as 1815 Spurzheim asked whether tissues could increase with exercise, because blood is carried in greater abundance to parts that are excited, and nutrition is performed by the blood. He thought that this principle might certainly apply to the brain

1

as well as to the muscles. Charles Darwin in 1874 noted that the brains of domestic rabbits were considerably smaller than those of the wild rabbit. He wrote that the differences might be attributed to their having been closely confined during many generations so that their intellect, instincts, sense, and voluntary movements were not exerted. In other words, the domestic animals did not have to face the natural threats of life in the wild. These are but a few early examples predicting that the structure of brains can change depending upon the input from the environment.

We now have evidence to illustrate the details of the anatomical changes that do occur with modifications in the environment. This evidence addresses many of the questions that concerned the early sociologists and educators, including the effects of the environment on the young as well as the elderly, sex differences, and the effects of nutritional deprivation, isolation, or crowding. It is now clear that the brain is far from immutable.

Documented speculations about brain changes in response to factors in the environment are not new. For example, in 1819, it was reported that an Italian anatomist, Malacarne, postulated that experience could alter brain structure (2). A century later, in 1911, a Nobel Prize-winning anatomist, Ramon y Cajal, suggested that "cerebral exercise" could establish new and more numerous connections between nerve cells in the brain (3). He realized, with the knowledge available at the time, that no new nerve cells would be formed after birth in the cerebral cortex, but he proposed that cells become bigger from use. Just over 50 years later, our neuroanatomy group at Berkeley measured a greater cortical thickness and larger nerve cell dimensions in the brains of rats that had spent some time in stimulating, interesting environments than in the brain of their brothers living in impoverished conditions. These were the initial experiments that set the stage for the production of this book.

The effort providing the background for our environmental studies extended over several decades. In the 1920s, in the psychology department at Berkeley, Professor Robert Tryon noted that some rats ran mazes better than others (4, 5). He wondered whether he could establish a maze-bright strain by breeding the animals that ran the mazes well—and similarly, whether he could breed a maze-dull strain. After several generations of inbreeding, he did create his two desired strains, one maze-bright and one maze-dull. Over the following years, the two strains were maintained separately from each other in the department colony.

In the 1950s two Berkeley scientists, a psychologist, David Krech, and a Nobel-laureate chemist, Melvin Calvin, asked themselves whether the brain chemistry of these two strains of rats might differ. Before they could try to answer their question, they had to decide which chemical would be most significant to measure. At the time, few neurotransmitters in the brain were known; one was the chemical, acetylcholine. The two scientists—Krech and Calvin—reasoned that if the animals were "bright," they should have more of this chemical to facilitate transmission of an impulse across the synapse. Acetylcholine is very unstable and difficult to quantify, but its hydrolyzing enzyme, acetylcholinesterase, is stable at room temperature (at least up to 6 hours) and, thus, more easily measured. The scientists hypothesized that if there were more acetylcholine in the maze-bright animal, then there should also be more acetylcholinesterase to break down the acetylcholine after it had served its function. With this idea to work from, it was now possible to begin a team effort to study brain chemistry and behavior. Calvin suggested that Bennett, a neurochemist from his laboratory, collaborate as the chemist; and Rosenzweig, a psychologist, joined Krech to complement the psychology team. With time, the hypothesis of Krech and Calvin proved to be correct; there was more acetylcholinesterase in the brains of the maze-bright animals than in those of the maze-dull. This was the first evidence of a specific positive correlation between brain chemistry and learning ability (6).

In 1949, prior to these studies at Berkeley, Hebb, at McGill University in Montreal, had hypothesized that animals living in enriched environments early in life develop permanent brain changes that enhance problem-solving capabilities (7). Hebb had based his hypothesis on the fact that rats that had been used as house pets, and thus had experienced enriched living conditions, were better at running mazes than were confined, caged rats. In the early 1950s, several psychologists, stimulated by Hebb's hypothesis, began to ask how much enrichment in an adult animal was necessary to produce maze-learning abilities superior to those of a nonenriched animal. They learned that rats that had been exposed to enriched, rather than impoverished, environments early in life were better maze learners upon reaching young adulthood.

A logical next question was whether animals living in stimulating environments differed from animals living in isolated conditions not only in behavior but also in brain chemistry. The Berkeley team of scientists drew on the reasoning and techniques they had used to study the maze-bright and maze-dull strains and applied them to the brains of animals that had experienced enriched or impoverished conditions. They found that the brain acetylcholinesterase concentration was greater in the environmentally enriched rats than in the impoverished ones (8).

While working at Cornell University in upstate New York in the 1950s, I read about these studies that correlated behavior and brain chemistry and wondered if there might be measurable structural differences in the brains of rats with dissimilar behavior and chemistry. For example, did the maze-bright and maze-dull animals differ in morphology of the cerebral cortex? Were nerve cell processes restructured into new patterns in these strains of animals? Could we somehow demonstrate a connection between brain anatomy and learning? My resulting excitement about various possibilities was intense. This initial curiosity then led me on continuously for the next several decades, being rekindled with each set of new data. As with most research, each answer led to a dozen more questions; to stop at any one point was tremendously dissatisfying.

Several preliminary studies were undertaken before we embarked on the long series of investigations dealing with the anatomy of the developing and aging brain and the environmental influences which changed the basic structural patterns. The first dealt with the localization of acetylcholinesterase in various cellular layers of the cortex in maze-bright and maze-dull animals. After identifying enzyme differences between the two groups, we counted cerebral-cortical nerve and glial cells in several maze-bright and maze-dull strains of rats to learn how the number of cells correlated with the enzyme distribution. We found no significant correlations. Cells were counted in acetylcholinesterase-high and -low strains of rats as well. Again no significant findings were obtained. Undoubtedly, differences were present at the level of the connections between cells, but from our results, not in cell number. But these initial experiments helped organize our thoughts for the major thrust of our anatomical experimental work over the years ahead. We had a better idea of what kind of morphological measurements could help us answer the unending questions about the brain and the environment.

This book will present the knowledge gained from such experiments in two main sections: (1) normal forebrain development and aging, and (2) modifications of forebrain development and aging due to environmental factors.

For many years after we began to study the effects of the environment on the cerebral cortex, it was never clear how the data fit into the lifetime continuum of brain development and aging. No baseline for the dimensions of the rat cortex, for example, was available for the young, adult, and old-aged animal. Roger Sperry, the Nobel laureate from California

Institute of Technology, once said, "Marian, all you are doing with your enriched environments is stimulating the maturation of the cortex." We did not know whether he was right or not. Were the stimulating environmental conditions increasing a growing, maturing cortex, or a cortex which had reached a plateau, or a decreasing, shrinking cortex? When does the cortex stop growing, and how does it age under "normal" laboratory conditions? In order to answer these questions, we accumulated, over a 7-year span, information on the patterns of development and aging in the male and female cortex and other forebrain structures. We wished to learn about the cell populations in the cortex over a lifetime. Not only was it important to examine the cortex as a whole, but we wondered whether the right and left cortices followed similar patterns during development and aging because new information was accumulating about functional differences in the two hemispheres of human beings. Would structural differences help us to understand the basis of the functional aspects?

In recent years a great deal of evidence has been offered indicating that the separate hemispheres of the brains of human beings serve different functions. It has been said that the right hemisphere is concerned especially with spatial mapping, processing information holistically and simultaneously, and with artistic and musical functions, whereas the left is involved in more analytical, sequential processing and in the production and understanding of language. Admittedly, such precise functions cannot be attributed to locations in the rat cortex, but with the knowledge that differences between the hemispheres exist, we thought it imperative to look at the asymmetrical structure of the two hemispheres and to learn how the separate patterns are maintained during the lifetime of the animal. By examining asymmetrical patterns in the rat, we hoped to gain an understanding of factors responsible for creating asymmetry.

Since sex differences in thickness of the outer layers of the brain were becoming more obvious with each type of measurement, the role of the sex steroid hormones in creating these differences demanded attention. Markedly different patterns of asymmetry in thickness were noted between the male and female rats. Aging had a specific effect on asymmetry. In order to learn what structures were responsible for these thickness differences, neuron and glial cell counts were made on samples of the right and left cortices in males and females. Were the numbers of neurons and glial cells partially responsible for thickness differences?

Investigators have reported that both male and female rat cortices contain estrogen receptors. We were interested to learn whether these receptors were equally concentrated in the hemispheres of the male and female rats. If not, was it possible that they played a role in establishing brain asymmetry?

It was becoming clear that cortical asymmetry was related to sex hormones. But in 1980 some French scientists found that asymmetry was also related to other factors. These investigators had discovered that lesions in the left cerebral cortex affected the immune system differently from lesions in the right cortex. However, they did not confine their lesions to specific regions in each hemisphere of the cortex, but performed extensive cortical removal. They did not make refined lesions because they were using the cortex as a control and had not expected to alter the immune system with decortication. We then attempted to benefit from their findings and tried to localize more specifically which cortical areas were playing a role in this reported cortical immune response. One important question arose from their results: If we could alter the cortex with stimulating environments, could we then someday carry out experiments which would strengthen the immune system with "enriched" conditions?

The results of our experiments dealing with cerebral development and aging indicated that mammalian cortical nerve and glial cells are subject to structural changes due to age, sex hormones, and immune response. But what about other forebrain structures? We learned that areas such as the hippocampus, entorhinal cortex, amygdala, and corpus striatum differed considerably from the cerebral cortex in their developmental and aging patterns. Each will be discussed briefly to indicate the importance of referring to a specific forebrain region rather than to the whole brain when dealing with growth and aging studies.

Once we had accumulated fundamental information, or baselines, on the "normal" laboratory rat forebrain, we were prepared to investigate how alterations in the environment could induce modifications in the structure of rat brains. We were interested to learn how the thickness of the young cortex was affected by enriched and impoverished living conditions. Once we had established that, we made more refined anatomical measurements, such as neuron number and size, glial cell number, and blood vessel size. We examined the effects of enrichment during the cortex's natural growing process, and then throughout the long period of natural decline in cortical thickness.

During the first postnatal month—the growing period of the cortex—the pups had to live with their mothers in either enriched or impoverished conditions. The experimental manipulations we made and the measurements we took during this time indicated whether these conditions were affecting maturation or not.

The most common experimental design used for decades in our laboratory was that provided for the already-weaned rats, those that no longer lived with their mothers. For the majority of these experiments, three basic environmental conditions were used: enriched (12 rats per large cage, 70 × 70 × 46 cm, plus toys); standard colony (3 rats per small cage, 20 × 20 × 32 cm, with no toys); and impoverished (1 rat per small cage and no toys). The cerebral-cortical thickness was measured on rats that had lived in these conditions for varying periods of time ranging from 1 day to 160 days. We were interested to learn whether the cortex could change both for animals as young as 14 days of age and for animals as old as 904 days of age, the latter roughly equivalent in the lifespan of rats to 90 years for a person. Not only were cortical thickness modifications measured in the brains from animals living in various environmental conditions, but nerve and glial cell counts were taken as well. The dimensions of the nerve cells were measured, including the size of the nerve cell body and its nucleus, the number and length of dendrites, the number and distribution of spines, and the length of the postsynaptic density. We also examined the internal and external skull dimensions to determine whether the anatomical and neurological changes within the brain affected the skull.

Since there has been much interest in training one side of the brain separate from the other, we wished to determine whether our multisensory environmental conditions altered the cortical thickness of one hemisphere differently from the other.

Both males and females were exposed to their enriched or impoverished conditions for similar periods of time. In addition, the brains of males living only with males during the enrichment period were compared with those of males living with females. Cortical thickness measurements were made on these groups of rats.

Nutritional effects on brain development and aging are of ongoing concern as we attempt to learn about conditions that best facilitate brain function. Our laboratory has collaborated with one investigator who carried out a set of nutritional experiments dealing with protein-deficient mothers and their nutritionally and environmentally rehabilitated offspring. Environmental enrichment proved to be an important factor even with the nutronally deficient animals.

While the above nutritional experiments were in progress, we became interested in the relation between glucose metabolism and environmentally enriched conditions. In collaboration with Dr. Carolyn Smith at the National Institute of Mental Health in Bethesda, Maryland, we carried out a study to learn whether the metabolic rate of the brains in rats in enriched environments was greater than in the standard colony animals. The results from this experiment were quite the opposite from our predictions and reminded us of the importance of doing experimental work to substantiate hypotheses. One cannot always foresee the many variables involved.

In the fall of 1985, we were invited to China to lecture, and I wondered what experiment with our rats might be of interest to our hosts. With their problem of overpopulation, perhaps the effect of crowding during brain development would be of interest. We conducted an experiment for which we used 36 animals in the enriched cage instead of the usual 12 and later measured the cortical thickness changes in them compared with the standard animals.

Is it possible that factors such as air ions could affect the outer layers of the brain? We were most fortunate to have one of the world's experts on air ions, Albert Krueger, working down the corridor at Berkeley (one of the precious advantages of being at this remarkable university), and we collaborated with him and his group on experiments dealing with the effects of air ions on cerebral-cortical structure and chemistry. Once we learned that ions did alter the cortex, we became interested in their effect on the immune system, specifically in the way they alter white blood cell counts. The complexity of the many interactive factors in the body and the environment was becoming more evident and intriguing.

Most of our efforts have focused on understanding the changes produced by environmental enrichment and impoverishment in the brains of animals exposed to those conditions. However, we have also been intrigued by the question of the possible transmission of the changes from these animals to their offspring. In other words, was it possible to detect morphological changes in the brains of future generations? Admittedly, this question suggested a possible Lamarckian view, but several factors could be involved which needed to be explored.

All of our brain measurements—whether of cortical thickness, dendritic branching, dendritic spines, or synaptic length—have little meaning without an index of behavioral changes. Our laboratory has not maze-tested the enriched or impoverished rats. But psychologists from many other laboratories have studied such rats in several different kinds of mazes and have found evidence of behavioral changes that correlate well with our anatomical brain results. (The data will be discussed in Chapter 9.)

Our ultimate goal in studying the brains of rats is to gain a better understanding of the human brain. Obviously, for ethical and practical reasons, we cannot completely control the environmental input into human brains, nor are we able at present to make precise anatomical measurements of identical areas of the brains of human subjects over time. Even the scanning techniques of computerized tomography (CT) and positron emission tomography (PET) do not give sufficient resolution, and besides, these methods are not safe to use for repeated measurement of living, healthy human brains. In the future, the noninvasive technique of magnetic resonance imaging (MRI) may offer more discriminating measures for detailed anatomical study of the healthy human brain. In the meantime, we use animal models; we can control the environment with animal subjects, and we can very precisely measure cortical dimensions on preserved animal brain tissues.

One question which is invariably raised about the study of rat brains is, How are the results applicable to humans? Needless to say, one cannot make direct extrapolations from the many variables involved, but several of the basic principles which are established from rat work can be applied to humans. For example, whether we are dealing with rats, cats, dogs, monkeys, or human beings, the brain consists of nerve cells and glial cells. Investigators have shown that the number of neurons in a single column of cortical nerve cells is the same in rats, cats, dogs, monkeys, and man (1). Furthermore, in all these species most nerve cells have branches that we call *axons* and *dendrites*. It is the pattern and the quantity of these branches, i.e., the complexity of the circuitry, that account for some of the differences among species. The cell bodies and branches of the neurons communicate with each other through functional junctions called *synapses*. As far as we know at present, the numerous chemical neurotransmitters located in the billions of synapses in the brain are of a similar nature in rats and man.

Nerve cells are designed to receive stimuli, store information, and transmit impulses, and this is true in both rats and man. Furthermore, much of what we know about the human reproductive system and its hormonal relationships has been established from studies with rats. In essence, most of what we have learned about the normal functioning of the human nervous system and its associations with the reproductive hormones has been learned from animals.

The kinds of brain measures used on our rats and the accompanying results are basic to the understanding of neural structure and function whether we study rats or man. Our findings may have wide enough application to encompass mammalian nerve cells in general. Both the human brain and the rat brain are very immature at birth, especially in the cerebral cortex, the structure which has received most of our attention. As will be described in more detail in Chapter 2, the cortex grows at an explosive rate immediately after birth, but the patterns of development are different for males and females—a finding which cannot be easily measured in humans with present technology.

There are many reasons to believe that data collected from rat brains can be useful in establishing guidelines for studying events occurring in the human brain. Accepting the vast complexity of the human brain, I only hope that this collection of information from controlled rat experiments and from a few studies on human brains will eventually serve in directing others toward a better understanding of the potential of the human brain . . . and thus, to greater efforts to improve upon the human condition.

2

NORMAL FOREBRAIN DEVELOPMENT AND AGING

The massive right and left cerebral hemispheres account for about 85% of the total human brain and about 45% of the rat brain. The outer few millimeters of nerve cells on these hemispheres constitute the cortex, commonly referred to as the cerebral cortex ("cortex" means "bark"). In actuality, there are three divisions of the cortex: the three-layered archicortex; the five-layered paleocortex; and the six-layered neocortex. The neocortex was of greatest interest to me not only because it is the seat of higher congnitive functions but because it is one of the last structures to develop embryologically and is one of the most recent phylogenetically. The neocortex of the human brain is a structure whose abilities are unique in the animal kingdom. (The term cortex or cerebral cortex will be used to refer to neocortex unless otherwise specified.)

Before we could make sense of our measurements of the cortices of enriched and impoverished rats, we first had to map the normal developing and aging pattern of the cerebral cortex for use as a standard for comparison. To obtain this standard, or baseline, we measured the thickness of the cortex on both female and male Long-Evans rats that had lived 3 per cage for varying periods of time to attain different ages. In our early work (1) we had dealt mainly with rats between 25 and 105 days of age and did not know whether the cortex was normally increasing or decreasing during this period. We realized what an important consideration we had overlooked and proceeded to gather data from the developing and aging cortex.

First, let us look at the cortex through data from both hemispheres combined to obtain the overall cortical developmental events. Figure 1 illustrates the location of brain samples removed for microscopic examination of the frontal, somatosensory, and occipital cortices, from anterior to posterior. The numerical designations according to Krieg (2) are placed on the left side of the hemisphere: Very brief functional descriptions are offered: area 10 represents the frontal cortex, an area in the human brain used for sequential planning; area 4 represents the motor cortex; areas 3 and 2 designate general sensory areas; areas 18 and 18a are visual association areas; and 17 is the primary visual cortex. Area 39 represents a multisensory integrative area.

Figure 2 shows a transverse section of the rat brain illustrating divisions of the occipital cortex as an example and how the thickness was measured on lines extending from the surface to the underlying white matter. The sections were cut at 20 micra (a micron or μm is one one-thousandth of a millimeter). We have learned that several cellular features

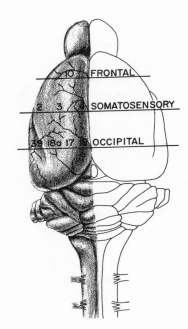

FIGURE 1. Dorsal view of rat brain indicating regions sampled for study. (Right) Frontal, somatosensory, and occipital sections are illustrated. (Left) Numerical designations of Krieg (2).

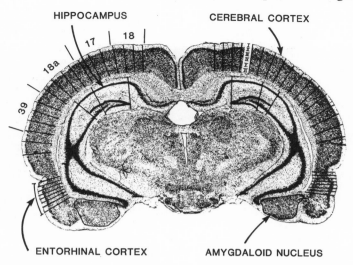

HIPPOCAMPUS   CEREBRAL CORTEX

17   18

18a

39

ENTORHINAL CORTEX   AMYGDALOID NUCLEUS

FIGURE 2. Transverse or coronal section of rat brain indicating areas studied.

account for cortical thickness, such as nerve cell density and size and glial cell number. The cortical cell layers I through VI are also shown.

Differences between Male and Female Cerebral Cortices

Figure 3 represents a growth curve of the frontal, somatosensory, and occipital cortex from 6 days to 400 days of age based on an average of 15 to 17 male rats per age group (3). This figure shows that the most rapid growth of the male rat cortex occurs between 6 and 10 days after birth. The cortex continues to grow until it reaches a peak, and a general decrease in thickness begins, sometime between the ages of 26 and 41 days. The early postnatal cortical increase in the male rat amounts to almost 45% before the peak is reached. Though not shown on this graph, a 9% decrease occurs between the ages of 41 and 650 days. After day 650 all cortical areas continue to decrease, but the occipital cortex decreases more steeply than the other regions until the last measurement at 904 days. These developing and aging cerebral cortical data fall into two basic slopes on the graph: a positive one before 41 days of age and a negative one throughout life after 41 days. Our challenge is to see whether environmental input can alter these slopes.

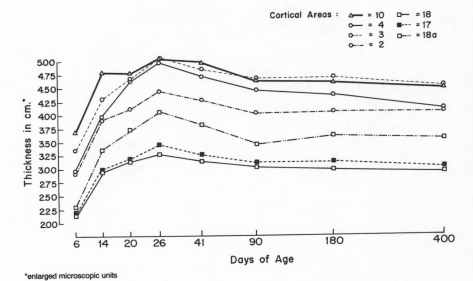

Cortical Thickness (cm) — Development and Adulthood in Male, Long-Evans Rats (N = 15-17 / age group)

*enlarged microscopic units

FIGURE 3. Cortical thickness (cm): development and adulthood in male Long-Evans rats (N = 15–17/age group).

In turning to the female cerebral cortex (Figure 4), we find a different developmental pattern from that of the male. The female frontal lobe is already fairly well developed at birth and grows only 15% in the first few weeks until it reaches a peak and then begins to decrease. The female somatosensory cortex is also more further developed at birth than is that of the male. In the female a major sensory integrative area, area 39, grows by 45% during the first week alone and does not reach its peak until close to the age of 45 days (see Figure 4). We do not have this precise measurement for the male. The two areas—frontal (10) and somatosensory, show clearly that the female cerebral cortex has a developmental pattern quite different from the male. In general, the female's cortical thickness is greater at birth than the male's, but by 3 weeks the male's cortex is thicker than the female's and the difference in thickness holds as the animals age. The occipital cortex in the male becomes markedly thicker than that of the female. Yanaid (4) found that the rate of neonatal proliferation of cortical cells in the male is slower than in the female. He suggests that such a phenomenon may represent "delayed maturation" of the male brain as compared with the female. It may be

Cortical Thickness (cm) — Development and Adulthood in Female,
Long-Evans Rats (N = 10-20/age group)

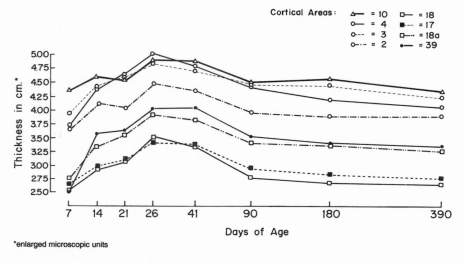

FIGURE 4. Cortical thickness (cm): development and adulthood in female
Long-Evans rats (N = 10-20/age group).

assumed that females have a higher rate of proliferation of brain cells at
a prenatal stage.

If natural selection operates in such a way as to ensure the reproduction of the species, it must promote the survival of young members of
the species. It is possible that the female cortex is more highly developed
at birth to ensure a better start. The human female, for example, ovulates
only about 420 times during her life, whereas the human male discharges
over 2 hundred million sperm with each ejaculation. The fact that she
has fewer opportunities to reproduce suggests the importance of the early
well-being of the female as she adapts to her environment.

Just as different regions of the female cortex develop at different rates,
they also age differently, at least up until the age of 390 days—the age
of the oldest group we have yet measured. In females between the ages
of 26 and 390 days, cortical areas 4 and 18 decrease in thickness by as
much as 22 to 31%. At the same time areas 10, 3, and 2 age only by
half as much, by 11 to 15%. During the second week, we have seen that
the frontal lobe increases by 6%, at the same time that area 39 increases
by 45%. In the male all areas of the cortex increase by 28 to 46% during
this same period of time. It appears that, on the whole, the separate

regions of the female cortex develop and age in a less uniform pattern than those of the male.

As stated earlier, most of our work has dealt with the rat brain, a fact which evokes the usual cautions about extrapolating from rats to man. And indeed there are differences on many levels. In the cerebral cortex of the rat, neuronal cell division is complete shortly after birth; it is followed immediately by profuse dendritic branching. Our results have shown that this rapid cortical development in the rat occurs during the first 40 to 45 days postnatally, with slightly different patterns in the male and the female. In contrast, cell division in human brains continues for about 1 year postnatally (5). But in human brains, also, rapid dendritic growth takes place during the first 3 to 4 postnatal years; as Dobbing and Sands point out (6), at least five-sixths of human brain growth by dendritic branching is postnatal and "in this respect humans resemble rats more closely than formerly thought."

Some very recent results on the developing human cortex support the notion that human brain growth follows the general developmental pattern seen in the rat cortex. From over 100 children with various neurological disorders, investigators selected 29 children (age 5 days to 15 years) who had suffered transient neurological events that did not measurably affect their normal neurodevelopment (7). The brains of these children were studied with 2-deoxy-2-[^{18}F]fluoro-D-glucose and positron emission tomography (PET scan) to plot the functional development of the brain. By examining the resulting human growth model, we learned that the absolute values for cortical glucose uptake were low at birth and rapidly increased up to the age of 3 to 4 years. These high rates of glucose uptake were maintained until about the age of 10 years, when they began to decline (8).

However, the authors of this study grouped their data on 3- to 8-year-olds into a single sample. When we examine separately the actual data points on their graphs, it appears that the cortex is beginning to decrease after the age of 3 to 4 years, and so including the 3- to 8-year-olds into one sample masks the initial stages of the decrease. Looking at the measurements for each year, we see a pattern similar to that found in the rat. The basic cortical developmental pattern shows a rapid increase after birth followed by a decline one month later in the rat or about 10 years later in the human brain. These new findings with the human cortex provide additional support for using rat data as a guideline to mammalian cortical morphology during developing and aging. We can therefore obtain knowledge from animal models about the human cortex.

Asymmetry and Sex-Hormonal
Influences on the Cerebral Cortex

Even though scientists were aware from about the middle of the nineteenth century that the two halves of the human brain were linked to some specific behaviors such as speech and awareness of body image, most rat brain scientists did not consider brain asymmetry in their chemical or anatomical studies until recently. It was not until 1975, when we were studying the normally developing and aging Long-Evans rat cortex, that we decided to make detailed comparisons between the hemispheres (9). We learned that in the male rat the right cerebral cortex was thicker than the left.

The male's right cortex was also thicker than the left in the S_1 strain (maze-bright) rats from the Berkeley psychology colony. [By using two strains, we established that the cortical asymmetrical pattern in the male rat brain was not peculiar to only one strain of animals.] To determine the cerebral-cortical thickness, we measured three representative transverse forebrain samples; in accordance with our usual procedures, we obtained our representative sections by utilizing subcortical landmarks for maintaining constancy. For example, the frontal cortical sample was taken immediately anterior to the genu of the corpus callosum; the somatosensory sample, at the crossing of the anterior commissure; and the occipital sample, at the level of the posterior commissure. These landmarks where chosen to allow us to compare regional degrees of asymmetry. (The regions included 10, 4, 3, 2, 18, 17, 18a and 39, according to Krieg's designations; see Figure 1). In order to understand whether asymmetry is present in the young and continues throughout the lifetime of the animals, we measured sections taken from male rats from birth to 904 days of age (the age of the oldest rats we have had).

Figure 5 presents the percentage differences between the right and left cerebral-cortical thicknesses in preweaned (6 to 20 days), adult to middle aged (90 to 400 days), and old aged (900 days) male Long-Evans rats, using 7 to 15 rats per age group and a total of 93 animals. The newborn male showed a similar right-greater-than-left pattern, but the data are not presented here. It is clearly evident that at every age and in every region except one, the right cortex is thicker than the left, with the differences ranging from 1% to 8%. Out of the 49 areas measured in all age groups the differences were statistically significant in 31 of them, or 63%. Some of the statiscally nonsignificant differences were in areas which did show asymmetry in some animals. But the failure of

Percent Difference Between Right and Left Cerebral Cortical Thickness in Young Adult and Old Aged Male Long-Evans Rats

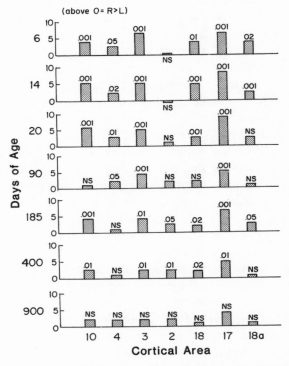

FIGURE 5. *Percent differences between left and right cerebral-cortical thickness in young, adult, and older-aged male Long-Evans rats.*

some, especially the very old, animals to exhibit any significant asymmetry partially explains the relatively low overall percentage difference in asymmetry.

For example, area 3, a general sensory area, and area 17, the primary visual cortex, showed the most marked right-greater-than-left differences consistently at every age. On the other hand, there was an apparent lack of asymmetry in area 2—another general sensory area, which in the rat receives input from the whiskers and from other sensory receptors—until the animal reaches 185 days of age, at which time it shows a statistically significant difference. Such a finding is intriguing in light of the marked asymmetry in the area adjacent to area 2, namely, area 3. Both regions are reportedly somatosensory areas. These data indicate that the sensory input from the whiskers, or the way that input is processed, differs from other sensory input in that it requires similar handling by both the right and left hemispheres.

In the male Long-Evans rat, the clearly defined asymmetry or laterality in some regions appears to be governed by testosterone. When the cortex was measured at 90 days of age on rats from which the testes had been removed at birth, the sections through the frontal and parietal cortex showed that the left cortex had become thicker than the right, a pattern similar to that of the intact female. However, in the occipital cortex, the right side retained its original dominant size. From these results, it becomes evident that some regions of the male cortex are governed by testicular hormones, though in others, perhaps, the thickness is determined more by genetic factors. Evidently, cortical asymmetry, as noted in the young and adult male rats, is essential for specific behavioral patterns during most of the animal's life. However, in the very old male rat (900 days), the right-dominant pattern is no longer statistically significant. Even the occipital cortex, which retains its laterality when the testes have been removed at birth, shows no significant right dominance in the very old animal.

After studying the asymmetry in the Long-Evans rats, we utilized data from male rats of the S_1 strain which were obtained from some of our other experiments. Again the right hemisphere was on the average thicker than the left in most areas. Areas 18 and 2 were the exceptions; there the two hemispheres were equal. In areas medial 10, 4, 3, 17, 18a, and 39, the hemispheric differences were statistically significant. By presenting these more detailed data from two strains it is possible to determine which areas demonstrated consistent asymmetrical patterns. Data from the two strains were similar for all areas except area 18, a visual association area; the results for area 18 were right greater than left in the Long-Evans strain and right equal to left in the S_1 strain.

In comparing the growth rates in the right and left hemispheres from 6 days to 90 days in the Long-Evans strain, we found the patterns to be very similar. They essentially paralleled each other. In comparing the left and right cortices in the S_1 strain between different age groups ranging from 55 days to 105 days, we observed a less consistent asymmetry pattern. For example, between 55 and 64 days of age the right hemisphere increased; it then decreased until 105 days of age. The left hemisphere did not follow a parallel developmental course in areas medial 10, 4, 17, 18a, and 39. Since the S_1 strain was bred specifically for maze-bright experience, it is possible that the right-dominant visual cortex was especially susceptible to stimulation at a time near sexual maturity.

A separate but similar study was made of the right and left cortical thickness patterns in the cerebral cortex of the Long-Evans female rat. We found quite different asymmetrical patterns from those seen in the Long-Evans male (10). (See Figure 6; also see note 49 for statistical tests used on our data.) The female did not show the strong asymmetries. (In sampling the female brains, we did not use as great an age span as with the males, only 7 to 390 days. The 900-day-old animals in the male study were a recent addition; we are at present attempting to raise the females to 900 days.)

In our earlier studies with 54 measurements of right-left differences in the female cortex, few statistically significant differences were found, but the left cortex was thicker than the right in 35 of the measurements, a 65% difference. We have since studied additional age groups (11). Using female brains from 18 to 41 days and as a result including 9 new measurements, making a total of 63 measurements, we found the right

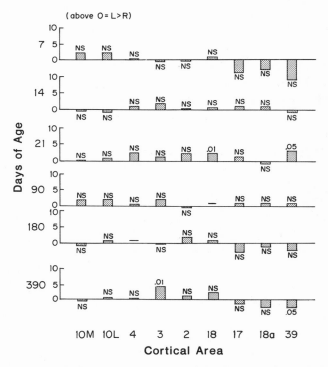

FIGURE 6. *Percent difference between left and right cerebral-cortical thickness in young, adult, and older-aged female Long-Evans rats.*

to be nonsignificantly greater than the left in 65% of the cases. From examining all these female data, it appears that the female cortex is not significantly asymmetrical. Yet, evidence to be discussed later shows that, for example, the estrogen receptor concentration and neuron and glial cell counts do follow the left-dominance pattern in the female, at least for certain age groups.

In comparing the male and female asymmetrical cortical patterns, sex differences are evident. The male shows quite significant right dominance in many areas, while the female shows no significant dominance. Our data suggest that the male loses significant cerebral dominance in old age, which may indicate that his brain becomes more like that of the female. Could these changes in cerebral dominance patterns be partially responsible for the decline in aggression seen in the older male? It has been reported that the older human male has more "domestic qualities" and prefers to stay closer to the "hearth" than the younger male (12). Once again the rat data offer directions for future studies of male human brains.

Most male rats are superior to most females in visual-spatial ability, which may be related to the greater importance of spatial perception for territoriality in the male (13, 14). Right structural dominance in the visual-spatial region of the cortex provides a basis for a key to understanding male behavior. In fact, Greer Murphy (15), working in my laboratory and utilizing the asymmetrical guidelines offered by the male rat, examined 31 human visual cortices and found the same trend as seen in the rat. He measured the volume of area 17 and learned that the right cortex was about 5% (p < 0.05) greater than the left.

The male's greater asymmetry in other cortical regions as well as the visual cortex may give him an ability to focus his attention more intensely, and this ability may be related to testosterone levels. As shown previously, a severe reduction in testosterone due to removal of the testes alters the male cortical dominance pattern in certain regions.

Our data showing that female rats lack significant asymmetry in the cerebral cortex are paralleled by recent findings regarding the human female brain. Here two fiber bundles connecting the two halves of the forebrain, the large corpus callosum (16, 17, 18) and the smaller anterior commissure (19), are measurably larger in the female than in the male. The corpus callosum, consisting of about 300 million fibers, connects the right and left cerebral cortices. Male and female differences have been demonstrated on preserved material from both fetal and postnatal human brains. Other investigators, utilizing magnetic imaging on live human brains, do not agree with these findings (20). But I have examined carefully de Lacoste's study on the fixed corpus callosum and have observed the sex differences on the enlarged photographs of the anterior commissure, which connects not only right and left cortices but the olfactory bulbs as well. Both these examinations lead me to agree that these structures are larger in the human female than in the male.

Speculations with regard to the meaning of these female brain data are enticing. The female rat results revealing no significant cortical asymmetry and the human female reports showing a thicker connecting link between the hemispheres indicate that it is important for a more balanced distribution of information to pass between the female's two cortices. What might be an advantage for a lack of prominent asymmetry in the female? Possibly marked asymmetry might make the brain less flexible in responding to new situations. Asymmetry might be more of a hindrance than a benefit to the female, confining her range of behavior so that protection of the immature young would be too limited as they explore their new surroundings. The structure of the female cortex suggests that it allows for a "free flow" of information to occur between the two sides of the brain, providing a more diffuse response to the input from the environment.

This lack of a pronounced cerebral asymmetry in the female's cortex may be the "natural" state, but we have shown that internal environmental influences, such as levels of sex hormones, can alter her basic patterns. For example, in the brains of female rats that had been ovariectomized at birth and were later studied at 90 days of age, we found that the right cortical mantle was thicker than the left in 7 out of 9 regional comparisons, with significant differences in areas 17, 18a, and 39. Specifically, the right hemisphere was greater in area 17 by 3%, in area 18a by 5%, and in area 39 by 5%. In other words, without her ovaries for 90 days, her cortical thickness pattern became very similar to that of the male at 90 days of age with his testes intact. These data support our hypothesis that the ovarian hormones play a role in establishing and maintaining cerebral dominance.

By once again examining the data in Figure 6, we see a right-dominant pattern developing in the occipital cortex of the 180-390 day old female. These data suggest that by obtaining further old-age data, we may encounter an even stronger right-dominant pattern in this region of the brain. Does the female brain become more like the male with aging? It has already been shown that the 904-day-old male loses his significant cortical dominance with aging, thus becoming more like the female. If all goes well, we will have new data on the cortex of the very old female in the not too distant future.

With the knowledge that sex steroid hormones can alter cortical structure and that the hemispheric asymmetry patterns are different in male and female rats, we continue to pursue an understanding of asymmetry in the cortex. It has been demonstrated that estrogen receptors are present in the cerebral cortex of both sexes for the first 3 weeks of postnatal life (21, 22, 23). But no one has reported whether the concentration of these receptors differs between the right hemisphere and the left. If the sex hormones do play a role in establishing hemispheric differences, knowledge of estrogen receptor concentration is important.

We found, in newborn rats that estrogen receptors are more highly concentrated in the male left cortex than in the right. Exactly the opposite pattern characterizes the female cortex. These data were discovered by using radioactive estradiol to determine the concentration of the receptors in the cortex during the first month of postnatal life (24). The results presented in Figures 7 and 8 clearly indicate that the concentration of these receptors is highest immediately after birth, rapidly decreases during the first month, and then essentially disappears.

We postulate that the presence of estrogen receptors during the development of the cerebral cortex may play a role in establishing the hemispheric asymmetrical patterns, for the following reason. In previous ex-

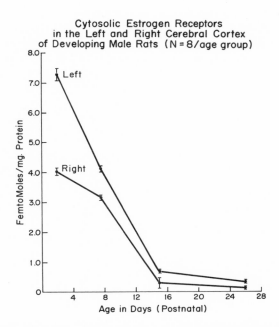

FIGURE 7. *Cytosolic estrogen receptors in left and right cerebral cortex of developing male rats (N = 8/age group).*

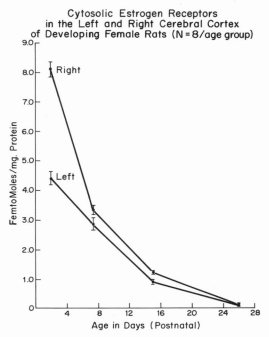

Cytosolic Estrogen Receptors
in the Left and Right Cerebral Cortex
of Developing Female Rats (N = 8/age group)

FIGURE 8. Cytosolic estrogen receptors in left and right cerebral cortex of developing female rats (N = 8/age group).

periments, we demonstrated that exogenous estrogen administered to adult female rats decreased cortical thickness (25). If estrogen acts on early postnatal cortical cells in much the way it does on adult cortical cells, then one might hypothesize that the hemisphere with the greater number of estrogen receptors will have the thinner cortex. This is precisely what we have found. Estrogen receptors are found in different concentrations in the right and left cortices in male and female rats.

In order to study the estrogen receptors in this first study, total samples of dorsal cortex were excised from each hemisphere. The kind of large tissue sampling used did not indicate a precise cortical location of the receptors. More recent preliminary results (26) have shown that the female right somatosensory cortex has a higher concentration of estrogen receptors immediately after birth than the right frontal or occipital regions.

Having found these sexual dimorphic patterns of asymmetry in the cerebral cortex, we then wished to learn whether similar dimorphism existed in several subcortical areas which have rich fiber connections with the cortex. If some structures do not possess asymmetry, it might offer a clue to the reasons for asymmetry in the areas where it does exist.

On the same tissues we had used for collecting the cortical-thickness development and aging data reported in 1975 and 1985, we turned to several subcortical regions and measured the thickness of the hippocampus, a region dealing with recent-memory processing, sexual behavior, and spatial mapping; the area of the amygdaloid nucleus, a region concerned with emotional behavior and reward systems; and the area of the corpus striatum, a structure which modifies movement as well as pain thresholds (see Figure 2. The corpus striatum is not shown in this posterior section. It is found more anteriorly beneath a frontal cortical section. Fig. 1)

On drawings from projected microslide images, we measured the hippocampal thickness (see Figure 2) on a total of about 100 male rats ranging from 6 to 900 days of age. Figure 9 illustrates the percentage of right-left differences in hippocampal thickness in rats up to 400 days of age (27). It is evident from this figure that in the male rat, the right hippocampus is significantly thicker than the left for the first 21 days of life. During the period of early sexual maturity, the significant differences between the right and left hippocampi disappear, only to appear again at the age of 185 days. Measurements on the 904-day-old male rat hippocampus indicate that the significant asymmetrical pattern is lost at this time. That is, the right hippocampus is still thicker than the left, but the

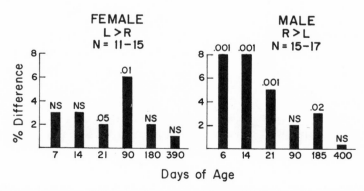

FIGURE 9. Percent difference between right and left dorsal hippocampal thickness in Long-Evans male and female rats.

differences are not statistically significant. The Long-Evans rat becomes sexually mature before 60 days of age, and it is about this time that the asymmetrical pattern in the male hippocampus first becomes reduced.

The reason why the right hippocampus is larger than the left, especially at the beginning of the animal's life, is not known. But we were curious to learn whether testosterone played a role. For this experiment, the testes were removed at birth, and the brains were studied 90 days later. The results showed that the left hippocampus was significantly larger than the right, but only by 2% ($p < 0.05$) in the 18 male brains measured. At 90 days of age in the intact animals, the right hippocampus was thicker than the left by 2%, but the difference was not significant. Perhaps 90 days is too long to wait to take the measurements. In the future, it will be necessary to remove the testes at birth and then examine the right-left differences in the hippocampus during the early period of the animal's life.

Because the right hippocampus and the right cerebral cortex of the intact male are each thicker than the left, the visual-spatial roles of the two areas may be closely related. O'Keefe and Nadel (28) have proposed an internal cognitive map theory correlated with hippocampal function. They hypothesized that the cells in the hippocampus encode the animal's specific position in its environment. We have already addressed the role of the right posterior cortex in visual-spatial acuity. The evidence points in the direction of a possible close functional relationship between these two forebrain structures during the early stages of the animal's life.

In the female, the right-left differences in hippocampal thickness were the opposite of those found in the male. The left hippocampus was found to be thicker than the right in female animals from 7 to 390 days of age with 11 to 15 animals per age group (Figure 9), but only at 21 and 90 days of age were the differences statistically significant. Thus, marked asymmetrical differences became more obvious at the time of female sexual maturity, again suggesting the possibility of a relationship between sex hormones and asymmetry.

In order to test that possibility, hippocampal thickness was measured in female rats that were ovariectomized at day 1 and autopsied at 90 days of age and was compared with the hippocampal thickness of 90-day female controls. In both groups the left hippocampus was thicker than the right. These data showed no evidence of a gonadal hormonal influence on the female asymmetry. Thus, removal of the ovaries at birth appears to have less of an effect on the hippocampus than on the cerebral cortex. It may be that the hippocampus, a phylogenetically older structure, does not alter its structure as easily as does the more recent cerebral cortex.

The marked asymmetry seen in the young 'animals declines with age in both the male hippocampus and the male cortex. The female also experiences a reduction in asymmetry in the hippocampus as she ages: from 90 days to 390 days her hippocampus showed a decreasing left-dominant pattern.

The next structure which was examined for right-left differences was the amygdaloid (almond-shaped) nucleus (Figure 2). This nucleus consists of numerous individual nuclei and is associated with many different functions, including expression of rage, aggression, sexuality, and reward mechanisms.

The amygdaloid nucleus is unique so far in our measurements in that it shows both strain differences and right-left pattern differences. In the Long-Evans male rats, the amygdaloid nucleus was symmetrical (29). The left-versus-right percent differences were nonsignificant in every case from the age of 6 days to 400 days. This was the first forebrain structure in the male Long-Evans rat where we did not find asymmetry. However, the male amygdaloid nucleus in the S_1 strain of rats showed significant asymmetry, with the right greater than the left (8 to 9%, $p < 0.01$). Replication measurements verified this strain difference. None of the scientists with whom we have discussed these findings have yet suggested an interpretation.

In summary, our experiments revealed asymmetry patterns in the male and female forebrain structures measured, with but one exception: the amygdaloid nucleus. In general the male showed marked right dominance early in life and the female displayed either no significant dominance or a left-dominant pattern.

Forebrain asymmetry in certain brain regions is not unique to the rat. There are isolated reports on brain asymmetry as one moves up the phylogenetic scale. A group of nerve cells called the habenula (Latin, "rein," the strap of a bridle) in the posterior thalamus of amphibians and fish has been noted to be asymmetrical (30). In the cat, fissural pattern differences exist in the hemispheres (31). In the great apes, the end of the Sylvian fissure on the surface of the hemispheres is longer on the left side than on the right (32). Such asymmetry is also evident in the human brain. The occipital lobe protrudes farther posteriorly on the left than on the right, and the posterior horn of the lateral ventricle is longer on the left side than on the right.

Though there is evidence of asymmetry throughout the animal kingdom, we do not fully understand why the brain developed this way. We can shed some light on the subject by examining language areas in the human brain. Motor speech activities are primarily governed by the left hemisphere in most right handed people. Hence, the left hemisphere is referred to as the dominant hemisphere for speech. The area in the right hemisphere comparable to the one on the left for motor speech, processes the emotional component of speech. Thus, this example suggests that lateralization allows for specialization of function. Both hemispheres deal with speech but each contributes a separate component to the process. Undoubtedly, as we learn more about each hemisphere individually, we will understand more about how integration of their outputs occur.

Our work has shown that the sex hormones can alter the asymmetry patterns in male and female rat brains. We may better understand the significance of brain asymmetry once we have had a chance to study behavioral deficits after the asymmetry patterns have been reversed for a considerable period of time. We will also need to study the effects of asymmetry on other body systems. We used to believe that there were paired structures in the brain to serve as a safety factor in case of the destruction of one part, but now it appears that the paired brain structures combine two different functions that are eventually integrated for more elaborate processing. Possible asymmetry exists to allow one side to function more efficiently independent of the other prior to integration. It is to the advantage of the animal—whether rat or human—for one side to develop rapidly, namely, the side governing the function most important for the animal's survival. For example, we could suppose that the visual-spatial role of the right cortex is essential for maximum survival of the male; then we could explain why nerve cells are present in the right cortex of the male than in the left. Similarly, since left-hemisphere dominance shows up early in the female, we could hypothesize that the early development of language skills contributes to her survival.

Cortical Structure and Altered Sex Hormone Levels

In light of what we knew of the impact of sex hormones on forebrain asymmetry, we were encouraged to consider their significance in the development of the cortex as a whole, including its cells and synapses. Knowledge of the relationship between gonadal hormones and the cerebral cortex is not as extensive as knowledge of the relationship between these hormones and other regions of the brain. The hypothalamus and preoptic area of the brain are important in mediating the effects of gonadal hormones on their target organs. Gonadal steroids influence sexual differentiation of the hypothalamus at a critical period in the development of the animal. In rats, the first 5 days after birth represent the critical time in the development of the hypothalamus. During this period, the pattern of the male hypothalamus is established by the action of testosterone that has been converted to estrogen. If the male is castrated at birth, the hypothalamus retains the female pattern. In adult female rats, the hypothalamus regulates the secretion of gonadotropic hormones in a cyclic fashion, resulting in the rhythm of ovulation and formation of corpora lutea in the ovary. Knowledge about the function of the hypothalamus in males and females has accumulated steadily over the years and is fairly well accepted. However, few investigators have examined the effects of gonadal steroids on the physiology and anatomy of the cerebral hemispheres.

We first became interested in the interaction of the ovarian hormones with the cerebral cortex when we were tabulating the results from experiments dealing with pregnant rats in the late 1960s and early 1970s. We had not studied the brains of female rats prior to this time, because we wished to avoid the additional variables that might be introduced by the estrus cycle. Actually, we learned about the influence of the sex hormones on the female cortex quite by accident. We were interested in the pups from parents living in different types of environments. In order to carry out the study, it was essential to mate males and females that had lived in either enriched or impoverished conditions. A puzzle emerged from the experiments involving the female rats living in enriched or impoverished conditions during pregnancy: we learned that the usual cortical thickness differences between the enriched and impoverished animals were not present. Upon close observation of the data, it was apparent that during pregnancy the brain of the impoverished female had increased to dimensions equal to those of the enriched animal. With this finding, we then began to study more closely the relationship between the ovarian hormones and the development of the cerebral cortex.

Information that is slowly accumulating shows that estrogen plays a role in shaping the structure of the cerebral cortex. Estrogen has been reported to alter the incorporation of amino acids into the neurons of female animals. Litteria and Thorner report that chronic injections of estradiol in adult ovariectomized rats depressed incorporation of tritiated amino acid into proteins in the cerebral cortex (33), as did injections given at 24 hours and 72 hours after birth (34). However, others find the opposite effect: single injections of estrogen into ovariectomized animals increased incorporation of tritiated amino acids into proteins and increased the protein content of the cerebral cortex (35, 36). It is possible that the dosage and time factor could be responsible for these opposing results. Nevertheless, estrogen clearly plays a role in cortical metabolism, though it may not be as pronounced as its role in other areas.

In the same year that we published our paper on the effect of pregnancy on the rat cerebral cortex (37), Presl et al. (38) found estrogen receptors in the cerebral cortex of young rats from 5 to 50 days of age. A perinuclear localization of the receptors was identified. In the same year, Kato et al. (39) found that at birth the concentration of estrogen receptors in the anterior pituitary was about 3 times as great as in the cerebral cortex; at day 45 the estradiol concentration was lower in the cerebral cortex than in any other part of the brain. These results indicate that estrogen receptors do exist in the cortex, but there are fewer of them there than in other regions.

Although estrogen receptors disappear from the cortex after the first postnatal month, we found that the brains of 116-day-old pregnant rats had thicker cortices than those of nonpregnant animals. Was it possible that estrogen could influence cortical structure in older animals even in the absence of receptors? A series of experiments were planned to learn whether the removal of the ovaries at various times during the life of the female altered cortical structure. The times chosen were (1) at birth; (2) during the early sexual reproduction period, at 90 days of age; and (3) later in life, at 300 days of age.

For the study of the impact of ovariectomy at birth (40), two females from each litter were ovariectomized and two served as sham controls, their ovaries having been exposed surgically but not removed to expose both sets of rats to similar stress. For each of the experiments, the females lived in standard colony cages for a 90-day period following the surgery—the first 21 days with their mothers, and then three ovariectomized females (or three controls) per cage.

The ovariectomized rats were found to have a thicker cortex in certain areas than the control, intact rats. The area which showed the most consistent increase was area 4 (see Figure 1). In the first experiment, this area was thicker in the ovariectomized rats than in the controls by 3% ($p < 0.05$), and in the replication experiment by 6% ($p < 0.05$) (40). That area 4 should show such responses to ovarian hormonal deprivation was unpredicted, because this area is reportedly associated with motor function. Admittedly, it is known that on the average females do not possess as great a muscular strength as males. These results suggest that a dampening of the motor cortex in response to ovarian hormones may diminish the output from the cortex to the nerves innevating the skeletal muscles, thus reducing the strength of contraction.

In order to determine whether changes had occurred in the neuronal dimensions of area 4 as well as in its cortical thickness as a result of the reduction in ovarian hormones, we measured the area of the neuronal perikarya and nuclei. For these measurements, the tissues were photographed and the cells were magnified (1500 ×) so the outlines could be accurately traced with a planimeter. We learned that the perikarya and nuclei were larger in the ovariectomized rat than in the control by 12% ($p < 0.01$) and 6% ($p < 0.01$), respectively. In addition, the control rats had a 17% greater cell density ($p < 0.001$), signifying fewer dendrites, than the ovariectomized rats. Here was the first evidence that removal of the ovaries at birth changed not only the thickness of the cortex in area 4 three months later, but the dimensions of the nerve cells as well.

In an attempt to determine more specifically whether these changes were occurring in the upper or lower cortical layers, the cortex was divided into equal halves between layers II and VI. We learned that the lower half changed dimensions significantly more than the upper half. Sheridan (41) later demonstrated that estrogen receptors were predominantly located in layers V and VI in the 2-day-old rat. Despite differences in methodologies and in the ages of the rats used in the two experiments, both our findings and Sheridan's indicated that estrogen was affecting the neurons in the lower layers of the cerebral cortex.

The fact that ovariectomy at birth changed the structure of the cortex attests to the significance of the ovarian hormones. But perhaps their significance is not lasting; perhaps they play their part in cortical formation during the animal's early growth. To consider this possibility we had to study rats whose reproductive organs were sexually mature (as they usually are by 60 days of age) before we removed the ovaries. For our experiment, female Long-Evans rats were ovariectomized at 90 days of age and lived without their relatively high concentrations of ovarian hormones for 90 days, or 3 months, before cortical thickness measurements were made. In these rats, which were 180 days old when we made the measurements, half of the measures showed the ovariectomized rats' cortices to be thicker than the controls'. But there were no significant differences.

In the third experiment of this type, ovaries were removed from rats at 300 days of age in an attempt to learn the effect of diminished ovarian hormones on the cortex of female animals one-third of the way through their normal lifespan. There were no significant differences between these older ovariectomized rats and their controls, but in 13.5 (1 was equal) out of 18 areas measured in the right and left cortices, the ovariectomized animals had thicker cortices than did their controls.

The above results indicate that the cerebral cortex is most responsive to ovarian hormonal deprivation in the early stages of postnatal life, but that some influence is evident in the older animals, where slight increases in cortical dimensions are noted after ovariectomy. If the older animals had lived for longer periods of time without their ovarian hormones, one wonders whether the differences would have become more marked.

Since ovarian hormones are used as contraceptives, we have good reason for wanting to understand the effects of these hormones on cerebral-cortical structures and functions. The rat results provide evidence that ovarian hormones can alter the outer layers of the brain. More recent experiments indicate that ovariectomy influences cortical cells at the synapse, the specialized apparatus for transmitting an impulse from one nerve cell (the presynaptic nerve cell) to another (the postsynaptic cell) across an intercellular space called the synaptic cleft. A synapse is composed of synaptic vesicles; presynaptic electron-dense projections; the presynaptic membrane; the synaptic cleft; and the postsynaptic membrane and its accompanying electron-dense material, which makes up the "postsynaptic density" (see Figure 10). When an organism receives input to one of its senses, the information is recorded as a nerve impulse, which is conducted to the synapse. Since the synapse does not involve a physical contact between neurons, a chemical carrier—a neurotransmitter—is generally required to bridge the synaptic cleft. Synaptic vesicles in the presynaptic terminal store quantities of the transmitter. Energy for the release of the transmitter is generated in the mitochondria of the terminal. Binding of the neurotransmitter to receptors of the postsynap-

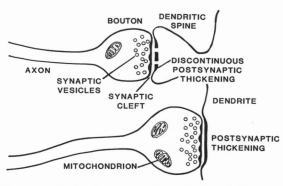

FIGURE 10. Synapse, (below) on a dendrite shaft and (above) on a spine. Axons are drawn to show the synaptic vesicles and both the presynaptic and the postsynaptic thickenings. Upper synapse has discontinuous postsynaptic thickening.

tic membrane produces changes in this structure that enable the impulse to continue into the adjacent neuron.

Pfenninger and Rees (42) demonstrated that during the formation of the synapse, the postsynaptic density is the first of all the synaptic membrane specializations to develop. With this finding, it was reasonable to consider the presence of an altered postsynaptic density to be a qualitative indicator of a possibly altered synapse and a criterion for quantification of its dimensions. Many investigators have measured the length of the postsynaptic density as representative of the length of the synapse with the assumption that it affects the overall efficacy of the synapse. More recent evidence has supported the hypothesis that discontinuities in the postsynaptic density may characterize more mature synapses.

Peters and Kaiserman-Abramof (43) took serial cross sections of synapses and observed cases in which a single synapse exhibited both a postsynaptic density with gaps and one with no gaps. One might consider that split synapses were simply immature, incompletely formed synapses. However, since the gaps have been observed exclusively in the larger, and therefore probably more mature, synapses, this possibility seemed unlikely to those of us studying postsynaptic densities. Furthermore, evidence by Dyson and Jones showed that the number of synapses with discontinuities in the postsynaptic density increased with maturation (44). Greenough et al. investigated the frequency of split synapses in the cortices of rats reared in enriched and nonenriched environments (45). These authors termed the gaps "subsynaptic plate perforations" and found that the relative frequency of the perforations increased dramatically in rats between 10 and 60 days of age. They also observed that rats reared in more complex environments had postsynaptic thickenings with a significantly greater number of perforations than rats raised in isolated conditions. (The synapses in the occipital cortex were measured to obtain this finding.)

That the discontinuous synapses increased with maturation and with stimulating environments suggested that this type of synapse did represent a more highly developed or more mature structure. Also, as previously mentioned, ovariectomy increased cortical thickness as well as the dimensions of the neuronal soma and nucleus. Therefore, in our experiments dealing with the effects of ovariectomy on cortical structural changes, it appeared most reasonable to choose discontinuous synapses for our next measurement.

In our attempt to learn whether the increased cortical dimensions after ovariectomy represented a more mature cortex, we not only quantified the discontinuous synapses, but we also analyzed the curvature of the synapses as a function of maturation. Dyson and Jones distinguished among positively curved, negatively curved, and flat junctions between pre- and postsynaptic bindings (44). Positively curved synapses were defined as those in which the postsynaptic density curved into the presynaptic terminal; negatively curved synapses were those in which the postsynaptic density curved toward the postsynaptic ending. These researchers found an increase in the frequency of flat junctions with age. They also discovered that a larger proportion of the synaptic curvatures were negative in young animals. With these facts, along with evidence that anesthesia produced a preponderance of negatively curved synapses, Jones and Dyson proposed that negatively curved synapses indicated nonfunction, and positively curved synapses, function. They also suggested that the flattening that occurred in more mature synapses represented an adaptation through which a "finer control of the neural network system" was accomplished.

In order to obtain synapses for our study, 7 littermate pairs of 1-day-old rats were separated. Under cryogenic (cold) anesthesia, one was ovariectomized and the other served as a sham-operated control. At 90 days of age, the animals were coded so the investigator was unaware of the treatment each rat had received. On photoelectron-micrographs, synapses were analyzed in layer II of the right medial occipital cortex, or area 18 (46). The total magnification was $34,000 \times$. Only axospinous synapses were analyzed. Both continuous postsynaptic thickenings and discontinuous synapses on dendritic spines were quantified. For the frequency of occurrence of the split synapses, chi-square tests were used; these revealed that the ovariectomized animals had significantly more split synapses (20%, $p < 0.05$) than the sham-operated rats. The discontinuous postsynaptic densities occurred in both groups, but more frequently in the ovariectomized one.

A significant difference was observed in the frequency of occurrence of positively and negatively curved synapses between the sham-operated and ovariectomized animals. The ovariectomized group had significantly fewer negatively curved synapses (63%, $p < 0.05$) and more positively curved synapses (19%, $p < 0.05$) than the sham-operated control. Accepting Dyson and Jones's hypothesis concerning the meaning of synaptic curvature, we can conclude that the ovariectomized animals had more functioning synapses (positively curved) and fewer nonfunctioning synapses (negatively curved) than their sham-operated littermates. Though no one has established any definitive functional implications of the difference between discontinuous, positively-curved synapses and negatively-curved synapses, these results on the effects of ovariectomy on cerebral cortical structure all support the available information indicating that a cortex from an ovariectomized rat is in a more mature state of development than one from an intact female.

Hormone Replacement

Ovarian hormone replacement seemed a logical next step to us in continuing our search for the relationship between cortical development and ovarian hormones. First, female rats that had been ovariectomized at birth were given estrogen in the form of ethinylestradiol, starting at day 40 and continuing until day 90 (dosage: $1\mu g/kg$) (47). The results obtained from cortical thickness measurements indicated that the ethinylestradiol-treated rats had a significantly thinner cortex than the oil-injected sham ovariectomized controls. The measured cortical areas with significant differences, ranging from 4 to 6%, were areas 4, 3, 18, and 17. Again, area 4 showed a response to ovarian hormones, as it had with ovariectomy, but, as might be predicted, in the opposite direction. In a preliminary study, the same dose of ethinylestradiol from day 69 to day 90 had produced no significant differences in cortical thickness. Evidently either 21 days is not a sufficiently long period for cortical change to occur, or the age at which hormone replacement begins plays a crucial role, or possibly both age and length of exposure are important.

Progesterone is known to have an antiandrogenicity effect, so one might hypothesize that progesterone might increase cortical dimensions. To study the effect of progesterone on the cortex, rats ovariectomized on day 1 were treated with progesterone from day 40 to day 90 (dosage: 2 mg/kg) (47). In comparing the cortical thickness of the ovariectomized rats receiving progesterone with the sham-ovariectomized rats, we found that the cortex was thicker as a consequence of progesterone treatment. In general, progesterone had an effect opposite to that of ethinylestradiol. The cortical areas which showed significant increases (ranging from 3 to 5%) were areas 10M, 10L, 4, 3, 2, and 18. In the previous studies with ovariectomized rats without hormonal supplements area 4 showed a consistent response to altered ovarian hormonal levels. With progesterone, this area increased by 3% ($p < 0.05$) compared with the intact controls. According to a one-way analysis of variance test, area 4 demonstrated a significant level of difference from the control in each of the experiments with changed concentrations of ovarian hormones, whether ovariectomy alone or ovariectomy with ethinylestradiol or progesterone.

On the tissues from the ovariectomized rats that we had used for cortical thickness studies, we also measured both the hippocampus and the pyriform cortex (see Figure 2). There was no significant difference in hippocampal thickness between ovariectomized females *not* given re-placement hormones and the control. However, the hippocampus was significantly thinner, by 3% ($p < 0.01$), in the ovariectomized rats re-ceiving ethinylestradiol than in the controls. As occurred in the cortex, the estrogen compound reduced the thickness of the hippocampus; but progesterone had no significant measured effect on this part of the fore-brain. The ovariectomized females and the ethinylestradiol-treated fe-males showed no significant differences from the controls in the pyriform cortex. The pyriform cortex was not measured in the progesterone-treated rats.

In summary, these studies clearly indicate that the structure of the rat cerebral cortex and hippocampus can be significantly altered by var-ious levels of female sex steroid hormones under certain conditions. Therefore, we have reason to believe that the normal course of cerebral development, and some of the differences between the male and female brains, are shaped by the sex hormones.

Growth and Aging Patterns in Subcortical Structures

Not all forebrain structures develop and age at the same rate. This section will deal with regions of the forebrain that differ from each other in development and aging patterns—including the hippocampus, the en-torhinal cortex, the amygdala, and the corpus striatum (see Figure 2); corpus striatum, however, is not shown, as mentioned previously in Chapter 2 (48). Attempts to understand these normal distinctive aging styles in the rat forebrain allow us insights into regions that may be involved in abnormal aging. In addition, some regions of the forebrain are more susceptible to environmental influences than others, as will be seen in Chapter 4. By examining areas with different aging patterns and different responses to the environment, we may find some clues to the interaction of aging and environmental stimulation and, in turn, shed light on possible neural patterns of disease processes.

The occipital cortex, located in the back or posterior region of the cerebral cortex (Figure 1), processes visual information; damage to this area results in partial or complete blindness. This region is offered as an example of the phylogenetically more recent six-layered neocerebral cortex.

The entorhinal cortex (see Figure 2) is also known as the *transitional cortex,* because this five-layered paleocortex arises in the phylogenetic scheme between the archicortex and the neocortex. The entorhinal cortex constitutes an important site of convergence for information from many sensory systems and for pathways concerned with memory processing.

The hippocampus, named for its physical resemblance to a sea horse, is found deep below the cerebral cortex and represents the three-layered archicortex (see Figure 2). A single, precise role of the hippocampus has not been pinpointed, but present information suggests that it is involved in such functions as learning and memory processing, emotional reactions, sexual behavior, and spatial mapping.

Both the hippocampus and the entorhinal cortex are of particular interest at present in our society, now that more people are living to old age. These are sites of abnormal formations, such as neurofibrillary tangles and plaques, which are characteristic (and indeed are the only certain diagnostic features) of the dreaded Alzheimer's disease. There is apparently no adequate animal model for this disease. But by observing the developing and aging patterns of these regions in an animal (because we cannot make such precise measurements in human brains), one can gain an insight into possible areas of specific variations.

The amygdaloid nucleus (see Figure 2), consisting of a conglomerate of nuclei, is so named because it appears almond-shaped in the human brain. This nucleus is located within the temporal lobe and is of interest because it plays a part in regulating such functions as aggression, sensory integration, responsivity to reward, and sexuality.

The corpus striatum is commonly called the basal ganglia, because it consists of masses of nerve cell bodies found in the base of the cerebral hemispheres. Its growth and development deserve attention because of its role in skeletal muscle control (it programs the inception and termination of motor activity) and because of its modification of pain. In addition, it has high quantities of various neurotransmitters compared with other areas of the forebrain, such as the cerebral cortex, suggesting a continuously active functional role.

In order to determine the growth and aging curves of these forebrain structures, we measured the thickness of the occipital and entorhinal cortices, as well as the hippocampus, on transverse histological sections of brains from male Long-Evans rats. The rats lived as littermates with their mothers until 22 days of age in small colony cages (34 × 20 × 20 cm) and then were housed in groups of three or four in similar colony cages. Seven to 16 animals were studied in each of the following age groups: 26, 41, 108, 650, and 904 days of age. The measurements of the area of the amygdaloid nucleus were made on 9 to 15 rats per age group at 6, 26, 55, 90, 185, and 400 days of age. For the measurements of the area of the corpus striatum, 7 to 15 animals per age group were used at 6, 10, 14, 20, 26, 41, 55, 77, 90, and 108 days of age.

The results from the occipital and entorhinal cortices and from the hippocampus are presented in Figure 11. Here it is clearly demonstrated that the hippocampus continues to grow slowly from 26 to 904 days of age. The increase is gradual throughout this time, providing an overall increase of 10%. Both the entorhinal and occipital cortices decrease with aging, however, but their patterns of aging differ. Sometime between 26 and 41 days, the occipital cortex begins to decrease steadily until 650 days of age, by approximately 10%. Between 650 and 904 days of age, there is a steep decline of another 11%, giving a total decrease between 26 and 904 days of about 21%.

Though the entorhinal cortex also decreases over time, its most dramatic decrease, by 8%, occurs between 26 and 41 days of age. From 41 to 904 days there is only another 5% reduction in thickness. While the occipital cortex is changing so dramatically between 650 and 904 days of age, the entorhinal cortex is not showing any significant change. Thus, it is clear from Figure 11 that these three regions of cortex follow quite different patterns during aging (when the animals live three to a cage in a controlled laboratory environment).

The growth and aging pattern of the amygdaloid nucleus offers yet

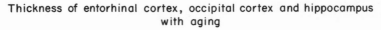

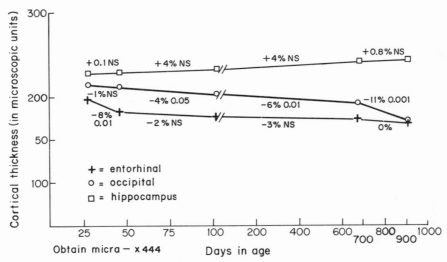

FIGURE 11. Thickness of entorhinal cortex, occipital cortex, and hippocampus with aging.

a different picture. After reaching a growth peak between 26 and 55 days of age, the amygdaloid nucleus decreases until sometime between 90 and 185 days of age, when it once again continues to increase. After 185 days it begins to diminish again until 400 days, the oldest age for which we measured this structure. Its aging pattern appears independent of those of the other regions measured.

The corpus striatum was not measured for as extensive a period as were the other forebrain regions. Yet, for the short period for which its dimensions were recorded, it also follows an aging pattern different from the surrounding regions. The corpus striatum increases greatly from 6 to 20 days of age, and from then on the increase is more gradual until 77 days of age, when it appears to peak. Though more points at later dates are needed to confirm this apparent peak, the development and aging pattern of this region is different from that of the others.

Because the various regions of the forebrain age at different rates, it is not precise enough to speak about an aging brain without defining the region involved. Whereas the hippocampus is steadily increasing in dimensions throughout a lifetime, the entorhinal cortex and occipital cortex display decreasing trends. These latter, more recently evolved cortices of five and six layers, are possibly more subject to the consequences of aging as they are to the environmental conditions to be mentioned in Chapter 4, than is the older three-layered cortex. The amygdaloid nucleus offers yet another aging pattern quite different from the three cortical regions. We have yet to identify the factors that influence these patterns.

3

DEVELOPMENT AND AGING OF CORTICAL NERVE CELLS AND GLIAL CELLS

It is well known among life scientists that not only are brain nerve cells formed at rapid rates during embryogenesis, but large numbers die during this time as well. Some investigators have stated that as many as 50 to 65% of the newly formed nerve cells are lost before birth. Most lay people believe that they are losing nerve cells in the brain as they age. Postnatal brain cell loss is a real concern. In fact, a very common question asked by a lay audience is, How many cells do I kill everytime I take my martini? Not only can we not answer this question with accuracy, but until recently we could not answer questions about brain cell loss with "normal" aging. Only by examining the brains of animals in controlled environments could we obtain a reasonable answer to this last query. The usual factors, such as diet, genetic background, air quality, and the general environment, all have to be taken into consideration. In order to understand how the environment alters brain cells, it is first essential to obtain measurements of cell populations in standard laboratory conditions.

We learned that nerve cell counts in rats are fairly unstable during the first 108 days of postnatal life. It may have been that neuronal death was continuing after birth for a short period or that the cells were moving to different locations. But after 108 days and until 904 days of age, the nerve cell number per unit area was remarkably stable. In other words, the aging rats were not losing a significant number of neurons from the cerebral cortex. Our results indicate that if an animal is living in a healthy environment throughout its lifetime, the number of nondividing cells exhibits unusual consistency after early adulthood. The counts of the glial cells—the structural and metabolic support cells of the nerve cells—followed patterns very similar to those of the neurons.

In order to create a field large enough for the cells to be identified and counted by several investigators, we took photomicrographs of 1 mm^2 areas of the medial occipital cortex (area 18; see Figure 1), a visual association area (1). Each area was enlarged to create a field of about 1 m^2 (a single field is reproduced in Figure 12). Area 18 was chosen for our detailed cellular analysis because it appeared to be the most responsive to our varied external environmental conditions. It was the first area to demonstrate a structural change when the rats had been enriched for only 4 days.

By photographing four adjacent, overlapping columns of the cortex from the surface down to the underlying white matter (at a magnification of 640 ×), we gave ourselves an adequate sample of tissue for cell counts. A montage was created from the individual pictures, and a clear sheet of Plexiglas was placed over it (Figure 12). In this manner, the cell types could be identified and marked with a colored wax pencil directly on the

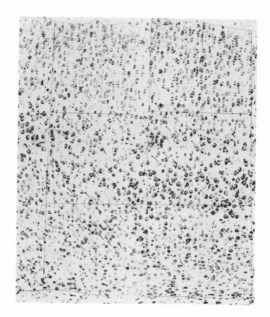

FIGURE 12. Montage of photographs illustrating neurons and glial cells in 1 mm^2 of cerebral cortex.

overlying Plexiglas. After all the cells in one sample were counted (there were approximately 600 to 725 nerve cells per square millimeter, depending upon the age of the animals), we replaced the marked piece of Plexiglas with a fresh one and made another cell count. The two completed sheets were then superimposed in order to declare a consensus on the counts.

The well-trained human eye connected to the discriminating brain has to decipher many variables in making a decision whether a cell should be counted or not. Not only are nerve cells of different shapes and sizes, but the several types of glial cells also display a variety of densities and sizes. The amount of overlap among all cell types is another consideration. When counting the neurons and glial cells, we do not wish to include the blood vessel lining cells, so they must be identified and excluded. No automatic scanner is yet sensitive enough to substitute for such judgments, even though many types of scanners are on the market.

Cells were counted on 6 micron (6 μm) sections beginning with 26-day-old male rats. With this thickness, we found we could not count the cortical cells prior to 26 days of age, because the cells had not grown enough branches to distinguish one cell from another (2). The density of cells per unit area was too great to allow us to see well-defined cell boundaries. After making counts on the 26-day-old animals' brains, we added additional age groups: 41, 108, and 650 days. All tissues were from our original longitudinal study with the Long-Evans rats.

At first glance, the results, shown in Figure 13, are consistent and revealing in one sense and very perplexing in another. Between 26 and 41 days of age, there was actually an increase in the number of neurons

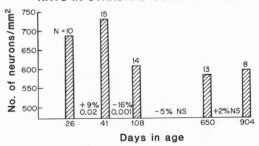

FIGURE 13. *Neuron counts with aging in occipital cortex of male Long-Evans rats in standard colony conditions.*

per unit area by 9% ($p < 0.02$). This increase can be explained by a decrease in total mass of cortex without a decrease in number of cells, which would reduce the connections between the cells and provide more cells to be counted per unit area. But between 41 and 108 days of age, a 16% ($p < 0.001$) decrease in neurons is seen. In this period of time, the cortex is also decreasing in thickness, and so this loss of cells could be a real one. The reason for these contradictory findings before 108 days of age is not absolutely clear.

If we had been comparing only the 26- and the 108-day counts, then a more satisfactory explanation could have been offered, since, as was pointed out, the greatest loss of neurons occurs during normal embryogenesis. A loss after birth could represent a continuation of the process that begins before birth, which could be explained as a tailoring of the nervous system to fit need and demand. Undoubtedly, as the animal is establishing a life pattern, the nervous system responds and molds its cell pattern and processes accordingly. Needless to say, more counts are necessary in the period between 26 and 108 days before any final conclusions can be made about neuron populations in the cerebral cortex during this postnatal period.

But between 108 days and 650 days of age, a more stable neuronal count is found with a nonsignificant loss of nerve cells of only 5%. This fact by itself is very encouraging to learn, that in a period of 542 days in the adult rat's life, no significant cortical neuron loss was measured in the occipital cortex. But still another remarkable finding was to emerge. The 650-day-old animals' cells were counted in 1977. In 1985, the counts on the 904-day-old animals' brains were completed (2, 3), and to our surprise, when all counts were tabulated, there was a nonsignificant difference between neuron counts at 650 and 904 days of age! The rat was not losing a significant number of neurons in the occipital cortex after early adulthood.

Table 1 shows a marked difference in the rate of neuron density changes between the upper layers and the lower layers of the occipital cortex between 26 and 650 days of age. For these counts, a grid overlying the photomicrographs was divided into two equal parts, upper and lower, between the beginning of layer II and the lower border of layer VI adjacent to the corpus callosum (see Figure 2 for a representation of the cortical layers). From 41 days to 108 days, the neurons in the lower layers decreased in density more markedly than those in the upper layers, a 24% decrease ($p < 0.001$) compared with a 9% decrease ($p < 0.01$). It is possible that the reduced physical activity experienced by the rats in their confined standard colony cages was influential in bringing about a

TABLE 1

Differences in Neuron Numbers in Upper and Lower Halves of the Rat Medial Occipital Cortex

AGE (DAYS)	NUMBER OF RATS	NUMBER NEURONS ($\bar{X} \pm$ S.D.)	DIFFERENCE BETWEEN AGE GROUPS (%)	p
Upper half				
26	10	371 ± 27	(+) 5	NS
41	15	388 ± 33	(−) 9	0.01
108	14	352 ± 30	(−) 7	NS
650	13	327 ± 37		
Lower half				
26	10	309 ± 34		
41	15	338 ± 37	(+) 9	NS
108	14	258 ± 21	(−) 24	0.001
650	13	255 ± 28	(−) 1	NS

reduction in neuron numbers. (The lower layers of cells project out of the cortex to subcortical structures or to the spinal cord. If less motor activity is taking place, fewer cortical cells are needed to innervate the motor cells in the spinal cord.) For the other age comparisons, no significant differences were found in neuron density changes between upper and lower layers.

The cell count data clearly indicated that after 108 days of age, the male rats living in our standard colony conditions, receiving healthy, protein-rich diets, breathing relatively good laboratory air, and drinking tap water, did not lose a significant number of nerve cells. In other words, if the brain was given an adequate support system as it aged, the number of nerve cells in the cerebral cortex was quite stable. Other investigators have shown similar results in the somatosensory cortex: no significant loss of neurons during aging after adulthood has been reached (4).

We have already demonstrated that the cortical thickness decreases slowly with aging. However, according to this new knowledge, there is no significant loss of cortical neurons between 108 days and 904 days of age. It would seem, then, that the decrease in cortical thickness can be attributed to a loss of dendrites.

In addition to counting the numbers of neurons, we measured the area of the perikarya (cell bodies) and nuclei of neurons from area 18 of the occipital cortex in the 26-, 41-, 108-, and 650-day-old rats. We used a microfilm reader to make projections of the negatives of some of the pictures used for cell counts, and from each frame we made tracings on paper of three well-defined neurons (neurons in which we could clearly see a nucleus, nucleoli, and Nissl substance dispersed throughout the perikaryon). The resulting total of 36 neurons per animal was measured with the aid of a planimeter. The total magnification from slide to drawing was 2000 ×.

Table 2 presents the data from the measured area of the perikarya and nuclei in area 18 from rats living in the standard colony conditions. Only the perikarya showed a significant decrease in area between postweaning and old age. As with the cell counts, the greatest decreases occurred in perikaryal area before 108 days of age, with a nonsignificant decrease during the next 542 days. It is important to stress that none of these animals was isolated; all were living at least two to three per small cage. Many other aging studies have dealt with animals housed alone and therefore in deprived sensory conditions; such studies have yielded smaller cell numbers and sizes than those reported here.

Glial cells are the second type of cell in the brain. Two kinds were quantified in our studies: oligodendrocytes (cells with few treelike processes) and astrocytes (star-shaped cells). The oligodendrocytes form myelin, the fatty sheath around nerve fibers which facilitates impulse conduction. Though oligodendrocytes are often found adjacent to the soma of the nerve cell or to capillaries, their function in these positions is not yet well understood.

Astrocytes are both structurally and functionally different from oligodendrocytes. Some of the processes of astrocytes terminate in expansions called *end feet*. These feet are found on blood vessels, on dendrites, or adjacent to the connective tissue membrane (pia mater) that surrounds the brain. One of their functions is to regulate metabolic and ionic conditions around blood vessels and dendrites; in connection with the covering around the brain, they serve a protective role.

TABLE 2

The Area of the Perikarya and Nuclei of Occipital-Cortical Neurons from 26 to 650 Days of Age

AGE (DAYS)[a]	AREA (IN.^{2}) ($\overline{X} \pm S.D.$)[b]	DIFFERENCE (%)	p
Perikarya			
26	0.459 ± 0.162		0.1
41	0.438 ± 0.146	(−) 4.5	0.01
108	0.394 ± 0.217	(−) 10.0	NS
650	0.385 ± 0.235	(−) 2.3	
Nuclei			
26	0.210 ± 0.145		NS
41	0.199 ± 0.111	(−) 5.2	NS
108	0.189 ± 0.104	(−) 5.0	NS
650	0.183 ± 0.134	(−) 3.2	

[a]N = 6 animals per age group with 36 cells per animal.
[b]Magnification = 2000×.

The stain that we used for neuron counts (a composite of Luxol fast blue and cresylect violet) is an excellent one to bring out the types of glial cells separate from the neurons. Though in the end the glial cells were counted on the same pictures as the neurons, we first identified them using the microscope to take advantage of the very precise color differentiation and then marked them on the photographs. The glial cells were shades of blue and the neurons were pink. Those glial cells which had small, pale-blue nuclei were counted as astrocytes. The cells we identified as oligodendrocytes had smaller and darker-blue nuclei than the astrocytes. Those cells with blue nuclei in between the two clearly defined glial types we counted as glial cells but of unknown designation. Figure 14 presents the values of total glial counts from 26 to 904 days of age.

The greatest decrease in density in these glial cell types occurred between 650 and 904 days of age. There was an increase in glial cell counts between 26 and 41 days that followed a similar pattern to the neuron counts. The similarity lends credibility to the counts, because the neuron and glial cell counts were made at different times but on the same tissues. The exact reasons for the increase in glial and neuronal numbers during this time period are still a mystery.

In the older age groups, we found that both the neurons and the glial

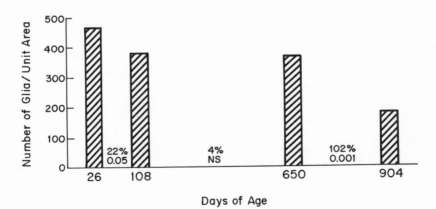

FIGURE 14. *Total glial numbers in Long-Evans male rat occipital cortex sample during aging.*

cells showed a density decrease by the same amount, 4 to 5%, from 108 to 650 days of age, and that both results were nonsignificant.

In summary, our results have shown a significant decrease in the density of neurons between 41 and 108 days of age, followed by a stability in number until 904 days of age. The density of astrocytes and oligodendrocytes decreased significantly from 26 to 108 days of age, yet no significant decrease occurred after this period until 650 days. Then a marked decrease took place between 650 and 904 days of age.

Having established methods for identifying neurons and glial cells in the cerebral cortex of the male rat, we next counted these types of cells in certain regions of the neurologically undamaged human male cortex. (We obtained the human brains from the Veterans Hospital in Martinez, California.) Glial cells reportedly increase in number as one ascends the phylogenetic scale. The hypothesis is that the more metabolically demanding nerve cells require more glial support cells. In other words, the number of neurons per glial cell or the neuron/glial ratio would be smaller in the more highly evolved brains.

We wondered whether the prefrontal lobe of the human brain was more highly developed and would have fewer neurons per glial cell than the inferior parietal lobe (Figure 15). The reason we decided to compare these two particular areas was that during evolution the prefrontal lobe of man has grown proportionately more than other lobes. But a neuroanatomist, Gerhard von Bonin, once proposed that the inferior parietal

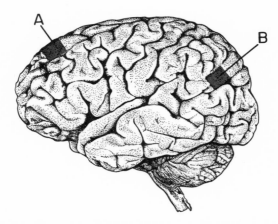

FIGURE 15. Lateral view of the human brain showing the position of the samples used for neuron and glial cell counts. (A) Superior prefrontal region (area 9); (B) Inferior parietal region (area 39).

cortex was also growing out of proportion to other cortical areas and was possibly "pushing" the frontal lobe forward during development. The inferior parietal region, like the prefrontal lobe, is an association cortex and does not receive primary sensory inputs from the external environment. These association cortices receive cortical input from the primary areas and other association areas. The inferior parietal cortex has frequently been called the "association area of association areas" because it receives information from several areas including the visual, auditory and somatosensory association cortices. Over the years, Professor von Bonin's comment had stayed in my mind.

We hypothesized that the region of the cortex that had more glial cells per neuron might prove to be the more highly evolved, or the more active, or both. With this hypothesis in mind, we began to collect cortical samples from neurologically undamaged male human brains from both the right and left prefrontal cortex (area 9) and the inferior parietal cortex (area 39) (see Figure 15). Sections of the tissue were prepared and stained in order to differentiate the glial cells from the neurons.

The results of the counts from 11 human male brains, ranging in age from 45 to 81 years, suggested that the prefrontal area had more glial cells per neuron than the inferior parietal lobe. These findings offer some support to our hypothesis that the prefrontal lobe is more highly evolved than the inferior parietal lobe.

We wanted to follow up our initial frontal and parietal human brain cell counts by studying an exceptional human brain, and we wanted to corroborate the results from our experiments on rats and those of others showing that glial cells increased with an enriched condition and did not increase with age in the controlled laboratory conditions (2, 3). Therefore, when we learned from an article in *Science* magazine in 1978 that no one had studied Albert Einstein's brain microscopically to compare it with "normal" male brains, we decided to request samples from Dr. Thomas Harvey, the pathologist who had obtained Einstein's brain at the time of autopsy in 1955. No one had attempted to make quantitative cell comparisons on Einstein's unique brain in over 25 years. After initially contacting Harvey in Weston, Missouri, we waited for three years before we received the small "cubes of brain" from the right and left hemispheres of Einstein's brain, including areas 9 and 39. The brain, when it arrived in Berkeley, was embedded in celloidin, a substance used to infiltrate tissue to harden it sufficiently to allow cutting micra-thin sections. Thus, the kinds of measurements we could attempt were very limited. Cell counts and cell size were among the few possibilities.

After completing the counts on Einstein's brain cells in a manner similar to that used for the 11 "normal" male brains from individuals ranging in age from 45–81 years (Einstein was 76), we learned he did indeed have more glial cells per neuron than the normal males had in each of the four areas sampled (7). In fact, in the left area 39, the differences were statistically significant. Since glial cells have been reported by some to increase with aging, we also compared his brain with the three brains in his specific age group. Einstein's brain had more glial cells per neuron.

Our carefully controlled glial counts on aged rats informed us that the number of glial cells not only did not increase with aging, but in the very old animals, actually decreased. Thus, using the results obtained from our enriched rats as a general principle, the glial cell counts on Einstein's brain lent support to the findings of our's and others showing that the more active cortex possessed more glial cells per neuron (2, 3).

Not only did we have Einstein's samples to compare with our normal data base of human males, but, unexpectedly, we learned that we had been given two human female brains from the pathologists. Unaware that these female brains had entered the collection, we counted their cells along with those in the male brains. It was only after the counts were completed that we learned that the female brains had been included. The results showed that the neuron glial cell ratios in the human female inferior parietal cortex (area 39) were smaller than those of the males. Since the samples from the females were so few, only the suggested trends are mentioned and no statistics are offered.

But these apparent sex differences in neuron glial cell ratios in area 39 in human beings led us to attempt to substantiate the results by counting nerve and glial cells in area 39, the inferior parietal cortex, in male and female rats. More stringent controls (such as uniform environments, diets, and temperatures) can be utilized with rats than with human material. Would we also see neuron glial cell sex differences in the rat cerebral cortex under these conditions? McShane et al. have completed the counts in area 39 of 90-day-old male and female Long-Evans rats (8). The initial results suggest that the female does have more glial cells per neuron than the male. A replication experiment is essential to confirm these preliminary results.

In conclusion, our counts on cerebral cortical nerve and glial cells indicate that after 108 days of age, the cell populations remain quite constant until very old age. Before 108 days postnatally, the fluctuations in our cell counts cannot be explained satisfactorily at the present time. If the cortical cells are not decreasing significantly in number with aging, then the decrease in cortical thickness, which was demonstrated previously in our development and aging curves, must be due to depletion of cell size expressed primarily in the numerous dendritic ramifications. That there are sex differences in cell counts in one cortical area not only needs to be confirmed, but such counts need to be taken from many cortical regions as we attempt to understand the structures behind the functions of male and female cortices throughout a lifetime.

4

THE EFFECTS OF ENRICHMENT AND IMPOVERISHMENT

The History of an Idea

Knowing the basic patterns of development and aging and some of the factors that influence the forebrain structures, we can now begin to approach more directly the correlations among brain chemistry, brain structure, behavior, and environment utilizing various experimental conditions. The Krech-Rosenzweig-Bennett team had demonstrated that some aspects of the chemistry of the cerebral cortex were related to learning behavior. They showed that the enzyme acetylcholinesterase, which is associated with the breakdown of the neurotransmitter acetylcholine at the synapse, is more concentrated in the brains of maze-bright animals than in those of maze-dull animals. Upon joining the team at Berkeley in the late 1950s, I asked whether the distribution of acetylcholinesterase through the cortical layers was also different between these two strains of animals with different learning abilities. (See Figure 2 for a location of the cortical layers.) Not only did we have the maze-bright and maze-dull animals to examine, but two strains of rats were specifically bred to yield high and low concentrations of acetylcholinesterase in the cerebral cortex. We were curious to learn whether these strains as well as the maze-bright and maze-dull strains differed in distribution of this enzyme through the cortical layers.

We thought that a reasonable bridge between the chemistry that was being measured by Bennett, Krech, and Rosenzweig and the anatomy that could be measured by my group would be a study of acetylcholinesterase concentrations in the anatomical layers of the cortex. Richard M. Diamond, a nuclear chemist-physicist, helped design a method utilizing radioactive copper (^{64}Cu) in place of the stable copper normally used in Gomori's thiocholine method to assay for acetylcholinesterase (1). In order to quantify the amount of acetylcholinesterase in the layers of the cortex, we took samples from rats with the different maze abilities and rats with the different enzyme concentrations. Cylinders of cortical tissue 2 mm in diameter were punched through the cortical surface down to the white matter. Frozen sections 25 μm thick were cut horizontally and were individually incubated with radioactive cupric thiocholine so that we could assess the acetylcholinesterase concentrations throughout the cortical layers, with the aid of a scintillation counter (2).

In the frontal lobe, the greatest differences in concentration of the esterase between the maze-bright and maze-dull strains were seen in the outer layers of the cortex—layers II, III, and IV—with the maze-bright having the higher enzyme concentration. In the somatosensory region, the greatest differences were also found in layers II, III, and IV. The finding that these layers, which are the last to develop embryologically and phylogenetically, reveal the greatest chemical change suggests that the cells in these layers are involved in the learning process.

Although this information was of immense interest, only later, by returning to the data after many years, could we put it together with other data to develop a complete story of the relationship between the chemistry of the layers and the accompanying cell counts. This chemical approach was no doubt fascinating, but I still wanted to learn more about the morphology of the cortex. How did brain cell structures differ?

Our laboratory spent the next few years counting cerebral cortical nerve cells and glial cells in the cerebral cortices of several rats of the maze-bright and maze-dull strains, as well as in high-acetylcholinesterase and low-acetylcholinesterase strains of rats. We found that the neuron–glial cell ratios between the strains were not significantly different. In counting cells we check only the nerve cell bodies and the nuclei of the glial cells. We did not measure the dendritic branches. Much of the cortex is occupied by the nerve cells' branches, which in turn are responsible for most of the acetylcholinesterase. Thus, as we look back, counting cell bodies was perhaps not the best indicator to determine areas of high or low enzyme concentrations in the cortex. After these studies were completed, we then turned our attention to the effects of different environmental conditions on brain anatomy.

As mentioned in Chapter 2, it was Donald Hebb at McGill University who began experiments dealing with the effects of stimulating experiences on behavior. He showed that rats living in enriched conditions were better learners than those which had not benefited from such experience. The exciting results from his report led to the quantitative study of the chemistry of the brains from enriched and impoverished rats which was initiated at Berkeley.

What is meant by an enriched or impoverished condition for rats? At Berkeley, an enriched environment contained many animals in a large cage with a variety of novel objects for the rats to explore, whereas the impoverished animals were caged singly and had neither the objects, nor the large living space, nor the companions. In essence, an enriched environment is one which introduces more stimulation to the body's surface receptors than does an impoverished one, whether it be for rats or human beings. For obvious reasons, the feral condition, the natural outdoor environment for the rat, could not be duplicated. The laboratory condition is sterile, controlled and protective by comparison, and even at the very best, not like living in the rats' natural habitat. Therefore, all types of laboratory environments have to be considered relative to the natural one. Nonetheless, the results from the experimental conditions in the laboratory can be validly compared to each other; one condition is more enriched than the other.

The experimental paradigm used for these initial environmental experiments was designed accordingly by Krech et al. in the Berkeley psychology laboratory (3). Twelve male animals were taken from their mothers in standard colony cages at 25 days of age and were housed together in a large cage (64 × 64 × 46 cm). Two different wooden "toys" from a set of seven were put into the cage each day. There was also a small wooden maze in the cage which the rats used as a nesting box. For 30 minutes each day, the rats were allowed to explore a Hebb-Williams maze with many partitions, in a box about a square meter in area. The pattern of barriers was changed daily. At about 50 days of age, formal maze training began in several other types of mazes, all providing different levels of problem solving. Glucose pellet rewards were given. The rats could normally take food and water ad libitum. Figure 16 illustrates the enriched, standard colony, and impoverished conditions we now use: the cages are built of sheet metal and metal mesh, and metal toys have replaced the wooden ones, which the rats used to chew upon.

Simultaneously, at 25 days of age, the littermate of each of the enriched rats was placed in the impoverished condition, consisting of pri-

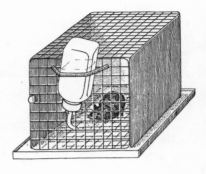
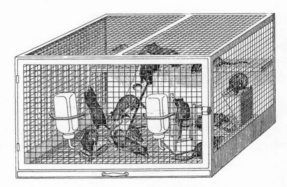

FIGURE 16. Illustration of environmental conditions: (below) enriched, a large cage with 12 rats plus toys; (upper left) standard colony, a small cage with 3 rats; (upper right) impoverished, a small cage with 1 rat.

vate cage (28 × 20 × 20 cm) with solid metal walls on three sides. (In later experiments the cages were all wire mesh or Lucite depending upon the experimental conditions, and the dimensions were slightly altered.) Food and water were available ad libitum, and every rat was given a glucose pellet each time its enriched littermate was rewarded with one. The impoverished animals did not see or touch another animal, nor were they handled during cleaning of the cages; but all animals in both groups were weighed at weekly intervals. After the animals had lived in their respective environmental conditions for the required period of time, all rats were coded so the anatomists were not aware of the previous experimental conditions, in order to prevent bias during the histological brain measurements.

The results indicated that either enriching or impoverishing the environmental complexity and training of rats caused measurable changes in brain chemistry and brain weight (4). More specifically, some of the results demonstrated that the cerebral cortex of rats subjected to enriched or impovrished environmental conditions showed not only differences in the synaptic enzyme, acetylcholinesterase, but also the wet weight of samples removed for chemical analysis. It was the weight differences which concerned us as anatomists. Though small (8% in the samples from the visual cortex and 3% in the samples from the somatosensory cortex), the differences were consistent and could be replicated. The cortical weights from the enriched animals exceeded those from the nonenriched in 79% of the cases for the visual area and 64% for the somatosensory area.

Though cortical weight differences were found between the two experimental groups, no significant changes in the weights of the subcortical tissues were seen. More recently, others have found no environmental effect on total hindbrain weight (5, 6). Floeter and Greenough (7) did, however, clearly demonstrate neuronal differences in a hindbrain structure—the cerebellum—between the enriched and the nonenriched rats, but no brain weight changes were measured. Also, in the Berkeley experiments in the early 1960s, where the animals lived in their environmental conditions for 80 days, the body weights of the isolated or nonenriched rats were greater than those of the enriched by about 7%. The body weight gains were in the opposite direction from the cerebral-cortical gains. Here was an interesting paradox: the cerebral cortex weighed more in the enriched animals, yet their body weights were less. In other studies where we measured the dimensions of some subcortical structures, including the diencephalon, we learned that the areas of these regions were more positively correlated with body weight than were our cortical measures. The findings indicate the importance of quantifying differences in specific regions of the brain rather than taking whole brain measurements as many earlier studies did.

For example, total brain weight differences between the enriched and impoverished animals after 80 days in their respective conditions were only 1% ($p < 0.01$) with 175 pairs of rats (8). With a larger sample of animals, 200 pairs, ranging in age from 18 to 530 days, Walsh et al. (6) found a mean difference of 3%. Others have also shown significant differences in rat brain weights between the two groups (9, 5). These total brain weight differences were so small, in part, because the major percent changes were localized. Since many brain regions were unaffected by these environmental conditions, whole-brain weight measures masked the localized changes.

Within the cerebral cortex, the largest brain weight changes were seen after 30 days of differential rearing (8). In male rats after 80 days, the occipital cortex showed a 6% difference in wet weight; at the same time, the somatosensory cortex showed only a 2% difference. This regional difference between the occipital cortex and the somatosensory will become of greater interest when cortical sex dissimilarities are reported in Chapter 6. Female rats were not used regularly in the early days of these experiments.

Wet- and dry-weight assessments were made in order to determine whether the difference in cortical weight was due to an increase or decrease in tissue fluid. By measuring both wet-weight and dry-weight brain samples from enriched and nonenriched rats, three separate investigations concluded that the experimental differences between the two conditions in rats were the same whether the tissues were wet or dry (10). Accumulation of fluid did not seem to be the factor causing the difference in brain weight.

Various investigators followed their brain weight measurements with macroscopic measurements of the cerebral cortex, such as cortical length and width. Reportedly, rat cerebral growth in width is essentially complete by 20 days after birth, but the length continues to grow at least to the age of 90 days (11, 12, 13). Altman et al. found that they could alter the length, but not the width, of the rat cortex by exposing the animals to 3 months of environmental complexity (12). Evidently, 3 months, or 90 days, was sufficient to show such a change, but 30 days proved an insufficient time to induce similar results (14). However, Walsh et al. chose a period in between, namely, 80 days, during which there was a highly significant change (2.5%) in length; whereas, with only 30 days, they found but a 1.2% difference in length of the cortex between enriched and nonenriched (13, 15). Others continued with this experimental approach and found that exposure to enriched conditions from 18 days to 530 days increased cerebral length (16, 17, 18, 19).

Walsh (15) pointed out that the length effect was limited to the anterior regions, and cortical weight effects were more marked at the posterior, and that they might therefore be largely independent of one another. This hypothesis would be consistent with results showing that weight and length effects appear to follow different temporal patterns depending upon the period of exposure to the experimental conditions (13, 18).

Prior to these experiments, the brain had generally been considered incapable of macroscopic physical changes as a consequence of alterations in experience. Here now was the opportunity to document weight and length increase in the cerebral cortex with quantitative anatomical microscopic measures.

Anatomical Changes
Within the Brain

When we were designing the first experiments on the Berkeley campus in the early 1960s to deal with the enriched and impoverished environments, it was not well established how long it would take to bring about measurable brain changes. Eighty days was the first time period we chose. Also in those early experiments, the rats were given maze training as part of their enriched conditions. This aspect of the enriched condition was dropped after 1965, when we found that it was not an important factor in producing the effects associated with enrichment.

In our first, and later replicated, enriched-impoverished anatomical experiment in the early 1960s, littermate male S_1 (maze-bright) rats from the psychology department colony were used (20). At 25 days of age one animal from each pair, chosen at random, was placed in the environmental complexity and training group (ECT). The littermate was assigned to the isolated-condition group (IC).

The simplest microscopic anatomical measurement we could make to compare the brains of the enriched and impoverished animals was our basic cortical thickness measurement. We measured it on transverse-cut sections 20 μm thick, utilizing subcortical landmarks to ensure uniformity in sampling from one rat to the next. Samples were taken from both the somatosensory cortex and the occipital cortex. For these early measurements of cortical thickness, we used an ocular micrometer, a small calibrated scale placed in the eyepiece of the microscope, to measure the distance from the beginning of layer II through layer VI on the brain slices (see Figure 2). We took differential counts of neurons and glial cells directly in the microscopic fields; in addition, we counted the numbers of blood vessels and classified them by size.

The results of these earliest experiments revealed significant differences in the thickness of the occipital cortex between rats living in enriched and impoverished environments for 80 days (see Table 3). In both the original and the replication experiments (Experiments I and II, respectively), the occipital cortex from the enriched rats was significantly thicker than that of the impoverished animals (6%, $p < 0.001$) (20). The results from both right and left hemispheres were combined to obtain these values.

TABLE 3

Thickness (μm) of Occipital Cortex from Enriched and Impoverished Rats (Excluding Layer I)

Experi-ment	N	ECT $\overline{X}$	ECT S.E.	IC $\overline{X}$	IC S.E.	p ECT/IC	p ECT vs. IC	p ECT > IC
I	11	1332	17	1271	22	1.048	< 0.001	7/11
II	9	1404	29	1298	27	1.082	< 0.001	9/9
I + II	20	1364	16	1284	17	1.062	< 0.001	16/20

ECT = Environmental complexity and training; IC = isolated condition.

Layer I was not included in these results because separate measurements of this layer alone in enriched and impoverished animals showed no significant differences. According to Eayrs and Goodhead (21), layer I shows very little change during the postnatal growth of the rat cerebral cortex. This fact alone is of interest when considering the dynamics of cortical development. Layer I is one of the early layers to form in the developing cortex; it receives terminal dendrites from cells in each of the underlying layers as well as axonal endings. These dendritic and axonal branches form a dense fiber plexus which constitutes layer I. Layer I apparently is not measurably altered in structure with our multisensory input: either our methods for determining morphological differences in this layer were not sophisticated enough or indeed no changes occur. The precise function of this layer, like that of many other cortical layers, is not known.

In the measurements of weight differences between the enriched and impoverished rats, the results for the somatosensory cortex had been smaller and less clear-cut than those for the occipital region. This finding was noted again in the present measurements of cortical thickness in the male S_1 rats. Although some differences in the somatosensory cortex were displayed between enriched and impoverished male rats, as seen in Table 4, the differences were not as striking as in the occipital cortex.

In an attempt to understand what cellular changes were responsible

TABLE 4

Thickness (μm) of Somatosensory Cortex from Enriched and Impoverished Rats (Excluding Layer I)

Experi-ment	N	ECT $\overline{X}$	ECT S.E.	IC $\overline{X}$	IC S.E.	p ECT/IC	p ECT vs. IC	p ECT > IC
I	10	1962	18	1825	22	1.075	< 0.001	10/10
II	8	1975	40	1985	38	0.995	NS	3/8
I + II	18	1968	20	1896	21	1.038	< 0.01	13/18

for the cortical thickness differences, cell counts were taken. In our first experiments, nerve cell and glial cell counts were made in each microscopic field, reading vertically from the pial surface of the cortex down to the underlying white matter. In the occipital cortex, the neurons per microscopic field were less numerous by 17% ($p < 0.01$) in the enriched animals than in the impoverished ones. The mean distribution of neurons in the rat occipital cortex from layers I through VI is shown in Figure 17 for the initial (I) and replication (II) experiments. The decreased number of neurons per microscopic field informed us that more intercellular material was present in the enriched animals than in the impoverished animals. It appeared that the nerve cells were not increasing in number but were getting larger by gaining more branches, so that their bodies were being spread farther apart and therefore the counts of nerve cells per microscopic field were fewer in the enriched animals. Since, at the present time, there is no evidence that the number of neurons increases in the cerebral cortex after birth, we conclude that any additional increase in cortical mass must be due in part to changes in the size of the nerve cells, including their dendritic branching.

The largest, most consistent differences between nerve cell counts in the enriched and the impoverished groups were apparent in the outer layers of the cortex, layers II, III, and IV (20). To be seen shortly, the greatest increase in the area of the neuronal soma also occurred in these

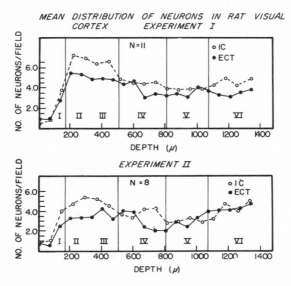

FIGURE 17. Mean distribution of neurons in rat occipital (visual) cortex showing the results in (I) the first and (II) the replication experiments.

layers. During embryological development, the lower layers of the cortex form first; each new group of cells has to migrate through the underlying layers to reach its outer position. In other words, an "inside-out" developmental pattern occurs. Our results indicating that the outer layers show the greatest plasticity suggest that those cells which are last to develop retain a greater ability to become modified in structure with an increase in new stimuli to the cortex.

It is clear from the above discussion that the animals living in enriched and impoverished conditions for 80 days, from 25 to 105 days of age, showed structural differences in the cerebral cortex. The enriched rats had thicker cortices, with the nerve cells spread farther apart, particularly in the outer layers. By counting the cortical cells per microscopic field, we did not record the total number of neurons and glial cells in a large cortical area but an average number in a single column of cells. With this method, no significant difference in number of neurons was noted between the enriched and impoverished animals. This was no surprise; we did not anticipate more neurons in the enriched rats because, to date, no cortical neurogenesis has been documented more than a few weeks after birth.

With our initial experiment in 1964 where we measured the area of the soma and the nucleus of the neuron by tracing their outlines from microscopic projected images, we found no significant differences between the size of the neurons from the enriched or the isolated rats. We were surprised with these results, for if we speculated that some of the thickness increases were due to a greater number of dendrites, then, in turn, we might expect a larger nerve cell body and nucleus to be supporting those dendrites. According to Glendinnen and Eayrs (22), the larger the neuron size, the more dendritic branching. All information suggested that we should be expecting larger neurons in our enriched rats.

For our later cell measurements, we turned to the negatives of the pictures previously used for cell counts. These negatives were projected through a microfilm reader; the final enlargement for the cells was 2000×. We expected these larger images to provide for a smaller margin of error in tracing the cell boundaries.

Since the photographs for cell counts were taken from the pial surface down to the underlying white matter, it was possible to divide the cortex (excluding layer I) into equal thirds in order to evaluate whether there was any difference in size between cells in the superficial layers and those in the deeper ones. The divisions were referred to as upper, middle, and lower. The results of the initial and replication experiments were that the upper division showed the greatest increases in both soma and nuclear size. In the combined experiments, the increase in perikaryal size for the enriched rats in the upper division was 18% ($p < 0.001$), and in nuclear size it was 20% ($p < 0.01$). Though the upper division showed the greatest increases, each division indicated a significant increase in the size of the soma and nucleus in the enriched animals compared with the isolated animals. Thus, all layers of the cortex included in these arbitrary divisions were showing differences, with the outer cellular layers indicating the greatest changes.

In 1966 Altman proposed that the outer layers of the cortex play a special role in central nervous system function (23). They exhibit slow postnatal growth, and an increase in number of cells as we ascend the phylogenetic scale. Their strategic position makes it possible for these outer cells to become the modulating influences on the input to and output from the cerebral cortex. Our data also indicate that the outer layers appear to show a greater response to the additional stimuli entering the cortex in an experientially enriched condition than in an isolated one.

By refining our methods, we were able to demonstrate the predicted differences in soma and nuclear size. (We do want to point out again that all of the tissues were coded to prevent bias during measurement. Otherwise, subconscious influences might play a role.) In a stepwise fashion, we have demonstrated that the enriched animals have larger nerve cell bodies and nuclei in all three levels of the visual association cortex, with the outermost level showing the greatest differences.

In the initial studies, we found not only fewer neurons per microscopic field, but fewer glial cells as well. We found the density of glial cells per microscipic field to be less in the enriched than in the impoverished rats by 7% in the occipital cortex and 6% in the somatosensory cortex. These findings indicated an actual increase in glial cell number, because the glial cell–neuron ratio was greater in the enriched animals than in the impoverished ones, and the total number of neurons was presumably constant. The density of glial cells through the cortical layers was so small that we came up with no significant findings in comparing the glial populations per layer between experimental groups. Table 5 illustrates the cell counts per unit area of occipital cortex in two experiments.

For the more detailed counts, the cells were not differentiated directly with the aid of the microscope as previously, but instead, photographs were taken of microscopic fields extending from the pial surface through the six layers of the cortex. We had previously reported a higher glial cell–neuron ratio in the enriched brain because the decrease in glia per microscopic field was significantly less than the decrease in neurons. Even

TABLE 5

Differential Cell Counts in the Occipital Cortex from Enriched and Impoverished S_1 Male Rats ($N = 17$ Pairs)

CELLS	ECT $\overline{X}$	IC $\overline{X}$	ECT > IC	% DIFFERENCE	p
Neurons	485.8	500.6	6/17	−3.0	NS
Astrocytes	87.0	83.0	9/17	4.7	NS
Oligodendrocytes	75.2	62.5	13/17	20.4	<.02
Indeterminate glial cells	23.4	17.2	14/17	35.5	<.01
Total glial cells	185.6	162.8	13/17	14.0	<.01
G/N	0.385	0.332	12/17	15.9	<.02

though we found this relative increase in glial cells, we were not satisfied with the results. Using our new, more refined techniques, we found an absolute increase in glial cells in the enriched brains, giving a higher glial cell–neuron ratio of 16% overall, with the enriched animal having the larger ratio in 12 out of 17 pairs ($p < 0.02$).

We found that the number of oligodendrocytes (a type of glial cell) increased (20%, $p < 0.02$) and cells with characteristics of both oligodendrocytes and astrocytes were proliferating (36%, $p < 0.01$). Nothing definitive can be said regarding the astrocyte counts, because in the first experiment the enriched animals had more astrocytes than the impoverished (27%, $p < 0.01$) and in the replication experiment the enriched animals had fewer by 7% (NS). By combining the results of both experiments, we arrived at an astroglial density that was greater by 5%, but this difference failed to reach significance.

A glial cell increase due to behavioral manipulation was reported by Altman and Das in 1964 (24), using similar but not identical enriched conditions and using radioautography to measure cell proliferation. These investigators did not attempt to differentiate types of glial cells but attributed an increase in labeled cells largely to cells situated in the cortical radiation and corpus callosum rather than in the cortical gray. We counted cells only in the cortical gray. Evidently, in a more recent communication with Walsh, Altman now thinks the cells he was identifying as glial were postnatally derived undifferentiated precursors of both neurons and glial cells. At the present time a clear conclusion about glial cell proliferation and enrichment cannot be drawn from his data.

Studies on whether adult cortical neurons can proliferate in superenriched conditions are in progress in our laboratory (25). York is attempting to demonstrate neurogenesis using ^{3}H to quantify dividing cortical cells. She hopes to differentiate between dividing neurons and glial cells between adult enriched rats and rats in standard colony conditions by labeling cells with ^{3}H-thymidine. Only by counter-staining the nerve and glial cells with a differential stain such as Luxol–Fast Blue–Cresylecht Violet will we really be certain that we are accurately separating the two populations of cells. This experiment has the potential to offer some clarification to the early experiment of Altman on whether the cells he identified were neurons or glial cells, though he was dealing with young animals and York (25) is using adult rats.

Since the early reports on glial cell counts, other investigators have also found increases in these cells with enriched conditions. In 1977, Szeligo and Leblond (26) confirmed our glial cell findings by reporting that 30 and 80 days of enrichment increased oligodendroglial densities by 27% and 33%, respectively, in comparison with those of social controls and isolated animals. (The glial cell counts of social controls and isolated animals did not differ significantly from each other.) Like us, they found that the differences in astrocyte counts were not as great as those in oligodendrocytes counts. Between animals experiencing their enriched and impoverished conditions for 80 days, the difference in astrocyte counts amounted to 13%. It has been reported that when neonates are handled in the first 10 days of life for a 15-minute period each day, the astrocytes increase by 12% but no significant changes are found in oligodendrocyte counts. But it is not clear what causes the astrocytes to be more susceptible to additional stimulation in the young and the oligodendrocytes to show a greater response in older animals. At one time, it was proposed that oligodendrocytes represented a later stage of astrocyte development; in other words, both came from the same stem cell but the astrocytes were younger than the oligodendrocytes. This theory has not been supported by additional experimentation.

Cummins and Walsh (27) continued to be intrigued with the role of glial cells and environmental input. They were able to demonstrate that the glial cell–neuron ratio was greater in the enriched brains by 8% after 90 days of rearing, thus supporting our original findings. However, in their experiments, it was the astrocytes that accounted for the increase in glial cell number. When such differences as these are obtained, it seems imperative for the investigators to collaborate and both count the same tissues to see where the differences lie. Since two groups—Szeligo and Leblond and Diamond et al. both showed that it was the oligodendrocytes that predominated following enrichment, it seems justified for now to accept these findings as the truer picture until proven otherwise. At least three groups of investigators have consistently reported an increase in glial cells in enriched conditions compared with impoverished. We must always consider when we compare only the enriched animals and the impoverished whether the enriched condition is only sparing or retaining the number of cells and not allowing them to decrease as they would with impoverishment. The ³H-thymidine experiments being carried out with standard colony and enriched animals should help to clarify this possibility.

What is the advantage for the nerve cell in having more glial cells? Numerous functions have been attributed to glial cells. Some of these have already been mentioned in Chapter 3. Different types have different functions, but by addressing them collectively one can say, in general, that they form myelin in order to facilitate impulse conduction along the axon; they regulate ionic movement between nerve and glial cells and the vascular system; they give metabolic support to the nerve cell in a manner not yet completely understood; they give additional specificity to synaptic membranes because of their close proximity to the synaptic junction; they assist with protoplasmic movement in the axon; they help regulate vascular flow; they supply either energy or substrate for energy for axonal function; and they serve as a scaffolding for early neuronal migration. Any or all of these functions may be demanding more glial cells for increased neuronal function in the enriched animals.

Besides counting glial cells and neurons, we also made quantitative measurements of the blood vessels in the cerebral cortex. Our results indicated that the somatosensory areas had more blood vessels than the visual area, a finding in accord with another investigator, Craigie (28). Our own findings are reported in Table 6. That the enriched group showed fewer capillaries per microscopic field was in agreement with our

TABLE 6A

Blood Vessels per Field in the Occipital Cortex from Enriched and Impoverished Rats in Experiment I

Type of vessel	N	ECT $\overline{X}$	ECT S.E.	IC $\overline{X}$	IC S.E.	ECT/IC	p	ECT > IC
Capillary	9	6.17	0.23	7.07	0.32	0.873	< 0.05	1/9
Over 5 μm	9	2.39	0.35	1.90	0.22	1.258	< 0.05	7/9

TABLE 6B

Blood Vessels per Field in the Somatosensory Cortex from Enriched and Impoverished Rats in Experiment I

Type of vessel	N	ECT $\overline{X}$	ECT S.E.	IC $\overline{X}$	IC S.E.	ECT/IC	p	ECT > IC
Capillary	7	8.00	0.54	8.67	0.72	0.923	NS	2/7
Over 5 μm	8	2.89	0.36	2.83	0.29	1.021	NS	6/8

findings of a smaller number of neurons per field, indicating again that the difference in the thickness of the cortex was due in part to an increase in the dendritic branching between both the nerve cells and the capillaries. The enriched group showed an increase in the number of larger vessels, those over 5 μm, presumably because this group required a greater blood supply (see Table 6). It is possible that all vessels increased in size with the enriched condition, thus pushing more vessels into the "above 5 μm" category. When the heart was examined after prolonged exercise, no new blood vessels were found, but it was shown that the existing vessels increased in diameter. It appears that a similar process occurs in the cerebral cortex.

The degree of vascularity corresponds directly to the degree of functional activity. In other words, a greater blood supply is necessary for higher metabolic activity. Thus, skeletal muscles need numerous blood vessels, in contrast to cartilage, which needs few. Dunning and Wolff (29) have reported that the vascularity of brain tissues varied with the number of synaptic structures and not with quantitative differences in nerve cell bodies. If an increase in cortical thickness is due to additional dendritic ramifications, which can account for more synapses, we would, in fact, expect an increased blood supply in the enriched brains.

After completing the nerve and glial cell counts and neuronal soma measurements, the next logical step in searching for anatomical changes due to modified environments led to the branches of the nerve cells, specifically dendritic and synaptic quantification. But before presenting these results, one study will be mentioned that provides beneficial background data for these more refined cellular measurements. We wanted to learn how much of a cortical area, such as area 18, was responding to our environmental conditions, the whole or only parts, by identifying and measuring areas including specifically active functional units called vertical columns.

Cortical cells are arranged in vertical columns with a width varying from 200 to 1000 μm. The nerve cells in a particular vertical column are related to the same peripheral receptive field and are activated by the same peripheral stimulus. Though our lines drawn to measure cortical thickness did not trace individual vertical columns precisely, by examining each line separately we would have a better idea on whether our enriched environments were affecting specific columns.

Figure 18 illustrates that whether the animals had been in their environments at age 60 to 64 days or age 60 to 90 days; each separate line showed a significant difference due to enrichment (additional data from these age groups will be discussed in Chapter 5). These more specific

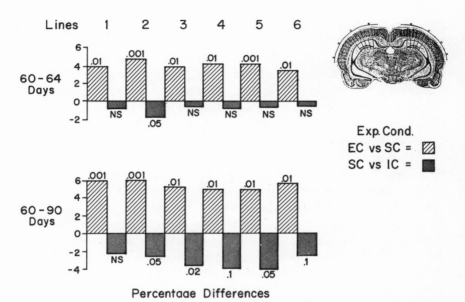

Measurements of Individual Lines in Areas 18 and 17

FIGURE 18. *Cortical thickness percentage differences between individual lines drawn on the cortex to determine if separate "columns" were responding to the environmental conditions. EC = enriched, SC = standard, IC = impoverished.*

data indicated that not just single columns of cells in the cortex were being affected by our environmental conditions: several millimeters of tissue were responding equally. This columnar information proved useful as we began to consider which nerve cell parts might be altered in their dimensions by the environment. Knowing that a large area of cortex was involved, we could now validly choose representative cortical cells from a broad region.

By this time we had thoroughly established that external environmental influences could alter the structure of the cerebral cortex, as shown by cortical thickness changes. Very early in our studies in 1964, we proposed that dendrites, the receptive extensions of the surface membrane of the nerve cell, were partially responsible for our cortical thickness changes. Small projecting receptive appendages on the dendrites called dendritic spines are known to be adaptable to severe deprivation, so these little projections seemed reasonable structures to quantify in our experiments. The functional junctions between the axon of one nerve cell and the dendrite of another, a synapse, were an obvious next choice for measurements in brains from animals exposed to stimulating or deprived environments. By examining each of these structures systematically, we could gain a clearer understanding of how the environment affects the morphology of the cortical nerve cell.

Changes in the Structure of the Nerve Cell

DENDRITE BRANCHING. The first recorded results showing that dendrites were indeed being modified by enriched and impoverished environments were made in our laboratory by Holloway in 1966 (30). He demonstrated that the dendritic branches' of stellate neurons (star-shaped nerve cells) in layer II of the occipital cortex (in area 18) were responding to the varied environmental conditions. He chose the stellate cells because they were more abundant in the outer layers of the cortex than in the lower layers. In the early description of our environmental results, we said that the outer cortical layers showed the greatest increases in neuronal soma size due to our form of enrichment. Holloway confirmed the prediction from our 1964 experiments; the changes in cortical thickness were due in part to changes in the dendritic branching or membrane arborization from the stellate nerve cells.

About 9 years after these results were obtained, the experiments of Greenough and Volkmar on small, medium, and large pyramidal neurons and on stellate neurons showed that enriched rats consistently had more higher-order dendritic branches than their impoverished littermates (31). In the pyramidal neurons, neurons whose cell bodies are shaped like pyramids, the branching differences occurred primarily in the basal dendrites, those extending from the base of the cell body (see Figure 19). Reportedly, these basal dendrites receive a rich input from nerve cells on the

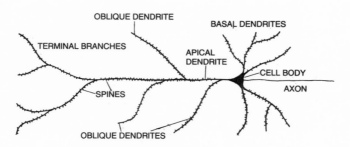

FIGURE 19. *Pyramidal nerve cell showing basal dendrites, an apical dendrite, and terminal branches, all with spines.*

same side of the cortex. That is, they do not primarily receive fibers from subcortical neurons or from nerve cells in the opposite cortex. It appears that they integrate information that has come into the same side of the cortex; this implies higher-order processing than would take place if the neurons were receiving information from subcortical areas, for example. No consistent differences in the length of branches were found either by Holloway or by Greenough and Volkmar.

The experiments of Holloway and of Greenough and Volkmar were carried out on neurons from the occipital cortices of young animals. It is possible that other regions of the cortex also change. In an attempt to find out, pyramidal cell dendrites were quantified in layers II and IV in the frontal cortex and layers IV and V in the temporal cortex (31). These investigators performed quite an elaborate analysis of the dendritic patterns. Their method was designed to give an accurate account of the number and length of dendritic branches and their location with respect to the cell body. Their type of analysis was reportedly more sensitive to the differences in higher-order dendrites than any previously used in the quantification of dendrites in the occipital cortex. The investigators found no systematic pattern of differences in dendrites from the frontal cortex between the enriched and the impoverished animals. However, in the temporal cortex, the effects of the two environmental conditions were clearly apparent in the higher-order branching of the basal dendrites. The enriched animals had significantly more basal branches on neurons in layer IV than their impoverished littermates. But the cells in layer V of the temporal cortex apparently had more basal branches in both the enriched and impoverished than in the standard colony group. The reason for this difference is not clear.

The investigations of dendritic patterns suggest that another factor to be considered in measuring dendritic branching is the variation of pattern between litters (31). These investigators found significant differences between litters in both the frontal and temporal cortices. Yet other investigators have noted the consistency of dendritic length between strains. It seems incongruous that litter patterns would vary yet strain patterns do not. Variations in dendritic responses were shown in the frontal and temporal cortical results. The fact that not all dendrites in the cortex respond equally to these experiential environmental conditions leads one to believe that the responses are specific to certain neuronal input patterns and not generally due to hormonal or nutritional factors, an observation made by Walsh as well (32).

If the dendrites could change in the young animals, we wished to learn whether they could do the same in the adult rats. A collaborative effort between our laboratories and those of Uylings et al. (33) was begun in the mid 1970s to study adult animals, 112 to 142 days of age. The results revealed that the basal dendrites in pyramidal neurons in layers II and III of the enriched and standard colony rats showed lengthening in the terminal segments of the dendrites as well as an increase in the branching relative to the baseline animals at 112 days of age. The first-, second-, and third-order terminal segments all increased in length significantly in the enriched animals compared with the standard colony animals. These findings strongly indicate that the new branches were mostly formed at a considerable distance from the tips of the terminal segments. Nonetheless, here was evidence that the dendritic structure of 142-day-old adult rats could be changed by enriched conditions.

Next we examined older animals. The dendritic measurements were made on the same 600- to 630-day-old enriched animals that had lived for 30 days with young rats (age 60 to 90 days), an experiment to be covered more thoroughly in Chapter 5 (34, 35). The only statistically significant difference in dendritic pattern between the enriched and standard colony 600- to 630-day-old group in this study emerged in the analysis of the sixth-order dendrites. The first branches off the nerve cell body are the first-order dendrites, the next branches are the second-order, and so on. The sixth-order dendrites were significantly longer in the 630-day-old enriched rats than in the 630-day-old standard colony rats ($p <$ 0.03). The mean length of the sixth-order segments from the enriched animals was 54 μm compared with a mean length of 29 μm for the sixth-order segments from the standard animals.

There are at least three possible explanations for the increased length observed in the enriched-environment animals: (1) a growth (elongation) of the sixth-order segments, (2) a retardation of the retraction process that occurs with age, and (3) a loss of segments which would result in greater internodal lengths and thereby artificially increase the remaining segment length. Neither the total number of terminal segments (34) nor the frequency of sixth-order segments (35) differed between the 630-day-old standard colony and enriched groups. Thus, it is unlikely that there was an artificial increase in length due to segment loss. Whether or not the increased length is due to a growth of the segment or a retardation of the retraction process cannot be clearly determined from these results. But recall that in the earlier study with Uylings et al., when a baseline group was available for comparison, the adult rat did show an increase due to enrichment and not just a maintenance of a status quo in dendritic length. Undoubtedly, for a final conclusion to be validated, another experiment will have to be done with a baseline group for the older animals to see whether the dendrites actually grew or maintained their original length. But whichever way this particular question is answered, the present study extended the findings of greater dendritic lengths in conditions of environmental stimulation from adult rats to middle-aged rats. It appears that the effect of the external environment on dendrites is still as important a consideration for the middle-aged rat as for the younger, adult one. It is possible that a longer exposure of the middle-aged animals to an enriched condition would result in a dendritic length change more similar to that observed in the adult animals.

Comparing our results on 630-day-old rats with those that Uylings et al. (33) had obtained in 142-day-old animals, we find that the lengths of segments of each order were markedly shorter in our study. Although our investigation used a different strain of rats, the differences in segment lengths were more apt to be due to the retraction of the dendritic length that occurred with age. Our belief that different strains of rats do not have measurable differences in dendritic lengths is supported by the similarity in dendritic lengths reported by Uylings et al. (33) and Lindsay and Scheibel (36).

Rats are not the only animals that experience brain changes in response to environmental conditions. Other species of rodents—mice and gerbils, for example—have shown occipital cortical weight and thickness changes as a consequence of exposure to various living conditions. Furthermore, the results from studies on monkeys have indicated that after 6 months of differential rearing, cells in the cerebellum, a more primitive hindbrain structure, also display differences (37). More specifically, the Purkinje cells in the archicerebellum, or old, vestibular cerebellum, displayed more extensive spiny branchlets in the enriched than in the nonenriched monkeys. The dendritic branchings from the smaller, excitatory granule cells of the cerebellum were not measurably affected. Perhaps of even greater interest, is the finding of changes in the old cerebellum, the nodulus and the paraflocculus. If one were to predict significant responses in a region such as the cerebellum, one might especially anticipate modifications in the neocerebellum, because of its rich associations with the cerebral cortex or neocortex, which have been shown to respond so readily to the enriched condition.

DENDRITIC SPINES. If the experiential environment can change the dendritic structure, it should be able also to modify the dendritic spines, the little appendages along the shafts of the dendrites. Spines were first described by Ramón y Cajal (38), who showed that they come in a variety of shapes. The classical spine structure with a thin stalk and a bulbous terminal ending showed a remarkable constancy in size (39). Ramón y Cajal suggested that the spines served to increase the receptive area of the dendrite. More recently, in the late 1970s, several workers reported that 85% of the synapses on the dendrites are found on the spines (40, 41). There can be as many as five or six synapses on a single spine, indicating that information could be integrated by a tremendous amount within the spine before being passed on to the dendrite shaft.

The density of spines over a given length of dendritic surface can vary widely. Many investigators have illustrated that changes in the density can occur under several conditions; for example, with prenatal ionizing radiation (42), undernutrition (43), or alterations in the amount of light entering the eye (44, 45, 46, 47, 48). But we were mainly interested in reports of changes in spine density associated with variation in the complexity of the environment (48, 49, 50) and with the age of the animals (51, 52). In order to study spines, a collaborative effort between the Berkeley laboratories and the University of California at Irvine (49) was established. Spine density was measured on pyramidal cells in the occipital cortex of male S_1 rats. Four replication experiments were designed to show the effects of 30 days (between 25 and 55 days of age) of differential experience between enriched and impoverished conditions on pyramidal cell spines in 40 littermate pairs. The spines were counted using the rapid Golgi method, which clearly demonstrates their structure. Also the lateral width of the basal dendrites was measured. The soma of the pyramidal cells being measured were in cortical layers IV and V.

The results of the counts showed that the density of spines on the basal dendrites was 10% greater ($p < 0.01$) in the enriched than in the impoverished rats (see Figure 19). The oblique dendrites, which arise from the apical dendrite, and terminal dendrites showed barely significant spine changes in favor of the enriched over the impoverished (4% and 3%, respectively, $p < 0.05$). No significant environmental effects were measured in spine densities on the apical dendrites.

These were the first results to indicate dendritic spine changes in response to stimulating experiential environments, but unfortunately, we made no attempt to differentiate between types of spines; all visible spines were counted. Later we were interested in quantifying types of spines, because of their different aging patterns, but the emphasis was on the effects not of enrichment but of impoverishment. For these studies, Connor counted two types of dendritic spines in three different age groups (53). First, spines were counted on dendrites from animals living in standard colony conditions from age groups of 90, 400, and 630 days. Spines with a "lollipop" configuration (a long stalk with a bulbous ending) decreased from 90 days to 400 days of age and then increased in density until 630 days of age. On the other hand, spines with a "nubbin" configuration (short, stubby, as wide at the top as at the bottom) were lowest in number in standard colony rats at 90 days of age and increased in density at every age period to a high at 630 days, the last age measured. Evidently, the two populations of spines have different aging patterns in the standard colony animal.

Next, Connor counted the two types of spines on dendrites from impoverished animals. The most consistent finding was a greater density of nubbin spines on all dendritic segments (oblique, apical, and basal) (see Figure 19) from the impoverished rats than from standard colony rats. Since both the impoverished environment and the standard colony aging process increased the number of the nubbin spines, it seems that this configuration might represent a degenerating spine or a spine remnant. Such an idea was proposed by Mervis (54) in his study of spines in the aging dog brain, where he found that the nubbin-type spine increased with age.

The lack of a long, thin stalk and a bulbous expansion that is characteristic of the nubbin spine could cause a significant reduction in the integration of afferent information passing into a given dendritic tree. It has been suggested that lollipop spines function to attenuate the post-synaptic potential, since the impulse would have to pass through the thin stalk to reach the main dendritic shaft (55). In addition, the thin stalk of the lollipop spine would effectively isolate the postsynaptic site from potential changes in the dendritic shaft (56). However, the exact significance of the nubbin-type spine is not apparent. Whether this type of spine is an actively degenerating spine, a spine remnant, or an immature spine (signifying an area of increased synaptic turnover) remains to be determined. But the fact remains that it is present more frequently in the aged and impoverished rat brain and consequently signifies some association with reduced stimulation of the nerve cells.

Besides measuring the effects of impoverished conditions and aging on the relative density of nubbin- and lollipop-type spines, Connor set out to determine whether spine density or type varied between superficial and deep layers of the cortex in impoverished animals. The fluctuations found in the density of spine types between neurons from different cortical layers suggest the need for treating the data from the various layers separately. For example, oblique dendrites in layer II had a greater density of nubbin-type spines on neurons from the impoverished animals than on those from the standard colony animals but this finding did not hold in layer III. In other words, a reverse pattern existed between layers II and III. The same discrepancy occurred for the basal segments in layers II and III. It is possible that if the results from layers II and III had not been treated separately, the results would have canceled each other.

The importance of comparing the effects of environmental input separately for the different cortical layers was also evident in layers Va and Vb, where a distinction in the response pattern between the standard colony and the impoverished animals was observed. Neurons in layer Vb from isolated rats had more lollipop-type spines on oblique segments than those of standard colony rats. This finding, coupled with similar data on dendritic branching (57), indicated an increase in the receptive area of neurons in layer Vb from impoverished rats compared with the standard colony rats. The same finding was not true in layer Va. Lorente de No (58) observed that axons from layer Va remained in the cortex, whereas axons from layer Vb left the cortex. From this information, one can speculate that the isolated rats can exhibit only a direct input-output type of behavior, whereas the standard colony rats can integrate the information entering their cortex before producing an output. In other words, in the standard colony rats more neuronal connections are involved before the neuronal output takes place.

With the exception of the above example, the lollipop-type of spine was remarkably constant on the dendrites from neurons from rats exposed to the two experimental conditions, the standard colony and the impoverished. This type of spine was much more prevalent than the nubbin-type on all dendritic segments in all layers of the occipital cortex.

To indicate the reliability of the spine counts (i.e., the total spine density per micron of dendrite), our study was compared with the only other quantitative spine study in old rats, that of Feldman and Dowd (52). The results indicated an almost exact agreement for basal (0.5 vs. 0.56) and oblique (0.07 vs. 0.76) dendritic spine densities. The apical shaft spine density per micron for our study (0.77) was well within 1 standard deviation of the apical shaft spine density of 0.92 reported by Feldman and Dowd. It is amazing how consistent spine counts can be when taken in separate laboratories across the country. This consistency offers a great reassurance for quantitative morphological studies of this type.

If spines can be changed in their morphological configuration after 30 days of environmental alterations, one wonders in how short a period does a spine change its dimensions. Van Harreveld and Fifkova (59) shed some light by comparing spines on the same dendrites of hippocampal granule cells after some had been stimulated and others had not. Two minutes after 30 seconds of stimulation, noticeable spine enlargements were demonstrated. These investigators suggest that the swelling was caused by a release of glutamate from the intracellular compartment into the extracellular space, which caused an uptake of water and electrolytes. If such increases were maintained long enough for protein synthesis to occur, this process might possibly explain spine growth as a result of experience. On the other hand, what happens when the spine is not stimulated or is deprived? The spine might be completely reabsorbed into the membrane of the dendritic shaft, or the molecular configuration of the membrane may become permanently changed at the position of reabsorption. If the latter is the case, then regrowth of spines may more readily occur at a previous site.

Thus, it is clear that dendritic branches are altered as predicted by Cajal in 1895 and by us from our results in 1964. The dendritic branching patterns of stellate cells in the occipital cortex were different between the enriched and impoverished animals. In our studies of the effects of enrichment on dendrite branching in pyramidal cells from the occipital cortex (area 18), we found increases in the number of middle branches—primarily third- and fourth-order branches—of basal dendrites in young and adult rats; and in older rats we found increases in the length of the terminal branches.

Dendritic spine counts showed that on the basal dendrites of pyramidal cells from young enriched rats there were significantly more spines than on dendrites of the nonenriched. Although similar differences were also seen on oblique and terminal dendrites, they were not as great. Types of spines were not counted separately in the young animal brains, but they were on the older ones, and in these it was the "nubbin" types, those with a base as broad as the head, that were more prevalent in the impoverished animals than in the standard colony animals. The "lollipop" types, with a thin stalk and large head, were more frequent in the older enriched animals. The evidence is clear that down to the level of the spines, the nerve cell shows great structural adaptability to its environment at any age studied this far, at least two-thirds of the way through the lifetime of a laboratory rat.

While teaching a group of 13- to 15-year-old youngsters in Shanghai about our work on the brain, I called on one poised young lady who stood up and asked the following question: "If most of our creative work is done before 40 and yet wisdom does not come until after 60, how do we explain this with regard to nerve cells?" Obviously, I had no real answer, but I immediately drew on the knowledge from our data. If I were forced to speculate, I would say that results from enriched-impoverished experiments tell us that it is the third- and fourth-order dendrites which increase in dimensions in the young rats. These are closer to the cell body and have a more limited expanse than the terminal dendrites and therefore may be dealing with more focused-creative activity. In the old rats, it is the terminal dendrites which show increases in length; they are broadly spaced and reach out widely. With such a massive extension, they sample more diffusely, making broad comparisons, and thus, allow for wiser judgment. The specific functions of the various levels of dendritic branches are not known at present; only further work will indicate whether there is a grain of truth in my speculation.

SYNAPSES. Since we had shown that both dendrites and spines change in response to environmental conditions and since both are sites of synaptic action, our next step was to study the effect of the environment on the dimensions of the synapse. It had been suggested that permanent changes occur in synapses as a result of stimulation and that these changes play some part in learning and memory (60). As we did in our earlier work when we were identifying ovarian hormonal effects on the synapse, we again chose to measure the length and number of postsynaptic thickenings, those structures which consist of a highly organized proteinaceous material immediately beneath the postsynaptic membrane.

Since we were ready to take a step in the direction of synaptic measurements when a medical doctor Møllgaard came to join our laboratory from the University of Copenhagen in Denmark, it seemed a reasonable project to offer to him. For the electron-microscopic study of synapses, we separated 12 newly weaned littermate pairs of 25-day-old male rats from the S_1 strain, placing one rat from each pair in the enriched condition and its littermate in the impoverished conditions. The rats were kept in the respective conditions until they were 55 days of age. Through all the anatomical procedures that followed, from sacrifice to completion of the measurement of synapses, the rats were studied as pairs. We sampled synapses in layer III of area 18 in the occipital cortex (61).

Measurements were made on the asymmetrical axodendritic synapses described by Colonnier (62). The great majority of dendritic spines are associated with asymmetrical synapses. The asymmetry of this type of synapse is characterized by the presence of postsynaptic densities of variable thickness that border on the postsynaptic membrane but not on the presynaptic membrane. Møllgaard measured only those junctions which reached an acceptable criterion of clarity in the photomicrographs. Curved thickenings were divided into smaller parts and the sum of the parts was taken. In some cases a large synapse had one or more discontinuities in the postsynaptic thickening; if the vesicles were uniformly distributed on the presynaptic side, the thickening was measured as one synapse in spite of the discontinuities. Serial sections and reconstructions have shown that such perforations are normally present in larger synapses (63). More recently, Greenough et al. (64) and Medosch and Diamond (65) reported that these discontinuous postsynaptic thickenings may represent more mature synapses, as discussed earlier. All of the synaptic measurements were done on coded prints so that the criteria of selection of synapses did not vary between the experimental groups.

In all, 2211 synapses were identified and measured, 1405 from the impoverished rats and 806 from the enriched animals. The number of synapses per print was 35% smaller for the enriched rats than for the impoverished in every pair. Though the enriched rats showed fewer asymmetrical synapses than the impoverished, the enriched synapses on the average were larger. After a cumulative frequency distribution of synaptic lengths was plotted for all enriched and impoverished rats, it was obvious tht the enriched rats had significantly fewer small synapses than the impoverished.

The total area of enriched and impoverished synapses was calculated, on the basis of measured cross-section diameters and numbers of junctions; that is, we assumed that the junctions were roughly circular. We calculated the area for each size of cross section, and then multiplied by the number of cross sections per size. From these calculations, it appeared that the total area of the synaptic thickenings in the enriched exceeded that in the impoverished by 40%.

There was a 4.0% difference ($p < 0.05$) in cortical thickness between the enriched and impoverished rats in this experiment, which was close to the 5% mean found in four previous experiments on rats that had lived in their conditions in the period from 25 days to 55 days. A high positive correlation (0.79, $p < 0.001$) was found between cortical thickness differences and synaptic length differences. The correlation was not significant between the differences in cortical thickness and the number of synapses.

Scientists have long speculated that long-term memory might involve changes in synaptic size and number. Almost as soon as the neuron doctrine was enunciated near the end of the nineteenth century, Tanzi (66) speculated that learning might involve the growth of new neuronal terminals, and Ramon y Cajal (67) supported this hypothesis. Hebb (68) postulated that learning might occur through formation of new synaptic connections. The opposite possibility, that learning involves selective *elimination* of neurons or synaptic connections or both, has received less attention, although Ramon y Cajal (69) felt that in embryological development there was a random selection among connections. In 1971 Dawkins (70) suggested that the relatively high continual rate of death of neurons did not occur at random but might be a mechanism of memory storage leaving those connections activated during memory consolidation. Other investigations (71) have considered whether learning and memory involve "growth just of bigger and better synapses that are already there, not of growth of new connections" (71). There were also those who doubted whether learning and memory involve any morphological changes; perhaps there are "only changes in physiological resistance and conductance . . . or various endogenous properties of neurons and glia" (72).

Our data demonstrated the presence of bigger synaptic junctions in the enriched than in the impoverished rats. The question which commonly arises in response to such findings is, Are bigger junctions more effective? It has been reported that the intensity of postsynaptic current increased with the local concentration of transmitter molecules and of available receptor molecules (73). If one hypothesizes that the amount of neurotransmitter liberated from the presynaptic terminal is proportional to the amount of membrane in which the receptors are localized, then the effectiveness of the synapse would increase as the size of the postsynaptic membrane increased. All of the morphological data collected on the enriched and impoverished rats support this hypothesis, as do the maze-testing data, which show that the enriched rats are better learners in many problem-solving situations.

Having found that the differences in synaptic measurements between the enriched and impoverished rats were very clear-cut, we had to ask ourselves, Was the difference in synaptic length mainly due to enrichment or impoverishment? In order to answer this question, another set of experiments (74) was designed to include not only the enriched and impoverished rats but the standard colony as well. We performed both initial and replication experiments, using littermate S_1 male rats that had lived in their conditions between 25 and 55 days of age, to replicate the setup of the original experiment we had done with Møllgaard. Measurements of the length of postsynaptic thickenings were taken from asymmetrical axodendritic synapses in layer IV of the dorsal medial occipital cortex (area 18). It should be noted that in the Møllgaard experiment it was synapses from layer III that were measured. After the publication of the results of the Møllgaard experiment (61), West and Greenough (75) reported that the enriched animal's synapses were longer by 10% in layer IV in cortices from four enriched-impoverished pairs. Since we were having some difficulty in replicating the large synaptic changes reported in

Møllgaard's results in layer III, we decided to increase the size of the sample used by West and Greenough and study layer IV synapses in our new experiment, as well as to include rats from the standard colony condition.

In the new experiment, we compared 675 synapses from enriched animals, 618 synapses from standard colony animals, and 680 synapses from the impoverished rats. We found an 8% difference ($p < 0.001$) in postsynaptic thickening length between the enriched and the impoverished rats that was primarily due to the effects of the impoverished condition. The number of synapses per unit area of neuropil was 15% more ($p < 0.01$) in the impoverished than in the enriched, and this difference was primarily due to impoverishment. The synapses in the impoverished brains were more in number but smaller—in essence a result similar to that found in the Møllgaard experiment but with a different emphasis where he noted fewer but larger synapses in the enriched compared to the impoverished.

A 7% ($p < 0.01$) cortical depth difference in area 18 was found between the enriched and impoverished animals used for synaptic measures; we could attribute it to either condition by comparing each with the standard colony rats. The effect of enrichment was about 4% ($p < 0.01$) and that of impoverishment about 2% (NS); but if the rats were older when entering their respective conditions, staying in them between the ages of 60 and 90 days, the effect of enrichment in area 18 was about 6% ($p < 0.001$) and that of impoverishment about 1%. The impact of enrichment is greater in the occipital cortex if the animals are older when placed in the enriched environment, while the effects of impoverishment are more significant earlier in life.

Thus, differential environmental experiences do significantly affect cortical thickness and synaptic length and number in the age groups measured in these experiments. In the Møllgaard experiment dealing with synaptic measurements, the differences between enriched and impoverished conditions were much greater than those found in our later experiments. In the Møllgaard experiment, layer III synapses were quantified, and in the more recent experiment it was the synapses in layer IV which were measured. In an earlier section, it was mentioned that the greatest differences in neuron dimensions between experimental groups were in the uppermost layers of the cortex. Is it possible that such large differences in synaptic dimensions as seen in the Møllgaard experiment were actually due to the presence of larger neurons found in layer III than those reported by West and Greenough and by us in layer IV? In the Møllgaard report, more synapses per picture were found in the impoverished rats than in the enriched ones. This finding was also encountered in the present investigation in layer IV, offering confirmation of some of the measures. Yet, Cummins (76), working with mice, has found a greater number of synapses in the enriched than in the impoverished. When we learned this, we asked to share photographs and compare measuring techniques and synapse identification criteria between our two laboratories. We could find no differences between our techniques, only in our results.

Aghajanian and Bloom (unpublished data), in a collaborative experiment with us in the late 1960s, found no synaptic changes in layer I between enriched and impoverished rats. We were not surprised by these findings, because layer I had not previously shown thickness changes in response to our environmental conditions. However, in 1972 West and Greenough showed synapses with greater lengths in layer I in enriched rats—thus adding ambiguities to these studies.

Like much of our work, our study of synapses requires additional data; ideally, we should compare synapses in all layers of the cortex, including layer I, in the same brains from animals exposed to these differential environments. Clearly, synapses are structurally modified by these environments, but we need much clearer and more detailed information on *how* they are modified before we can draw definitive conclusions. No one expected that the measurement of synapse numbers and dimensions would be simple—at least with regard to subtle environmental alterations. Severe environmental insults—such as reduction of visual input to the visual cortex—have been much easier to quantify. Synapses evidently change constantly, and to pick up the fine changes takes great patience and skill. With modern techniques using computer-integrated measuring devices, we should obtain better results in the future.

Other Brain Structures

Over the years, as we learned how readily the cerebral cortex responds to our external environmental paradigm, we wondered what other brain structures were similarly affected. Such structures as the corpus callosum, entorhinal cortex, hippocampus, amygdala, lateral geniculate body and cerebellum were examined in animals exposed to differential experiences.

Except for one area, lateral 10, of the frontal cortex, the increase in cortical thickness in our experiments was essentially the same in both hemispheres. Since the two sides were affected equally, we anticipated finding that enrichment causes an enlargement of the corpus callosum, the large fiber tract connecting the right and left cerebral cortices.

Though the tract has not been measured directly in our laboratory, there was one experiment that might indicate an increase in either size or number of callosal fibers or both. In the late 1960s, Leon Dorosz (77) set out to determine whether a transcallosal electrically induced response in the enriched cortex was different from that in the impoverished cortex. In his first experiment, he implanted electrodes directly into the cortices of the enriched and impoverished rats to record chronic activity at various times, only to learn that within a few days the enriched rats had chewed out each other's implants. (Group living and this kind of surgical intervention were not compatible.) He then performed acute preparations in which stimulation and recording were carried out directly from the brains just prior to the termination of the experiment. On one side of the cortex, he used a stimulating electrode, and on the other, he picked up the transcallosal response with a recording electrode. With this technique, he was able to demonstrate a significantly larger peak-to-peak amplitude in the occipital cortex from the enriched than from the impoverished rats after they had been living in their respective conditions for 80 days.

These results can be interpreted in one or both of the following ways: (1) the larger signals Dorosz was picking up resulted from the increased cellular dimensions in the occipital cortex, or (2) the fibers in the corpus callosum had increased in size or number. That they were due to an increase in callosal functioning, as suggested by Dorosz, was later substantiated by the work of Walsh et al. (78), which actually demonstrated a thicker callosum in the enriched rats than in the impoverished rats. Walsh et al. found that in the frontal region, but not the occipital, the lateral but not the medial, callosum was 14% thicker ($p < 0.01$) following environmental enrichment. With the hundreds of prepared tissues from rat brains in our experiments, this is one investigation we could easily duplicate.

All of our previous studies on enriched and impoverished environments have dealt only with the cerebral cortex and some of its related fiber tracts. But this does not mean that we have not tried to find morphological changes in response to the environment in other regions of the rat brain. None of the fifteen other areas of the brain which were sampled but the corebellum gave a significant indication of a specific localization of an enrichment effect as measured by tissue weight or acetylcholinesterase.

Nonetheless, we continued to look for anatomical changes due to altered environments in various regions of the forebrain, because there was a chance that small alterations might be evident that were not noted with previous wet weight or chemical measures. It seemed likely that other regions known to be involved in learning and memory should show differences, and so we obtained morphological measures for the entorhinal cortex and hippocampus as well as other forebrain regions, including the amygdala and the lateral geniculate body, the first three regions having been discussed previously with regard to growth patterns in Chapter 2.

Our attention was drawn in particular to the entorhinal cortex and the hippocampus because of their role in learning and memory. It was clear that the enriched condition facilitated learning in some way (for instance, the enriched animals were better maze learners), and so we expected that we might find some changes in these two forebrain areas. (See Figure 2 for identification of the areas and the manner in which their dimensions were determined.) We learned that the male entorhinal cortex exhibited a definite increase in thickness in response to the enriched conditions for two age groups, 60 to 64 and 60 to 90 days. However, in measuring the hippocampus on the same tissues used for both occipital and entorhinal cortical measurements, the environmental conditions did not significantly change the thickness of the hippocampus, for either the 4 or 30 day duration. In fact, totaling the results of our hippocampal thickness measures on as many as 231 pairs of male rats from enriched and nonenriched conditions, at no time were the differences significant. Since the entorhinal cortex showed changes in response to the environment and because it sends a major fiber tract into the hippocampus, we are still puzzled why changes of the magnitude found in the former did not create some measurable changes in the latter. We thought, perhaps, our measurements were not sensitive enough to detect the small changes in the hippocampus.

However, other investigators have noted some alterations by confining their measures to only the granular cell layer in the female hippocampal complex (79). They did find the anticipated increases resulting from the enriched environmental conditions, but only in the females. We looked for thickness differences in this layer in our oldest rats, the 904-day-old male rats, which are losing their asymmetry patterns to become more like the female pattern. Still we found no significant differences between male enriched and nonenriched rats.

These data suggest that there is a sex difference in the response of the hippocampal complex following differential experience. Since we do have brain sections from female rats exposed to either enriched or impoverished environments, we can measure the hippocampal complex in these brains to learn if our results concur with those of Juraska et al.

By providing greater detail on the changes in the male entorhinal cortex, we can see just how responsive it is in contrast to the male hippocampus. In our experiments S_1 males were maintained in enriched, standard colony, or impoverished conditions either between the ages of 60 and 64 or between 60 and 90 days of age. The entorhinal cortex showed a thickness 3% ($p < 0.01$) greater in the enriched rats than in the standard colony rats in as short a period as 4 days. The increase in thickness that occurred in this short period was of the same order of magnitude as the change that appeared during the 30-day period between 60 and 90 days of age. The entorhinal cortical change at 60 to 90 days was slightly less at 4% than the increase in thickness found in the medial occipital cortex at 5%. These results proved that the entorhinal cortex could show a definite structural change in response to our environmental conditions. Since the entorhinal cortex is known to be part of a memory pathway, this finding offers encouragement about the possibilities of improving one's memory through enriched conditions.

Scoville and Milner reported that the entorhinal cortex is related to memory in human beings and also stressed the importance of the anterior hippocampus and the hippocampal gyrus, which includes the entorhinal cortex, in retention of new experience (80). They claimed that if the medial temporal lobe was bilaterally removed in man, and if the removal of tissue extended far enough in the posterior direction to damage portions of the anterior hippocampus and hippocampal gyrus, a persistent impairment of recent memory would result. Stepien et al. (81) reported that monkeys that had undergone bilateral ablation of the hippocampus and hippocampal gyrus displayed a recent memory deficit in vision and auditory tests. These findings are supported by Drachman and Ammanya (82), who reported impairment in new-pattern discrimination in monkeys with lesions of the hippocampus and hippocampal gyrus. In the famous H. M. case so thoroughly studied by B. Milner in Montreal, bilateral removal of the temporal lobe caused him to lose recent memory permanently. And a study of eighty-five human brains from people with Alzheimer's disease, where clinical manifestations of recent-memory deficits are marked, revealed neurofibrillary degeneration within the neurons of the lateral entorhinal portion of the hippocampal gyrus, as well as in an area of the hippocampus (83). All of these reports made it seem imperative to understand the effects of an enriched or impoverished environment on the separate parts of the hippocampal complex.

In light of the close proximity of the amygdaloid nucleus to the hippocampus and entorhinal cortex in the temporal lobe, we continued our pursuit and examined the effects of our varied environments on this nucleus (84). We undertook this study even though we knew that bilateral excision of the tip of the temporal lobe, which includes the amygdala (another term for the amygdaloid nucleus) but not the hippocampus and entorhinal cortex, did not harm memory function in any way, indicating that the amygdala is not primarily concerned with memory processing. Nonetheless, the amygdala has been associated with both active and passive avoidance learning (85). In addition, because it is known to mediate arousal, we thought that it might vary among our environmental groups since animals must be aroused to interact with their environment.

Studies have shown the amygdala to be associated with territorial behavior. Furtermore, Sherman et al. (86) and Webster (87) reported that preferential processing of spatial information in the right cerebral hemisphere in rats may be important for territoriality. The finding that both the right amygdala and the right visual cortex were larger than the left, may signify an interaction between the two areas in integrating territorial behavior. Thus, like the hippocampus, another older part of the forebrain, the amygdala does not vary in its dimensions as a consequence of changes in our environmental conditions, whereas the cerebral cortex readily does. A more plastic visual cortex could provide more variety in territorial behavior, while the amygdala's role is more stable.

In continuing our search for subcortical changes, we studied the lateral geniculate body within the visual pathway (88). This study was done on very young animals—28 days of age—that had lived either in a multifamily enriched condition (3 mothers with 3 pups each) or in a unifamily impoverished condition (1 mother with 3 pups) for 22 days. (The other subcortical measures were performed on animals at least 55 days of age.) Like the cerebral cortex in these young rats, the lateral geniculate body manifested a significant response to the environmental conditions: 20% fewer neurons per unit area in the multifamily enriched rats than in the unifamily impoverished rats ($p < 0.01$). These results indicated that the neuropil, or fibers between the neurons, had increased in either size or number to "push" the soma or cell bodies, of the neurons farther apart. Here, then, was one subcortical structure that showed measurable variation with the degree of enrichment in the environment. However, because the lateral geniculate was measured in animals who had not yet been weaned and the other subcortical areas—the hippocampus and amygdala—were examined in animals who had been weaned, it is possible that the plasticity of subcortical regions depends upon age, declining as the animal ages.

In our attempt to localize more precisely the regions in the rat brain which were responding to the enriched condition, we mentioned earlier in this chapter that the cerebellum of rats in that condition did increase in weight. As Walsh mentioned (89), on theoretical grounds the cerebellum might be expected to play a role in response to enriched environments because studies have pointed to the necessity of active self-guided exploration and kinesthetic feedback for learning to take place (90). The cerebellum plays an important role in maintaining the position of the body in space, providing a rationale for the above behavioral patterns.

Active interaction with the toys was essential for the enrichment effect to occur in the cerebral cortex in our rats (91, 92). The animals climb, explore and balance on the ladders and wheels—all activities requiring cerebellar control. On the basis of what is known about the connections between the cerebral cortex and the cerebellar cortex, again one might predict cerebellar responses to the enriched condition. Floeter and Greenough (7) did find changes in the more primitive parts of the young cerebellum in enriched animals compared with the nonenriched. Between the overall cerebellar weight changes of Rosenzweig et al. (93) and these specific regional alterations reported by Floeter and Greenough, one is led to believe that even a hindbrain structure such as the cerebellum could show plasticity in young adult rats.

But we have the opportunity to study the cerebellum of the very old rats (904 days old) to determine whether an environmental response can be measured. The number of Purkinje cells and the thickness of the outer molecular layer, which is made up primarily of the dendrites from the Purkinje cells, are being measured in these old animals. Any proof that plasticity can exist in the aged cerebellum will be most comforting news to elderly people who are developing problems in balancing and coordination. Therapies designed to stimulate cerebellar function could be rationally encouraged.

Asymmetry

In our first enriched-impoverished morphological experiment carried out in 1964, on animals from the S_1 strain that had lived for 80 days in their conditions (from 25 to 105 days of age), we found that both hemispheres were affected equally by the environmental conditions (94). But having shown in our developmental studies that in the male Long-Evans rat the right hemisphere was significantly larger than the left in many areas, we wondered whether one hemisphere would be affected more than the other if we changed the age of the rats and the period of exposure to their respective environments. We carried out right-left comparisons on several groups of animals of the S_1 strain from which we had other enrichment data, including additional rats from the 25- to 105-day groups. The ages in days at commencement and termination of exposure to the environmental conditions were as follows: 25 and 55; 25 and 105; 60 and 64; and 60 and 90. A total of 267 rats from these various age groups were studied for these right-left comparisons.

Analyzing these data from the S_1 strain of rats for these left-right studies was useful in confirming other factors which had been found separately from combined right-left data. The statistically significant differences among the three conditions (enriched, standard, and impoverished) were confirmed for all regions measured. There was a statistically significant change in cortical thickness with age in all areas; from youngest to oldest, we found a general decrease in thickness, as was noted in Chapter 2 in connection with the development and aging study using the Long-Evans strain.

We learned that even with exposure to the different experimental conditions and for different periods of time, both hemispheres were still affected equally except for area 10 in the frontal cortex. Area 10, according to Krieg (95), is an association cortex; but according to Paxinos (96), it is also a motor cortex related to movement. We found that in medial area 10, the difference between the right hemispheres in the enriched and standard animals did not achieve statistical significance, although the right hemisphere differences between animals living in the standard and impoverished conditions did. It was the impoverished condition which decreased medial area 10 in the right hemisphere of these male rats. If one accepts the report of Paxinos, that the frontal cortex governs motor function then it is possible that without physical activity, as the rat lives in an impoverished condition, the right hemisphere decreases in dimensions. (It would be of interest to test whether the impoverished rats had changed a paw preference compared to the standard colony animals.) However, for the remainder of the cortex, one can conclude, in general, that with the multisensory environment provided by our type of enrichment, the hemispheres in the S_1 strain of rats are apparently affected equally.

These results do not lend support to Denenberg's report (97) on the effect of infantile stimulation and environment on brain lateralization in rats. He stated that the right brain was the repository for the interaction between environmental enrichment and handling in open-field activity. He concluded that lateralization of behavior occurred, and the effects of early experiences were asymmetrically distributed in the rat's brain. It is possible that lateralization of specific kinds of behavior occurs, but that the neuronal protein changes which record an activity in the brain involve neuronal interplay between both hemispheres.

The results with the S_1 strain of male rats supported our previous findings with the Long-Evans strain showing that the right hemisphere was thicker than the left in the majority of comparisons. In the male S_1 rat, the right hemisphere was on the average thicker than the left in all areas except 18, where the left was thicker than the right, and area 2, where the hemispheres were equal. In areas medial 10, 4, 18, 17, 18a, and 39, the hemispheric differences were statistically significant. A particularly striking aspect of our findings was that the effects were seen in a large sample rather than only among a few individual animals.

In our studies we have been particularly interested in area 18 of the cerebral cortex, because this area is most frequently affected by the enriched condition. In our shortest duration of exposure to enrichment, from 60 to 64 days of age, it was area 18 which showed the only significant increase in cortical thickness over standard colony littermates. In addition, for all long durations in the environmental conditions, area 18 always showed a significant change, whereas other areas were not so consistent. As we search for a meaning to the susceptibility of this area to the environment, we noted that area 18 in the left hemisphere of the S_1 strain always showed a tendency to be thicker than in the right irrespective of the environmental conditions. This area is known to be a visual association area, but many subcortical regions project to this area. Examining our most recent data from crowded-enriched Long-Evans rats (36 enriched rats rather than 12), we find that area 18 shows an even greater difference in favor of the left hemisphere than is seen in the standard colony rats.

This latter fact becomes useful as we try to gain some understanding of the meaning of asymmetry by following only one area in rats that come from one strain but from different housing conditions. If we examine the male Long-Evans rats that have been raised in the Berkeley colony for over 50 years, we find very marked right-greater-than-left differences in area 18. If we look at right-left differences in Long-Evans rats from our local distributor, where the housing conditions are not identical to those at Berkeley, we find that area 18 in the left cortex is thicker than in the right. If we enrich these Long-Evans rats from the local distributor, we find that area 18 begins to show significant left-greater-than-right differences. But most important, if we now provide an environment that is both enriched and crowded, the left-greater-than-right asymmetry pattern in area 18 becomes very significant. These findings were present in both an initial and a replication experiment. It appears that asymmetry patterns are subject to change in response to conditions as nonspecific, yet pervasive, as housing density.

Skull Size

Now that we had clearly demonstrated that the cerebral cortex varies in size in response to environmental variations, we wondered whether the intracranial capacity increases to accommodate an increased brain mass. We conducted experiments to study the skull dimensions of rats living in the different environmental conditions. The animals were exposed to their respective conditions—enriched or impoverished—for 77 days, from the age of 25 days to the age of 102 days. Roentgenograms for the initial and replication experiments were taken 8 days after the animals entered their respective conditions and again 69 days later (98). For our measurements, we used the methods established by Asling and Frank (99). The landmarks employed for the skull measurements on the Roentgenograms are shown in Figure 20. The results showed that the intracranial capacities of the two groups did not differ significantly. Evidently the two diverse environments did not alter internal cranial dimensions.

As was pointed out in Chapter 2, the cortex of the Long-Evans male laboratory rat reaches a peak in development sometime between 26 and 41 days of age and then begins to decline. We have one experiment (100) comparing the cortical thickness measurements of a baseline group at 112 days of age with those of animals from the standard colony and from the enriched group at 142 days of age. In this experiment we learned that growth of both the cerebral cortex and the dendrites did exceed the baseline as a result of enrichment. Here was evidence that enrichment actually caused the young adult cortex to grow and did not merely slow down or arrest a decrease in size. We can deduce from these data that an increased brain mass does accumulate with enrichment and as a consequence more intracranial space might be necessary. But our intracranial measurements show something different. It has been my fantasy that with further enrichment during early adulthood, an increase in cortical dimensions might produce the first cortical fold in the rat to accommodate more mass in a limited space. Cats, dogs, monkeys, and man all have folded cortices. Brain growth had to exceed intracranial dimensions to produce folds. There is no evidence of folds in the rat cerebral cortex. We need to find out more about the formation of the cranial cavity by examining the time factors involved in the formation of the sutures as related to brain development.

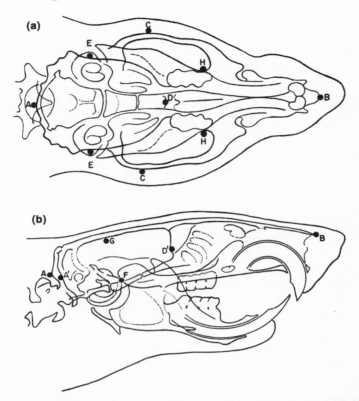

FIGURE 20. (a) Dorsal view of rat skull. (b) Lateral view of rat skull. Total skull length (A–B); maximum width (bizygomatic) (C–C); length of ventral neurocranium (A–D); external width of neurocranium (E–E); internal height of neurocranium (F–G); snout length (D–B); maxillary width (H–H); and lateral length of neurocranium (A'–D'). Neurocranium is that part of the skull which houses the brain.

According to Massler (101), the rat attains its maximum cranial width by 20 days of age, with the internasal and interfrontal sutures completed by 3 to 10 days and the sagittal suture completed by 20 days. The sutures of the calvarium, which are primarily responsible for cranial length, are completed by 40 days. From these data, it appears that the cranial size in our rats should have been well established approximately 15 days after the rats were put into the experimental conditions at 25 days of age.

However, Weidenreich (102) suggested that the problem cannot be solved merely on the basis of the conditions of the sutures. He pointed out that the brain and cranial cavity might enlarge even after the sutures were completely closed. He believed that it was possible for the cranium to grow by the *internal absorption of bone and the laying down of bone on the external surface.* Intracranial capacity might, thus, be able to increase in enriched young adult animals, which exhibit greater thickness and weight in the cerebral cortex. However, since no intracranial differences were found between the two experimental conditions, it appeared that either the slight growth of the brain could be accommodated by a decrease in the volume of cerebrospinal fluid between the meninges surrounding the brain, or the internal ventricles decreased in size, or the cranial cavity did enlarge but our methods were not sensitive enough to detect it.

Though the internal cranial dimensions were not measurably changed by the environmental conditions, the effects on the external skull dimensions were quite marked. The isolated animals had the larger external skulls. Even in as short a period as 8 days, there were two differences which were statistically significant at the 0.05 level: the width of the upper jaw (bimaxillary width) and the width of the cheek bones (bizygomatic width). After 77 days in the environmental conditions, both the bimaxillary and bizygomatic widths were greater in the isolated than in the enriched by as much as 10% ($p < 0.001$). However, these external skull dimensions simply reflected changes in body weight; not anything occurring within the brain was causing these changes. This fact was confirmed by the high correlations between body weights and facial bone measurements after both 8 and 77 days in the experimental conditions.

In other 80-day experiments (on rats that had lived in the experimental conditons between the ages of 25 and 105 days), the body weights of the impoverished animals were always greater than those of the enriched. It was only when the duration of the experiments was shortened to 30 days that the body weight differences disappeared. In this present experiment dealing with skull measurements, the impoverished animals were significantly greater in both body weight and size of the facial bones. Yet their intracranial dimensions were similar to those of the enriched rats.

An explanation for this regional difference in skull development is offered by Weidenreich (102), who reported a negative correlation between size of brain case and size of face: the larger the former, the smaller the latter, and vice versa. Since the jaw was the essential constituent of the face, he reported, a larger face implied the development of a large and strong masticatory apparatus. It is very possible that the isolated rats had little to do but chew on the cage as well as on their hard food pellets and, thus, developed a greater body weight with an accompanying larger jaw.

Not only were the facial bones of the isolated animals larger than those of the enriched rats, but the skulls of the isolated animals were heavier. The difference may have resulted from an overall increase in skeletal weight, which in turn may have accounted in part for the total body weight increase noted in the isolated animals. It is well known that restricted activity is a method used in agriculture to fatten animals, and obesity has been produced in laboratory animals by restriction methods (103). However, Donaldson (104) reported that isolated animals grow less well than those kept together. From our experiment, it is apparent that the isolated animal, in its smaller cage, becomes heavier in bone weight as well as in weight of soft tissues than the more active, enriched animal in the larger cage.

Our data indicate that the length of time the animals spend in their condition is important for the reliability of a study of body weight differences. Weight differences were considerably more marked in the initial experiment than in the replication. In the initial experiment the body weights of the two experimental groups diverged greatly after 8 days, whereas in the replication experiment the early separation did not take place. In an attempt to understand this apparent inconsistency between the data from the two experiments, body weights from two additional experiments were examined. In one, the body weight differences were obvious very early, and in the other, they were not. It appeared that no consistent large difference in weight existed in the early stages of the experiments, but that eventually each isolated group became significantly heavier than the corresponding enriched group.

Our skull measurements have indicated that the intracranial dimensions of enriched and impoverished young adult animals (25 to 102 days of age) are identical. When the animals are older (112 to 142 days), we have clear evidence from studying a baseline group that the cortex grows in response to an enriched environment. In our younger groups (e.g., those living in enriched or impoverished conditions between the ages of 25 and 105 days or 60 and 90 days), we do not have the baseline group for comparison. With the conditions we have studied at the present time, it can be said that though the intracranial cavity is stable in relation to environmental conditions, the cortex does have the capacity to increase in dimensions. Body weight is positively correlated with external skull dimensions but not with intracranial size.

5

ENRICHMENT AND IMPOVERISHMENT OVER THE LIFESPAN

The Prenatal Period

Because the brain is constantly changing through development and aging, environmental stimuli must have different effects throughout a lifespan. Now we had the opportunity to examine these effects based on the encouraging results obtained from our initial experiments. These findings in 1964, showing brain alterations after enriching or impoverishing the environment postnatally from 25–105 days of age, set the stage for the others to follow.

The first experiments established that many measurements taken on the cortex, from cortical thickness to glial cell number, neuronal cell size, and blood vessel dimensions, could change with experience during this particular time period. With our initial results in hand, we began to examine such factors as age, duration of exposure to different environmental conditions, and sex to determine the potential extent of brain plasticity under a wide variety of conditons.

To start with environmental influences during prenatal development, while the nervous system is actively forming, seemed a reasonable beginning. The concept of "intrauterine education" can be traced back many centuries. It is found in Chinese literature of over 2000 years ago. Today in Japan, women still practice *Taikyo,* a type of intrauterine enrichment which is believed to have a beneficial effect on the postnatal life of the yet unborn child (1). Our initial studies from the prenatal period have proved that it is possible to influence the structure of the cortex with environmental enrichment at this very young age.

We designed an experiment in the early 1970s to study the effects of enriched environments on the intrauterine development of our rats (2). Long-Evans rats used in this study were weaned at 21 days of age and then grouped three of like sex to single standard colony cages. At 60 days of age the animals of each sex were separated into enriched and impoverished conditions. At 90 days of age, males and females of like environments were selected at random and placed together in small cages, one pair to a cage, for mating. (Vaginal smears were taken after a few days to determine whether pregnancy had occurred. No significant differences in the first appearance of sperm were noted between enriched and impoverished animals.) After 5 days the male-female pairs were separated, and all animals were returned to their original conditions, either enriched or impoverished, for most of the 21-day gestational period. But one day before they were to give birth, the females from the enriched condition were placed individually into the standard laboratory cages to allow privacy during parturition. The females already in the impoverished condition during pregnancy remained in their single cages while giving birth.

The parents lived in the experimental conditions between the ages of 60 and 116 days, a total of 56 days. Maze experience was still being used as part of the enriched environment when this experiment was performed. We found it necessary to stop this experience for both the males and females after 15 days of enrichment, because the pregnant females climbed over the maze barriers and squeezed between the tops of the barriers and the metal screen covering the whole maze. We were not certain how this activity would affect the fetal pups, and so we terminated the maze running.

Immediately after birth, the pups, as well as the parents, from all conditions were sacrificed, and the brains were prepared for histological study. At the same time, the adults' adrenals, thyroids, and testes were weighed; no significant differences in these organ weights were noted between the enriched and impoverished rats. There were no significant differences in the number of pups produced by enriched and impoverished parents or in the number of implantation or reabsorption sites in the uteri of the enriched and impoverished mothers. Such sites are one of the things we examine in studying rat reproduction: occasionally an imperfect embryo is formed and the developing pup is reabsorbed, leaving an identifiable site.

Though there was a trend for the cerebral cortices of the neonatal pups from the enriched mothers to be thicker than the cortices of those from the impoverished, there were no significant thickness differences between the two groups of pups. However, the body weight differences between the pups from the enriched and impoverished parents led us to pursue this type of experiment further. The pups from the enriched parents weighed 6% more ($p < 0.001$) than those from the impoverished parents. This difference was identical in both the male and female neonate pups.

We initially speculated that we would find an accelerated somatic maturation to correlate with this greater body mass at birth in the offspring of the enriched parents. The advanced maturation, if it took place, might allow the offspring a greater opportunity to interact with the environment at an earlier age than was possible for the less mature offspring from the impoverished animals. If this too were true, we supposed we might be able to demonstrate an increase in cortical thickness in the pups from enriched parents resulting from early somatic maturation and, ultimately, from greater birth weight.

With this hypothesis in mind, we designed a new set of experiments. In the new experiments, we studied the brains of the first generation of pups (which we labeled the F_1 generation) from enriched or impoverished parents, but those of pups from the next two generations (F_2 and F_3 generations) as well (see Figure 21). The design of this new experiment was similar to that of the previous experiment but with several major differences: (1) The parents were enriched in similar enrichment cages for similar periods of time, 30 days, but no maze experience was offered, and no impoverished animals were studied. (2) Instead of examining the F_1 pups' brains on the first postnatal day, the pups were nursed by their

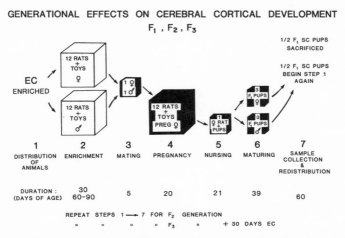

FIGURE 21. Experimental paradigm to show generational and enrichment effects on cerebral cortical development in F_1, F_2, and F_3 rats.

mothers now housed in individual cages until weaning at 21 days of age. The pups were then separated by sex and lived 3 to a standard cage until they were 60 days of age. (3) At the age of 60 days, half of the male and half of the female F_1 pups were placed into the enriched condition for a 30-day period to start the cycle for the F_2 generation. The other half of the F_1 animals we sacrificed in order to take the tissue samples needed for cortical thickness studies in their generation.

The cycle was repeated to obtain the F_2 generation and the F_3 as well. However, all of the animals of the F_3 generation were put into an enrichment cage for 30 days when the animals had reached 60 days of age. Since the F_3 animals were exposed postnatally to the enriched condition, they cannot be justly compared with the F_1 and F_2 animals that were not directly enriched. Nevertheless, the results from the F_3 animals are important in light of the results of our developmental studies showing that cortical dimensions normally decrease slightly between 60 and 90 days of age. Therefore, even though the F_3 animals were autopsied at an age 30 days older than the F_1 and F_2 rats, their results are included to demonstrate the cortical response in these slightly older rats after benefiting from their prenatal enrichment and from direct enrichment themselves.

The results from our continued breeding experiment before and during enrichment showed that between the F_1 and F_2 generations, it was the male pups that were affected the most. We found significantly greater thicknesses in the male F_2 cortex than in the F_1 in all three cortical sections sampled: frontal, somatosensory and occipital. Lateral area 10, in both right and left hemispheres, showed F_2 significantly greater than F_1 (by 5 and 6%, respectively); area 3, in both the right and left hemispheres, showed F_2 significantly greater than F_1 (by 4 and 5%, respectively); area 2, in both right and left hemispheres, showed F_2 was significantly greater than F_1 (by 7 and 13%, respectively) areas 4 and 39 in the right hemisphere showed F_2 significantly greater than F_1 (5% and 8%, respectively). There was a nonsignificant trend showing F_2 greater than F_1 in all other male cortical areas sampled.

In comparing the male F_2 and F_3 groups, we observed two different patterns of response. The effects of aging were apparent in the frontal and somatosensory areas; that is, the cortical thickness decreased between the F_2 and F_3 animals. Specifically, the frontal cortex of the F_3 animals was significantly thinner than that of the F_2 animals (by 6 and 8%, respectively in the left and right hemispheres). The somatosensory cortex of the F_3 animals was thinner than F_2 (by 2 to 4%) in both right and left hemispheres, with area 2, governing sensory mechanisms, showing a strongly significant difference ($p < 0.005$).

There were additional effects of the environmental enrichment in the occipital section, which was thicker in the F_3 animals than in the F_2 animals. For example, it was significantly greater in the F_3 generation in area 17, left hemisphere (6%) and in area 18, right hemisphere (4%). There was also a nonsignificant trend showing F_3 greater than F_2 in several other areas we examined in the occipital cortex.

The cortical differences between generations were not as marked in the females enriched in utero as in the males. In the somatosensory cortex, area 3 in the right hemisphere showed the only significant difference, a 6% greater thickness ($p < 0.01$) in the F_2 females than in the F_1; and in the posterior cortex, the only significant difference was in area 39 in both hemispheres, where the F_2 females also exhibited a 6% greater thickness ($p < 0.01$). Comparisons between F_2 and F_3 females revealed no significant differences, although some of the areas of the frontal and somatosensory cortex in the females did show positive effects of enrichment.

To summarize these results, the changes in the occipital cortical samples are particularly illuminating because of their consistency in the response to the experimental conditions. Figures 22 and 23 illustrate the F_1, F_2, F_3 enrichment incremental changes noted in the male and female Long-Evans rats for the right and left hemispheres. On the whole, it is clear that the male exhibited more extensive differences than did the female, both significant and nonsignificant.

A recent experiment by Kiyono et al. (3), has demonstrated that enriching the environment of the pregnant rat can enhance the maze-learning ability of the offspring. Their results suggest that the thicker cortex we found in successive generations in our experiments may contribute to better maze learning. It should be noted, however, that the parents in our experiment were exposed to 30 days of enrichment as adults as well as the enrichment the female subsequently received during pregnancy. Our females thus received twice the amount of enrichment that the mothers in the Kiyono experiment received. It is quite possible that our rats' maze-learning abilities would be even greater than those documented by Kiyono.

In order to assess the contribution of maternal care to the behavioral results they had observed, Kiyono et al. also cross-fostered the pups so that some were nursed by their enriched biological mothers and some by nonenriched foster mothers. The Kiyono group found that there was no

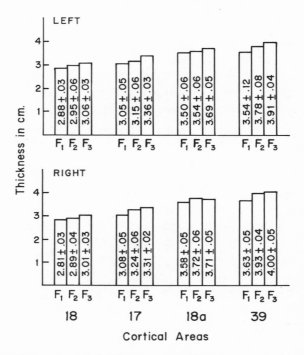

Cortical Thickness Values
in F_1 F_2 and F_3 Generations — Males

FIGURE 22. Posterior cerebral cortex (occipital cortex + area 39) in F_1, F_2, and F_3 generation males from enriched parents.

significant difference in the behavioral test results for the two groups of pups.

Other studies, however, suggest that there are lasting effects of both maternal care and enrichment in utero. Ivinksy and Homewood (4) put mothers and their pups into an enriched environment at different times between pregnancy and the time of weaning. When tested at 64 days of age, those pups exposed soon after birth to an enriched condition had significantly better scores on behavioral tests than controls.

To our knowledge, our experiments provide the first evidence that the dimensions of the cerebral cortex can be altered without directly enriching the offspring, i.e., by enriching the parents before pregnancy and the female during pregnancy. With the experimental design we used we still do not know whether the enrichment before pregnancy had any effect. The experiment should be repeated by separating the two variables, either enriching the parents or enriching the pregnant female.

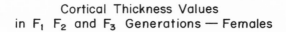

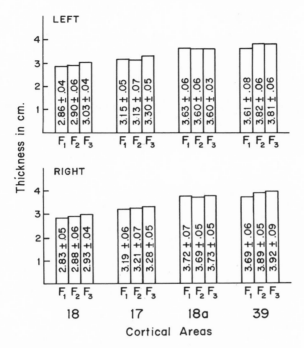

FIGURE 23. Posterior cerebral cortex (occipital cortex + area 39) in F_1, F_2, and F_3 generation females from enriched parents.

For these first experiments we were anxious to learn whether we could change the cortical thickness dimensions in the offspring of enriched parents and thus, gave enrichment in several stages, before pregnancy and during pregnancy. The results indicate that parental enrichment can produce positive results in some regions of the cortex.

For now, the hypothesis we offer to explain these effects is that the sex steroid hormones that are present at high levels in the mother during pregnancy might more readily cross the placental barrier if the mother is a more physically active, enriched female, thereby "priming" the cortex of the developing fetus. The enriched F_2 animals would then have an advantage over the enriched F_1 animals, having been subjected to higher than usual levels of sex steroid hormones during two pregnancies.

An explanation for the changes in the female fetal cortex is suggested by the results of Pappas et al. using young adult females. Pappas et al. injected exogenous progesterone intraperitoneally (2 mg/kg body weight) into neonatally ovariectomized rats from 45 to 90 days of age. They found increases in cortical thickness throughout the cortex, with significant differences in areas 10, 4, 3, 2, and 18. It is of interest to note that in our experiment, four of these same areas (area 18 being the exception) responded to the generational enrichment conditions in the male rat, whereas in the female area 3 was the only one to show significant differences. The results of Pappas et al. suggest that progesterone has an increased metabolic effect on cortical tissue and thus increases its dimensions. It is possible that such an effect occurred in the rats enriched in utero.

Other experimental results show that progesterone increases protein uptake in intact female rats. This interaction could help influence the increase in cortical thickness seen in our experiments.

The influence of either progesterone or estrogen on the developing fetus is obviously complex. The effect of these hormones on cortical development may depend on the age and sex of the animal being exposed, the duration of exposure, and the amount of maternal circulating hormone as well as existing ratios of progesterone and estrogen in the animal's system.

Factors other than steroids circulating in the blood play a role in altering the structure and chemistry of the developing brain. For example, direct maternal control of the fetal biological clock in utero has been measured in terms of the rhythm of glucose metabolism in a part of the brain called the suprachiasmatic nucleus (5). This nucleus is found in the hypothalamic region of the forebrain. Investigators have demonstrated that the mother coordinates the phase of the fetal biological clock to her own circadian rhythm, which in turn is determined by the ambient lighting conditions. If the mother can transmit something that indicates ambient lighting conditions to the fetus, it is possible that she also transmits something about the effects of other environmental stimuli she receives, for example, increased tactile stimulation. Our findings, which show significant generational increases in somatosensory areas 2 and 3 for the males and in area 3 for the females, suggest that extra tactile stimulation either in utero or during lactation can affect cortical development of the young rats.

We have no rational explanation for the responsivity of area 39 in both sexes to the generational effects, yet the differences seem too consistent to be accidental. It is just this area which responds most to enrichment in the youngest unweaned animals' brains that we have measured (after 8 days of enrichment between the ages of 6 and 14 days). This area, a lateral posterior part of the brain, continues to be responsive to the enriched environment until the animal is 105 days of age. But in the older animals, 185 and 904 days of age, no significant changes are noted as a consequence of living in the enriched condition. It appears that the young animal's responsiveness in area 39 is lost with age.

Although the F_1 and F_2 comparisons are the most valid to make because the experimental conditions were similar, the measurements made in the occipital region of the F_3 group were consistent with the pattern of incremental increases in cortical thickness observed in the first two generations. As mentioned earlier, the F_3 group could not be directly compared with the other two groups because the F_3s were exposed to an enriched condition between 60 and 90 days of age and thus the F_3 animals were older at autopsy. The impact of this exposure was evident in the fact that, despite their being older than the other two groups at autopsy, the F_3 rats' cortices were thicker in the occipital cortical sections.

Since the thickness of the occipital cortex normally decreases in animals living in the standard laboratory conditions between 55 and 90 days of age, the larger size of the F_3 cortex compared with that of the F_1 and F_2 was particularly noteworthy. The areas of the F_3 occipital cortex were apparently benefiting from the intrauterine effects or direct enrichment or both. It should be noted that it is the occipital cortex that most frequently increases in thickness during postnatal enrichment.

In conclusion, our experiments have demonstrated incremental increases in cortical thickness over two successive generations of rats experiencing parental enrichment and enrichment in utero. The third generation displayed some increases as well, albeit with additional exposure to the enriched conditions. Undoubtedly, many factors could be behind these findings. We have suggested the possible role of progesterone. The high concentration of nerve growth factor in the placenta might conceivably be another consideration in stimulating cortical dimensions in the fetuses of the enriched mothers with a possible increased placenta circulation. The role of nerve growth factor in cortical development is only recently becoming established. We are anxious to continue with these types of experiments to gain a better understanding of the mechanisms involved.

From Birth to Weaning (1–28 days)

Having found that it was possible to influence the prenatal cortex, we now wished to learn whether the early postnatal cortex (that of rats before the age of weaning) could also be affected by enriched or impoverished environmental conditions. (Weaning for these experiments was at 28 days rather than at 25 as for the others.) We have noted that the plot of normal cortical development has essentially two definite slopes. The first slope is a steep increase immediately after birth until the animal is 26 to 41 days of age; it reaches a peak and is followed by the second, a slow decline throughout the rest of the lifetime of the animal. We were now interested in determining whether we can change the cortex of rats during the normal increasing slope of the curve between birth and the age of 26 to 41 days. Usually, rats are weaned between 21 and 25 days of age.

In order to learn about the effects of a stimulating environment on the rapidly growing phase of the cortex, we conducted an experiment that required a new living arrangement: young animals had to be housed with mothers (6). Long-Evans male pups had an advantage at the beginning of these experiments compared to pups in the experiments after weaning because the litter size was reduced to three pups per mother at birth instead of the usual eight. When the pups were 6 days of age, three environmental conditions were formed: (1) One mother with her three pups remained in the standard colony cage; this condition was referred to as the unifamily environment. (2) Three mothers with three pups each were placed together in a single large cage, 46 × 71 × 69 cm (the multifamily environment). (3) Three mothers with three pups each were placed together in a single large cage with "toys" (the multifamily enriched condition). The toys were many different kinds of objects, such as ladders, small mazes, wheels, and swings (see Figure 24). Unifamily and multifamily enriched groups were sacrificed at 14, 19, and 28 days of age. The unifamily and multifamily but not enriched cohort was sacrificed at 28 days of age.

By the time one succeeds with an experiment it appears straightforward, but we arrived at the final experimental design just described only after several unsuccessful attempts. For example, in our first multifamily enriched environments, the three mothers with their three pups each were put into the enriched cage immediately after the birth of the pups. By the second day, the mothers had eaten the babies, possibly because of parental anxiety due to this unfamiliar grouped environment. Step by step we learned that not until the pups reached 6 days of age would the mothers tolerate the group enriched living condition.

Some behavioral observations of these groups were noted during the course of the experiment. The multifamily animals were more docile than those raised in the unifamily environment. Often isolated animals are quite disturbed when handled. During the night (the 12-hour dark pe-

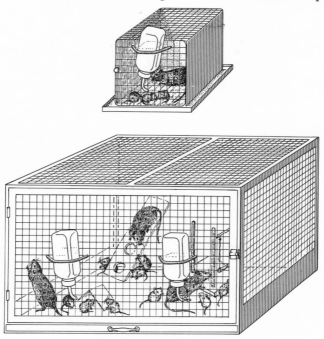

FIGURE 24. Living conditions for the unweaned rats: (below) multifamily enriched condition; (above) unifamily condition.

riod we subjected the rats to), the enriched multifamily animals explored their cages more than the unifamily animals; and like other multifamily animals, the enriched multifamily rats were more docile than the unifamily at autopsy. The greater interaction that the enriched mothers and pups had with other rats may have prepared them for more docile responses to the experimenters.

When we compared the rats housed in the unifamily condition with the multifamily rats, the former were significantly heavier (6%, $p <$ 0.05) in body weight than those living with several families. This is consistent with other findings that the body weight of small litters (5 rats) is greater than that of larger litters (8 rats) during the weaning period (7, 8). But there were no significant differences in adrenal weights and in the time of eye opening between the unifamily and multifamily pups.

At 14 days of age, the unifamily and enriched multifamily rats differed significantly in body weight, head-to-tail length, and testicular weight. The differences were 10% ($p < 0.05$), 15% ($p < 0.001$), and 7% ($p < 0.05$), respectively, the values for the unifamily rats always being greater. Rats become sexually mature by 60 days of age. Because of the increased testicular weight in the unifamily pups, it would be of interest to follow some of these little rats until sexual maturity to learn which group, the enriched or nonenriched, reached this stage first. When enriched and impoverished males were mated with enriched and impoverished female animals respectively, there were no significant differences in the time of the first appearance of sperm in the vagina, suggesting that exposure to the different environments did not produce differences in sexual maturation. In examining other endocrine organs, we found no differences in adrenal weights between the experimental groups, signifying that stress was not a major factor in these experiments.

The time of eye opening was observed carefully in order to determine the rate of maturation of the nervous system. Normally, rats' eyes open on day 14. However, the eyes opened on day 13 for the enriched multifamily rats and on day 14 for the unifamily animals. This one-day difference was statistically significant ($p < 0.05$). At least two factors can be considered here: (1) that the enriched condition was accelerating maturation, a conclusion supported by cortical thickness measurements (to be described shortly); and (2) that the possible increased androgen levels produced by the enlarged testes delayed the perforation of the palpebral fissure (between the eyelids), preventing early eye opening. Though either of these suggestions is feasible, the former is more strongly supported by our other experiments.

Body measurements were taken on the 14, 19, and 28 day groups of rats. Only the 14 day group showed somatic differences between the multifamily and the unifamily impoverished animals. In experiments with rats at 19 and 28 days of age, the somatic differences noted at 14 days were no longer exhibited. In these experiments, however, once again the eyes of the enriched multifamily rats opened earlier than did those of the unifamily animals, this time by 2 days ($p < 0.01$).

Cortical thickness measurements were taken on all of the pups in the various conditions. No significant differences were noted between the unifamily and the multifamily animals at 28 days of age. In other words, the animals (3 mothers plus 9 pups) living together in the large cage without toys did not develop cortical thickness changes which differed from the animals living in the unifamily condition (1 mother plus 3 pups). The importance of the presence of stimulus objects or toys with which the animal can interact will be borne out in the next comparisons.

In as short a period as 8 days (the animals were in the experimental conditions from 6 to 14 days), the somatosensory cortex of the multifamily enriched animals developed strikingly significant differences from that of the unifamily rats (Figure 25). The differences in thickness ranged from 7% ($p < 0.025$) to 11% ($p < 0.001$), with the enriched animals having the thicker cortices. The importance of the presence of toys in influencing cortical structure is clearly confirmed in this experiment. Interestingly, the visual cortical regions did not show significant differences at this early stage, when the rats were 14 days old. Evidently, since the eyes had not opened until 13 days of age in the enriched and 14 days in the unifamily group, not enough visual input had occurred to induce cortical changes between the two groups. But in the most lateral segment of the sample of the occipital cortex, area 39, a multisensory integrative area, by 14 days of age a thickness difference of 16% ($p < 0.01$) had developed between the multifamily enriched and the unifamily group. In these young rats receiving a good deal of input, clearly evident in the changes found in the somatosensory area, the active recruitment of information from many sensory regions apparently created the changes seen in area 39. This 16% difference in cortical thickness is the largest we have encountered in rats either before or after weaning.

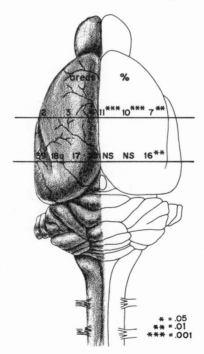

FIGURE 25. Percentage cortical thickness differences between multifamily enriched and unifamily rats living in their respective conditions from 6 days to 14 days of age.

By the age of 19 days, the enriched multifamily rats had significantly thicker somatosensory and occipital cortices than the unifamily animals (Figure 26). One area, area 2, did not show a significant change at this age. This area often does not follow patterns that other cortical regions show in response to development or environment.

In the animals autopsied at 28 days of age, all subdivisions of the somatosensory and occipital cortices showed significant differences in thickness between the enriched multifamily and the unifamily animals. At 28 days, the occipital cortex appeared to have shown more response than it had during either of the shorter periods. In fact, the differences ranged from 9% ($p < 0.05$) to 12% ($p < 0.001$), the largest changes seen throughout the occipital cortex with any age group, whether before or after weaning. The 16% change reported at 14 days was in one region only while other, adjacent regions were nonsignificant; in the 28-day-old group, the differences represent significant changes in three adjacent regions.

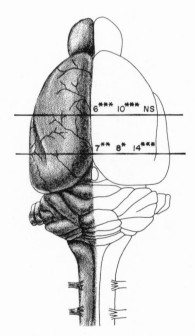

6-19 days of age

FIGURE 26. Percentage cortical thickness differences between multifamily enriched and unifamily rats living in their respective conditions from 6 to 19 days of age.

The cortical changes in these not-yet-weaned male rats indicate that it is possible to accelerate measurable morphological cortical maturation in very young animals. In many segments of the cortex, we achieved cortical thickness differences greater than those we have seen in animals past the age of weaning. The results also suggest to us that the somatosensory cortex is more plastic before the eyes open, but once visual input begins, it is the visual cortex that shows greater changes.

From Weaning to Adulthood (25–185 days)

In studying the impact of the environment on the cortex of rats during the period from weaning to adulthood, we wondered whether the age of onset of the experimental conditions was an important consideration. We made our first comparisons between animals living in their environments from 25 to 105 and from 105 to 185 days of age (9). In none of the cortical sections we compared was the change in thickness significantly different between the two 80-day groups. As we found when we established normal cortical thickness developing and aging curves, the cortex is decreasing during both of these age periods. Although one comes in the early phase of descent and the other a little later, the effects of different environmental conditions are similar in the two age periods in counteracting the decrease. Whether we started enrichment at 25 days or 105 days, the greatest changes occurred in the occipital cortex, with the magnitude of the change similar for the two groups, between 2% and 5 to 6% (see Figure 27). These results show that an 80-day exposure to enriched or impoverished conditions is as effective whether it starts during the early part of the decreasing slope of the cortical curve or 100 days later.

We also compared two other periods of onset, one at 25 days (25 to 55 day group) and the other at 60 days (60 to 90 day group). But in the experiments based on these starting ages, the animals were in their conditions for shorter periods of time, for 30 days instead of 80. The thickness of the cortex did not differ significantly between the groups with these two starting ages, with but one exception, the lateral occipital cortex (see Figure 28). Figures 28 and 29 include 10 sections through the cortex instead of the 3 shown in Figure 1. Even with a shorter duration (30 days), and with different starting ages (either 25 or 60 days), the enriched and impoverished changes were, in general, not significantly different. That is, the effects of the enriched or impoverished conditions

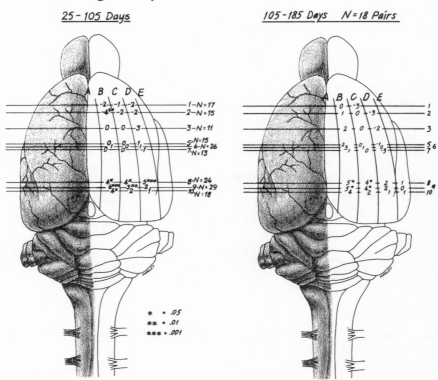

FIGURE 27. Cortical thickness percentage differences between enriched and impoverished rats living in their respective environments for 80 days, either 25 to 105 days or 105 to 185 days.

were not significantly different (with one exception) between the 25 to 55 day group and the 60 to 90 day group.

Figure 29 shows the effects of enrichment and impoverishment compared with standard colony conditions. For the younger 30-day group, subjected to the conditions between the ages of 25 and 55 days, the differences are primarily due to the impoverished condition. Slight enrichment effects are seen in the occipital cortex, sections 8, 9, and 10. It is apparently detrimental to isolate the young pup immediately after weaning at 25 days of age; at the same age, the effect of environmental enrichment is not very strong. But by waiting until the animals are 60 days old to place them in their respective environments for a 30-day period, we get a different cortical response. The effects of enrichment become stronger, especially in the frontal and occipital cortex, as do the effects of impoverishment. A reduction in stimuli to the cortex appar-

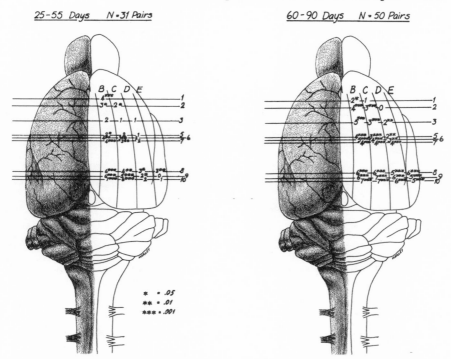

FIGURE 28. *Cortical thickness percentage differences between enriched and impoverished rats living in their respective environments for 30 days, either 25 to 55 days or 60 to 90 days.*

ently creates more deleterious effects than increased stimuli enhance cortical structure. In other words, the effects of impoverishment are stronger than the effects of enrichment in creating cortical structural changes in both the 25 to 55- and 60 to 90-day groups.

We have found that both 30-day and 80-day periods of enrichment or impoverishment alter the cortex, but is one duration as effective as the other? The younger 30-day group (25 to 55 days of age) did not differ markedly from the two 80-day groups (25 to 105 and 105 to 185 days of age). However, the older 30-day group (60 to 90 days of age) gave significantly greater measurements than both of the 80-day groups in several of the areas compared. From these results, we can conclude that the animals living for 30 days in their respective environments as young adults developed the most significant cortical changes. During the 80-day period, the rats may have become "bored" with the selection from a common pool of toys, and the cortex decreased in its dimensions

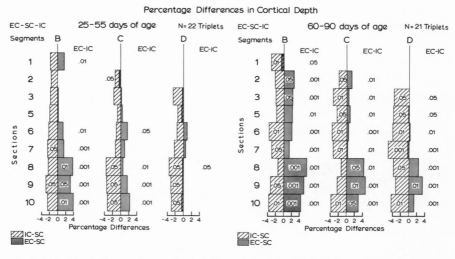

FIGURE 29. Effects of enriched and impoverished environments compared with a standard, 25 to 55 days or 60 to 90 days. Segments and sections are as illustrated in Figures 27 and 28.

as a result of a lack of stimulation. The importance of keeping new variety of inputs to the cortex to maintain its increased thickness became evident from these experiments.

In both 30-day groups (25 to 55 days and 60 to 90 days of age), the enrichment effect was mainly in the occipital cortex, including the primary visual cortex. However, some scientists do not believe that vision plays an important role in the effects of enrichment and impoverishment. Studies by Krech et al. (10) and Rosenzweig et al. (11) showed that cortical weight changes occurred even if the enriched and impoverished experiments were run in the dark or with blinded animals. Yet, in our study (6), when we examined the lateral geniculate nucleus, a thalamic way station in the visual pathway, we found the proportion of neuronal cells per unit area to be 20% less in the enriched unweaned rats than in the nonenriched. These results suggested that the lateral geniculate nucleus from the enriched animals possessed more fiber connections or neuropil separating the nerve cells from each other than that of the nonenriched animals. Our results indicate that the visual system is involved in the cortical thickness changes.

In addition, other results, from our studies on rats before the age of weaning, have shown that vision may play a significant role in altering the enriched occipital cortex. It will be recalled that if the animals were placed in the enriched or nonenriched conditions between the ages of 6 and 14 days, before the eyes opened, the primary visual cortex did not respond to the environmental conditions. If, however, the animals were placed in their respective conditions for the period between 6 and 19 days of age, which includes at least 5 days with the eyes open, significant differences between the enriched and nonenriched rats were found in the thickness of the visual cortex. Thus, two of our experiments offer evidence that vision plays a considerable role in promoting the cortical changes.

Because so many brain regions send fibers to the occipital cortex, at the present time it is difficult to attribute to any one functional unit the full responsibility for the cortical changes in response to the environment. Fibers other than visual fibers associated with the occipital cortex include those from the basal ganglia (12), hypothalamus (13), hippocampus (14), and nonspecific thalamic fibers (15, 16). From these various sources of input it is not possible to determine which specific pathways are being stimulated to increase the dimensions of the occipital cortex.

For all of these studies on rats between weaning and adulthood, the animals lived in their respective conditions for either 30 or 80 days. We wondered if we could shorten these periods and still find measurable cortical changes. In the next series (9), the rats were exposed to their environmental conditions for successively shorter times, i.e., for 15 days (from 25 to 40 days of age), for 7 days (25 to 32 days of age), for 4 days (26 to 30 or 60 to 64 days of age), and for 1 day (60 to 61 or 80 to 81 days of age).

No significant cortical thickness differences were noted between the enriched and impoverished animals that had lived only 1 day in their respective environments, whether from 60 to 61 or from 80 to 81 days of age. However, we learned that after 4 days of exposure to the different living conditions, the cortical thickness differences were highly significant in area 18, the medial occipital area, by 3 to 4% ($p < 0.001$). As mentioned previously in this chapter, it is this visual association area of the cortex which consistently responds to the enriched condition, for reasons that are not yet fully understood.

In the 4-day groups, the other areas of the occipital cortex also showed differences related to environmental conditions; these were most significant in the medial areas and progressively less significant in areas farther laterally. The experiments on animals in the 26- to 30-day age group caused cortical changes due primarily to impoverishment, whereas those on the 60- to 64-day age group created differences which were mostly due to enrichment. As mentioned earlier in this chapter, taking the pups away from the parent early in life after weaning appeared to be detrimental to cortical development. In the older animals, short-term exposure to the impoverished conditions did not negatively affect the brain structure, yet with longer-term exposure to impoverishment, detrimental effects became evident even in the older animals.

If the occipital cortex could change after 4 days in enriched or impoverished conditions, was the pattern of change any different after 7 or 15 days? Yes, after 7 days, the frontal, somatosensory, and occipital areas all showed statistically significant differences ranging from 2% ($p <$ 0.05) to 5% ($p < 0.001$). Area 18, the medial occipital cortex, showed a 4% change after 7 days of enrichment, as it did after 4 days of enrichment. After 15 days of enrichment, all regions of the cortex that were measured again showed statistically significant changes. After 15 days, area 18 (the medial occipital cortex) reached a larger difference, a 7% difference ($p < 0.001$), in contrast to the 4% seen during the shorter time periods. The animals living in their environments for 30 to 80 days also differed by 7 to 8% in area 18, if they entered their environments before 100 days of age. With our environmental conditions, cortical area 18 appears to be most susceptible to change and reaches its greatest thickness after two weeks of enrichment. The effects of the 30- and 80-day periods on the cortical thickness were no greater than those of the 15-day period.

Once we learned that young animals living in their environments for 30 days (from 60 to 90 days of age) experienced thickness changes throughout the cortex, we then wondered if it were possible to change the structure of the cortex in adult animals during a 30-day period. We carried out a study in collaboration with Uylings et al. at the Brain Research Institute in Amsterdam (17). The design was as follows: At the age of 112 days (considered young adulthood) 12 sets of triplets were divided accordingly: 12 animals were sacrificed to serve as a baseline for cortical thickness at this age, 12 were placed in the enriched condition, and 12 were separated 3 per cage in the standard colony condition. After 30 days, the cortical thickness was measured on the enriched and standard colony rats.

This was an important experiment for at least two reasons. First, it did prove that the adult cortex could change positively in response to an enriched condition in a 30-day period. The cortical thickness of the adult enriched rat was thicker than that of the rat living in the standard conditions at 142 days of age. Second, and perhaps even more important, it showed that enrichment was actually increasing the dimensions of the cortex and not only inhibiting the normal decrease in cortical thickness. The enriched rat's cortex at 142 days of age was thicker than the baseline rat's cortex measured at 112 days of age. This experiment, with its baseline control, thus offers sound evidence for actual growth due to enrichment in the adult animal.

Middle Age and Old Age
(400–904 days)

We were now interested in learning whether the brain in middle and old age could show changes similar to those seen in the younger brain. Several studies were made over the years from the late 1970s to 1985, including those of older animals at 444 days, two groups at 630 days and 904 days of age. (As we mentioned earlier, the Long-Evans rat has been known to live for as long as 904 days in our laboratory.) For the 444-day-old animals and the second group of 630-day-old animals which consisted of only the middle-aged animals in the enrichment cage, the results were similar to those in the younger adult animals (112 to 142 days of age); i.e., the thickness of the occipital cortex was greater in the enriched than in the nonenriched rats (18). Even the 630-day-old animals, which were over halfway through their lifetime, could develop cortical changes in response to the enriched living conditions.

The first 630-day-old group of animals need to be described in greater detail, for their experimental design was somewhat different from other enriched animals. It was our first aging experiment. For this group, only seven animals lived to be 600 days of age. Thus, it was necessary to redesign our experimental conditions to suit so few animals. We decided for the first time to mix age groups, to bring the number of animals in the enriched condition up to 12 by using four 600-day-old animals and eight 60-day-old animals. We put the remaining three 600-day-old animals in the standard colony condition. This way, we had the usual number of 12 rats in the enriched condition—four middle-aged and eight young—and we had three middle-aged rats in the standard colony condition. We had several cages of 60-day-old rats in the standard colony to compare with their littermates in the enriched condition. All rats lived in their respective conditions for 30 days, from 60 to 90 days of age for the young, and from 600 to 630 days of age for the middle-aged.

When the cortical thickness measurements were made at the end of the 30-day period, each of the four 630-day-old enriched rats' cortices was thicker than those of the nonenriched. Since there were so few animals, the differences were not significant, but this experiment demonstrated that the cortices of rats two-thirds of the way through a lifetime could still grow in response to a stimulating environment.

Though the middle-aged (630-day-old) rats showed a positive response to the stimulating environments, the younger rats living with the older ones differed in their response to enriched conditions from young rats living in enriched cages without old rats. The young enriched rats—the 60- to 90-day group—living with the older enriched ones showed no significant differences in cortical thickness compared with the young nonenriched rats. In other studies, large differences had developed when young rats lived only with their age-mates from 60 to 90 days of age. Apparently, it was the old rats that dominated the mixed environment. They were the ones that lined up in the front of the cage to see what new toys would be introduced for the day. While the old ones awaited their toys, the young ones slept in the back of the cage. It appeared as if a dominant hierarchy had been established whereby the old animals were interacting with the toys and preventing the young ones from doing so.

We later learned that rats could live to the age of 800 days under normal conditions in some German laboratories. Our 630-day-old rats were not old by comparison. We needed to change our laboratory rat-raising procedure in an attempt to get our rats to live beyond 630 days of age. For the next study, my long-time assistant, Ruth Johnson, and I decided to take care of the rats ourselves instead of leaving their upkeep to others (19). As we changed the toys and cleaned the cages twice a week, we provided a little more attention to the animals than was normally given. We held them up against our laboratory coats for a short period. Perhaps as a result of this extra attention, the rats lived up to the age of 766 days in their standard colony conditions. Until this age (over two-thirds of their lifetime) they had lived in the colony condition, three rats in each small cage, before some of them entered a new, stimulating environment.

Specifically, the rats were taken from their standard colony conditions at 766 days of age and separated into either the enriched or the standard colony conditions, with new living partners. After 138 days in their respective environments, when the rats reached the very old age of 904 days, the experiment was terminated. Upon examining the cortical thickness, once again we found that the enriched animals had a thicker cortex than the nonenriched, especially in area 18, where the difference reached 10% ($p < 0.05$) (see Table 7 and Figure 30). In fact, the differences in cortical thickness were as great as those seen in the young rats. But it is essential to point out that for these old animals, the experimental conditions lasted for 138 days rather than for the 30-day periods we used with the young rats. How much of a change would have occurred in the old

TABLE 7

Percentage Cortical Thickness Differences between 904-Day-Old Male Long-Evans Rats Exposed to Enriched and Nonenriched Environments

	AREA	ENRICHED[a] (N = 5)	NONENRICHED (N = 8)	%	p
Frontal cortex	10M	2.69 ± 0.187[b]	2.53 ± 0.114	6	0.03
	10L	2.97 ± 0.210	2.75 ± 0.136	8	NS
Parietal cortex	4	2.68 ± 0.076	2.55 ± 0.152	5	NS
	3	2.92 ± 0.236	2.76 ± 0.184	6	NS
	2	2.68 ± 0.306	2.49 ± 0.107	8	NS
Occipital cortex	18	1.61 ± 0.115	1.46 ± 0.117	10	0.05
	17	1.84 ± 0.077	1.73 ± 0.076	6	0.01
	18a	1.93 ± 0.053	1.86 ± 0.082	4	0.05
	39	2.09 ± 0.116	2.08 ± 0.147	0.4	NS

[a]Exposure to the enriched conditions was from 766 days of age.
[b]Values are $\bar{X}$ ± SD. Micrometers can be obtained by multiplying by 444.

rats after only the 30-day time period remains to be seen. Most important, however, the cortex of the very old animals did respond positively to the enriched condition.

We stopped the experiment when the rats reached 904 days of age because by this time we had lost two animals, both of them from the enriched condition. We were concerned that all of the enriched animals might die before we could measure their brains. But it was puzzling to find animals dying in the enriched and not in the nonenriched condition.

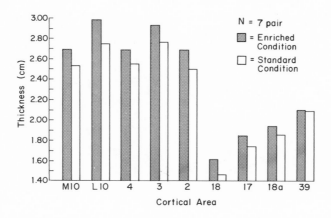

FIGURE 30. Environmental influences on the thickness of the cerebral cortex in rats exposed to standard or enriched conditions between 766 and 904 days of age.

We hypothesized that, perhaps, the stimulation of living in the larger group with the toys was not beneficial to such old animals.

It is possible that the old rats would survive better if they had access to more solitary living, free from interaction with other rats. Their food and toys could be in a large central enrichment cage with arms radiating to their more solitary sleeping quarters. With this experimental design, the rats could voluntarily seek solitude or only one or two partners. Group living for the old animals might be more stressful than living in the standard cages, as indicated by the loss of the enriched animals earlier than the nonenriched. We will have to complete a new experiment to determine whether providing an escape from the enriched condition will prolong the lifetime of the very old animals. For the present, we are satisfied that with the conditions used in our experiment we have shown that the old brain has the potential to respond to increased stimulation.

Since nerve cells in the cortex do not divide shortly after birth, the animals must live for a lifetime with the same nerve cells, in our experiment, for 904 days. Therefore, it is essential to maintain these cells by providing a healthy support system, whether it be the glial cells, the cardiovascular system, the urinary system or other systems of the body. If properly maintained, supported and stimulated, the cortical nerve cell possesses a unique potential for adaptation at any age.

The results of this study demonstrating cortical plasticity in the very aged animal contain both caution and promise for our aging human population. They caution us against entering into inactive life styles that reduce the sensory stimuli reaching our brains, and they provide hope, if we continue to stimulate our brains, for healthy mental activity throughout a lifetime.

6

THE INTERACTION BETWEEN SEX HORMONES AND ENVIRONMENT

Investigators have considered the impact of both the environment and sex hormones on the brain since the nineteenth century. Even as early as 1819, the Italian anatomist Malacarne postulated that experience could alter brain structure (1). And in 1885, Gowers noted that epileptic seizures, which frequently originate in the cerebral cortex, varied with the phase of the menstrual cycle (2). In spite of these very early reports, no one has put together an experimental program dealing with the interaction of the sex hormones, the environment, and the cerebral cortex.

Most of our early studies dealt with male rats so they would not be influenced by any possible variables such as that of the estrous cycle on the female cerebral cortex. We were trying to determine what purely external environmental influences existed and wanted to have as few variables as possible. It was not until 1971 that we published the first results on the anatomy of the female brain exposed to our different environmental conditions (3). We had learned how responsive the female cortex was to both the experiential environment and the level of the sex steroid hormones.

Like many scientific discoveries, knowledge of the impact of the female hormones on the cortex came quite by accident. We discovered it at a time when we were interested in learning the effect of the enriched environment upon the next generation. But before examining the brains from F_1 pups, we wished to confirm that morphological changes had taken place in the brains of their parents, both enriched and impoverished. The usual effects of the environment on cortical thickness were confirmed in the male brain, but an unexpected finding was that pr nancy also modified the dimensions of the cerebral cortex. Of course, a great many metabolic changes occur during pregnancy, and these could be responsible for the differences we were finding in the brains of the pregnant rats. But we began to turn our attention to the interaction of female sex hormones and differential environments in affecting cortical structure.

The following study provided the clue that the female sex hormones brought about changes in the environmentally enriched or impoverished cerebral cortex. We examined the cortical thickness in the brains of the following groups of Long-Evans rats: 24 male rats from enriched and impoverished conditions, 24 postpartum females from enriched and impoverished conditions, and a control group of 24 nonpregnant enriched and impoverished females.

The experimental procedures for these animals are those that were reported in Chapter 5 where the environmental influences on the prenatal pups were discussed. They will be described again here briefly as a background for these results on adult males and females. At 60 days of age both males and females were separated into enriched or impoverished conditions. At 90 days of age, males and females from like environments were placed together in standard cages for mating. All animals were returned to their original conditions, either enriched or impoverished, for most of the 21-day gestation period. But one day before they were to give birth, the females from the enriched condition were housed individually in standard-sized cages. The females that were already in the impoverished conditions during gestation remained housed singly in their cages during parturition. The period the parents were in the experimental conditions was the age span from 60 days to 116 days, a total of 56 days. Maze experience was terminated after 15 days of enrichment.

The control group of females was similarly divided between the enriched and impoverished conditions. But this group was treated differently from the preceding group of females once the 30 days of differential living conditions had ended. Instead of housing an enriched female with an enriched male or an impoverished female with an impoverished male, we housed this group for 5 days accordingly, two enriched females or two impoverished females to a standard colony cage. (A better control might have been to use a castrated male with the female during this 5-day period, but here we might have had to deal with effects of pseudopregnancy on the cortex.) The brain and organ weights from the nonpregnant females were used for comparison with those from the post-partum females and the males.

Immediately after the birth of the pups, animals from all conditions were sacrificed, and the brains were removed for histological study. Figures 31a, b, and c illustrate the results of these experiments with males (a), nonpregnant females (b), and postpartum females (c). There was an initial (I) and replication (II) experiment for each group, with I and II summed for the final results. As seen in Figure 31a, the cortical thickness differences in the Long-Evans male parents were primarily in the occipital cortex, a 7% difference ($p < 0.001$) in area 18; the frontal cortex also showed a difference, but to a lesser extent. In the male rat, the somatosensory cortex did not respond significantly to the environmental conditions during this experimental period. These data suggest that males are primarily visually responsive animals because their visual cortex changed so much compared to the rest of the cortex.

In summing experiments I and II with the 24 pairs of nonpregnant females, the occipital cortex did differ between the enriched and impoverished rats, but the differences were only 4% ($p < 0.001$) in area 18 (see Figure 31b). This difference was significantly smaller than the difference in this region between enriched and impoverished males. However, in

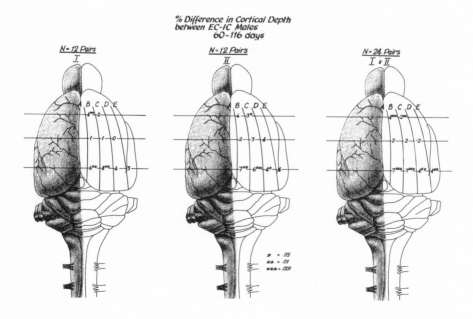

% Difference in Cortical Depth
between EC-IC Males
60-116 days

N = 12 Pairs   I

N = 12 Pairs   II

N = 24 Pairs   I & II

* = .05
** = .01
*** = .001

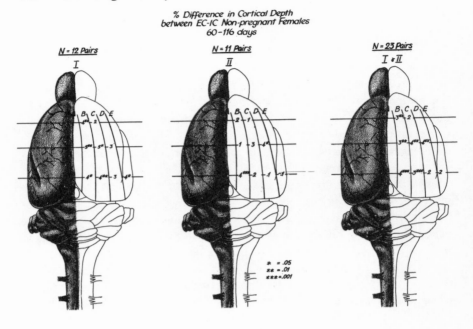

% Difference in Cortical Depth
between EC-IC Non-pregnant Females
60-116 days

the somatosensory cortex, which receives general sensory information, such as touch, pressure, temperature and pain, the differences between the enriched and impoverished females were significantly greater than those between enriched and impoverished males. The frontal cortex showed approximately the same amount of change in both sexes. The marked response in the somatosensory cortex of the female to the environmental conditions suggests that she is more "general sensory" responsive rather than visually responsive as the male. However, in a separate experiment, using female rats in their respective environmental conditions in the age span from 60 to 90 days and a more challenging arrangement of the toys, we encountered a cortical response more like that of the male. Having the females climb over a pile of toys to reach their food caused the occipital cortex to change as much as 7%. The results showed that it was possible, with female rats at a different age, dealing with a more encumbering arrangement of the toys, to produce changes in the occipital cortex identical to those of the male.

It was the pregnant females which exhibited the most surprising cortical changes after living in enriched or impoverished conditions. At first we believed that no cortical thickness changes had occurred between enriched and impoverished pregnant females, because both the initial and

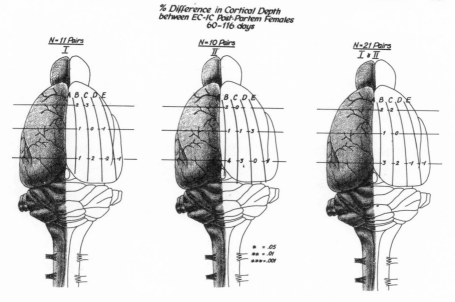

FIGURE 31. Percentage differences in cortical depth (thickness) between enriched (EC) and impoverished (IC) rats in their environments from 60 to 116 days, experiment I, experiment II, and experiments I + II: (a) males, (b) nonpregnant females, and (c) postpartum females.

replication experiments indicated no cortical differences between animals in the two experimental conditions (see Figure 31c). Upon careful examination, however, we noted that pregnancy had a marked effect upon the impoverished rat's cortex, actually increasing its dimensions to equal those of the enriched pregnant rat's cortex. In fact, with additional comparisons, in no instance did the cortical thickness measures of the impoverished postpartum female differ significantly from those of the impoverished male. The two had reached a comparable level of development.

The results on the pregnant rats showed that the female cortex definitely was sensitive to the interaction of pregnancy and the special living conditions. Several questions immediately arose in response to these results. We wondered whether there was a "ceiling" to the effect created by these conditions beyond which the cortex would not increase in thickness. On the other hand, perhaps we could find a way to induce the first cortical fold by combining sex steroid hormones with enrichment; since the mechanism is not known for folding and the intracranial dimensions were identical in enriched and impoverished animals. What could an increasing cortex do in a confined space? We now began experiments to examine some of the roles played by the sex hormones in the development of the cortex during varied environmental experience.

But before we continued with our study of the effects of sex hormones on the cortex, we found some interesting sex differences by examining the body weights of the males and females living in enriched and impoverished environments. No differences in body weight were noted between the enriched and impoverished males, or between the enriched and impoverished postpartum females; but between the nonpregnant enriched and impoverished females, there was a significant 6% difference in body weight in favor of the impoverished rats. It is of interest that this body weight difference should show up in only the nonpregnant females. In early experiments dealing with male animals that had been in enriched and impoverished environments for an 80-day period, the impoverished males were always of greater weight than the enriched males. But when the duration of the experiment was reduced to 30 days, the body weight differences disappeared. In the present experiment the time of exposure to the environments was 56 days, just about halfway between the 30- and 80-day periods, and only the nonpregnant female experimental group showed the weight gain. Unfortunately, no explanation is available why this one group showed a difference at this particular time period, but the information is presented because once again body weight responses to the environmental conditions can be quite different from those in the cortex.

We continued to attempt to understand how ovarian hormones interacted with environmental diversity to influence development in the cerebral cortex. We had already demonstrated that ovariectomy alone could increase cortical thickness. In a new set of experiments (4), twelve sets of quadruplet Long-Evans female rats were divided as follows: From each set of quadruplets two were ovariectomized and two were sham-operated at day 1. At 21 days of age, the animals were weaned and placed three or four to a cage. At 60 days of age, the rats were separated between enriched and impoverished conditions. In other words, 12 ovariectomized rats lived in one enriched cage and 12 sham-operated rats lived in another. In addition, 12 ovariectomized and 12 sham-operated were separated into impoverished conditions, one animal per standard cage.

As with the pregnant animals in the previous experiment, it was again the impoverished animals that produced the most unexpected results. The total thickness of the impoverished ovariectomized rats' cortices became much greater than that of their sham-operated impoverished littermates (see Figure 32). The percentage differences ranged from 3% ($p < 0.05$) to 10% ($p < 0.001$), with area 18 developing as much as a

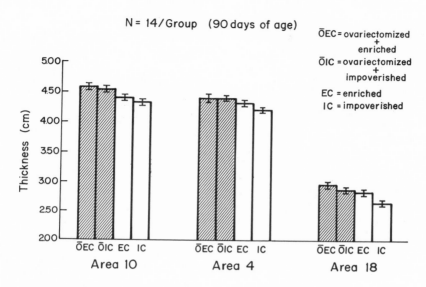

FIGURE 32. *Cortical thickness in female Long-Evans littermate rats experiencing differential environments with or without ovaries, N = 14/ group (ovariectomized day 1, autopsied 90 days of age).*

10% difference ($p < 0.001$) in 13 out of 14 cases. There was no doubt that something unusual was taking place in the impoverished animals' cortices in response to the changes in ovarian hormone levels.

One might offer the hypothesis that the impoverished rats, living by themselves, were under stress and that the adrenal hormones related to stress were responding differently when the ovarian hormones were altered. That stress might be a factor has not been borne out by a comparison of adrenal gland weights between impoverished intact animals and enriched intact rats. In order to be certain that stress is not a major consideration and that adrenal hormones have not been altered, we will eventually have to measure the plasma levels of the corticosteroids (hormones secreted by the adrenal cortex) under the experimental conditions.

Between the ovariectomized enriched and the intact enriched rats, the only cortical regions which showed a significant difference in thickness were those from the frontal cortex (3%, $p < 0.05$, to 5%, $p < 0.01$); none of the differences in samples from the somatosensory cortex or occipital cortex reached a statistically significant level. Figure 32 shows clearly that ovariectomy increases cortical dimensions in both enriched and impoverished animals. It is known that ovariectomized animals take in more food, show increased protein intake, and do little voluntary exercise (5). Protein intake is an important factor in contributing to cellular growth, whether it be dendritic length or cortical thickness (6, 7). Our results suggest that tissue synthesis could be increasing and producing larger neurons, accounting for the thicker cerebral cortex in the ovariectomized rats. If this were the case, one would find an overall cortical response, not one confined to the frontal cortex.

In these ovariectomized enriched and impoverished rats, we had another opportunity to look for a correlation between cortical thickness differences and body weight changes. We learned that the body weight of the ovariectomized enriched rats was 14% greater ($p < 0.001$) than that of the intact enriched rats. Yet the only significant cortical difference between the two groups of rats was seen in one region of the frontal cortex. On the other hand, when the whole cortex increased on account of a lack of ovarian hormones in the impoverished rats, the ovariectomized impoverished rats were also 14% ($p < 0.001$) heavier in body weight than the intact impoverished rats. These data support the previous findings with the pregnant enriched rats showing a negative correlation between body weight and cortical thickness, and the pregnant impoverished rats showing a positive correlation between body weight and cortical thickness compared with intact rats.

In examining differences and similarities between the sexes in the different environments, we also need to consider the effects of the interactions between males and females. Thus, we investigated whether the brain of the male increases more after living in the enriched condition with the female than when living only with other males. We planned an experiment in which 6 males and 6 females (the usual 12 animals) would live together in the enriched condition between the ages of 60 and 90 days. We chose this age and duration because we had previously learned that it is this age span with 12 rats of like sex living together that creates the most marked changes in the total cortical thickness. We knew that pregnancy would occur when males and females were placed together, whether or not toys were present, and the gestation period for pregnant female rats is only 21 days. We did not want the females to give birth in the enriched condition with all the other rats present, because six females with their litters plus the six males would undoubtedly cause problems, resulting in the loss of the pups and stress to the parents. Therefore we placed one group of six 60-day-old females with the six 60-day-old males for the first 15 days of the total 30-day period and then replaced these females (which we expected to be pregnant by now) with six new 60-day-old females for the last 15 days.

Pregnancy was confirmed, as anticipated, in all 12 females at the end of their 15-day term in the experiment. Since we already knew that pregnancy compounded the changes in the cortex of enriched females, we primarily compared the brain changes in the enriched males living with males and those in the enriched males living with females.

In both the right and left hemispheres, the frontal cortex was thicker in the enriched males living with females than in the males that had no female companionship. In the rest of the cortex, the trends were not as clearly delineated. The frontal lobe changes may have been caused by the close association of the rodent frontal lobes to the hypothalamus and its functions related to sexual behavior. A replication experiment is needed to confirm the trends of these results, since there were only six males in the enriched condition with the females, but these preliminary results do offer the first information indicating that living with females alters the structure of a male's cerebral cortex.

Our findings that pregnant and nonpregnant animals respond differently to the environmental conditions was our first clue that the sex steroid hormones could alter cortical structure. We then explored the role of the ovarian hormones and cortical morphology further, learning that removal of the ovaries at birth altered the cortical asymmetry pattern to resemble that of the male cortex. Removal of the testes at birth reversed the right-greater-than-left pattern in the frontal and somatosensory male cortex. This finding indicated that hormones from the testes can modify cortical structure. Now, we wondered what interaction testosterone might have with the different environmental conditions in their influence on structural changes in the cortex. We studied two groups of male animals, one castrated at birth, before the hypothalamus had adopted the characteristic male form, and one castrated at 30 days of age, after maleness was better established. After weaning, all animals lived three per standard colony cage until 60 days of age. Both castrated groups were divided between an enriched and an impoverished condition between 60 and 90 days of age. The resulting modifications in the thickness of the cerebral cortex were very similar to those found in the intact rats, whether the testes were removed at birth or at 30 days of age (see Figure 33a and b). Both the frontal and occipital cortex developed differences, of up to 4% and 8%, respectively, with the somatosensory cortex showing no significant changes. (See Figure 28 for the corresponding data for intact males.) Thus, it appears that the external environmental conditions rather than sex hormones are responsible for these cortical alterations in the male rat.

That removal of the gonads does not alter the cortex of the enriched or impoverished male but removal of the ovaries affects the female cortex

a.

Percent Differences in Cortical Depth between Neonate Castrates in Enriched and Impoverished Environments (N=11 pairs)

b.

Percent Differences in Cortical Depth between Rats Castrated at 30 Days of Age and placed in Enriched or Impoverished Environments (N=12 pairs)

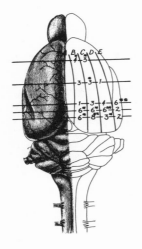
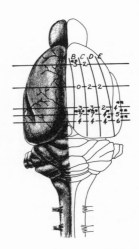

FIGURE 33. (a) Percent differences in cortical depth (thickness) between neonate male castrates living in enriched and impoverished environments between 60 and 90 days of age (N = 11 pairs). (b) Percent differences in cortical depth between rats castrated at 30 days of age and placed in enriched or impoverished environments (N = 12 pairs).

exposed to these environmental conditions enticed us to continue to study the female. After first learning that the female sex steroid hormones altered the structure of the cerebral cortex, we held a laboratory meeting to discuss the next step in our research. In the early 1970s over 50 million women in the world were on contraceptive hormones for birth control; we wondered whether these hormones could also be affecting cortical function. Undoubtedly, most people will agree that "the pill" is the most effective method of birth control, but we were absolutely ignorant about its effect on this quite plastic region of the brain, the cerebral cortex.

We designed an experiment to study one contraceptive hormone and its relationship to the cerebral cortex (8). We wished to ascertain whether norethynodrel, the progestin component of Enovid, at the time a widely used oral contraceptive, altered not only the thickness but also the electrolyte and water content of the cortex of rats exposed to different experiential environments. We used samples from the occipital cortex, because this region responds most frequently to our environmental conditions. We were particularly interested in the water and electrolyte measures, because we know these change during pregnancy but we did not know whether they were responsible for some of the cortical increases that resulted from our hormonal alterations.

Norethynodrel did alter the response of the cortex to environmental enrichment. In the animals we treated with this hormone, some areas of the cortex were thinner than the corresponding areas in non-treated animals in the enriched condition. One area in the somatosensory cortex and one in the occipital cortex were found to be significantly thinner, and 15 out of 15 or all the other cortical areas measured showed a trend in this direction.

Not only did norethynodrel reduce the enlarging effect on the cortex, but it had previously been shown to reduce protein synthesis in the brain (9). Furthermore, norethynodrel has been reported to have a slight but significant anesthetic effect on the central nervous system (10). Thus, it was possible that norethynodrel was dampening the brain's excitability, preventing the animals from responding to the stimulation of an enriched environment, as reflected in the thinner cortex.

In addition to possessing cortical thickness differences, the norethynodrel-treated animals in the enriched condition had significantly less cortical sodium, a trend toward both less chloride and higher potassium. There were no differences in electrolytes and water between animals kept in the impoverished condition whether they received norethynodrel or served as controls. If norethynodrel was acting to dampen the response of the cortex to environmental stimulation, these results would be expected. The impoverished environment, by definition, is a low stimulation environment, and norethynodrel would be expected to have a minimal effect. The finding of no difference in cortical water between the experimental groups of animals is consistent with the work of Bennett et al. (11).

We also learned that the sodium concentration in the occipital cortical samples of rats kept in the enriched environment was greater than in the cortices of those animals living in the impoverished condition. It has been proposed that the concentration of intracellular sodium correlates positively with the excitability of the nervous system. It is thus possible that animals in the enriched environment may have a more excitable nervous system than the animals in the nonenriched condition. This hypothesis was supported by the work, reported in Chapter 4, of another student, Lee Dorosz, who demonstrated a greater peak-to-peak amplitude in the electrically stimulated cortex of the enriched animals compared to the impoverished (12).

What we have learned of the relationship between sex steroid hormones and the asymmetry of the cerebral cortex opens new horizons. It suggests that neuronal and glial cell counts and thickness measurements in male and female human brains should be examined carefully to help us understand some of the biological basis for behavioral differences as well as similarities. The irregularities in the thickness of the human cortex will make the measurements more difficult than they are in the rat. In addition, the range of male and female behavior is extensive, and overlaps exist; but by accumulating data on human brains, scientists can obtain average values as we did for the rats. Very little knowledge is available on the effects of sex steroid hormones on the cerebral cortex during a lifetime, whether female or male.

In summary, the studies reported in this chapter clearly indicate that the cerebral cortical structure responds not only to the sex hormones, but it responds differently depending upon the environmental conditions. If male and female rats experience similar enriched or impoverished environments during the same period of adulthood, the male occipital cortex responds significantly more than that of the female; whereas, the female somatosensory cortex responds more than that of the male. However, if the female is further challenged in her enriched environment, her occipital cortex responds as much as does that of the male. Male rats living with female rats show a greater frontal cortical response than do males living only with males. Pregnancy increases the dimensions of the adult cerebral cortex, as does ovariectomy at birth. Apparently, the cerebral cortex is very susceptible to changes in the concentration of the sex steroid hormones and sometimes in most unpredictable ways. Teasing apart the roles played by the ovarian hormones from those played by the hormones of the adrenal gland will be a challenge for the future.

7

OVERCOMING
DEPRIVATION
AND STRESS

A few studies have illustrated that an enriched environment can overcome either deprivation or possible stress to the brain. Malnutrition, one form of deprivation, was examined in a recent collaborative investigation on brain development. In this study enriched diets and enriched living conditions were provided in an attempt to help the brain compensate for the detrimental effects of a protein deficient diet during pregnancy and lactation (1). Nutrition plays a critical role in human brain development and thereby in intellectual prowess because food supplies the nutrients that catalyze the chemical reactions underlying mental activity. But we are surprisingly ignorant about how this process operates.

In the late 1960s, Winick and Noble reported that malnutrition during the "critical period" of brain growth resulted in a permanent reduction of brain cells (2). This frightening news focused attention on the potential of the prenatal brain to grow during several stages of its development, not only the very early "critical period." Many subsequent human and animal investigations have dealt with behavioral measures following nutritional restrictions, but such measures were difficult to reproduce because the findings were often inconsistent. Human studies suffer from the same limitations in interpretation as do animal studies when the behavioral testing is done on the very young. With the young child it is difficult to use the results of any test as an index of future performance. In the early 1980s studies on both animals and humans demonstrated the apparent effectiveness of enriched living conditions in alleviating some of the behavioral deficits brought about by early nutritional deficiences. Though the behavioral manifestations are an ultimate concern, our present attention is focused on neuroanatomical changes related to malnutrition and subsequent nutritional and environmental enrichment.

Such an anatomical study, conducted in collaboration with a Peruvian graduate student in Berkeley's Department of Nutrition, Arianna Carughi, revealed that rehabilitation through enriched diets and enriched living conditions could overcome some of the deficiencies in the brains of offspring whose mothers were exposed to protein deficits during pregnancy and lactation (1).

Carughi's experimental design was as follows. Pregnant Sprague-Dawley rats were fed a 17% protein semipurified diet from day 13 to day 17 of the 21-day gestation period. At 17 days, the pregnant rats were paired by weight and randomly assigned to one of two groups: (1) controls, receiving 17% protein diets, and (2) protein-restricted females, receiving 8% protein diets. These two dietary conditions were continued throughout the rest of the pregnancy and the following 21-day lactation period, during which the litters were reduced to 8 pups per mother.

At weaning, the male pups from the control litters were placed either 2 to a standard cage or 12 in the enriched cage, and all of them had access to the 17% protein diet. The pups from the protein-restricted mothers were paired by weight and randomly assigned to one of four groups, with groups 1 and 2 as the protein rehabilitated animals and groups 3 and 4 as the low protein animals: (1) a group maintained on a 17% protein diet while being housed in a standard condition, (2) a group maintained on a 17% protein diet and housed in an enriched condition (in these experiments, the enriched condition consisted of the usual 12 rats with "toys," but the toys were changed daily instead of two times each week as with the other experiments), (3) a group retained on a 6% protein diet and housed in the standard condition, and (4) a group retained on a 6% protein diet and housed in an enriched condition. The standard colony animals were housed two per cage rather than the usual three as in our other experiments. After the animals had lived for 30 days (from 21 days after birth to 51 days) in their respective environments, the brains were collected for measurement of either cortical thickness or dendritic branching. The dendritic measurements were taken from pyramidal cells in layers II and III, where, as previously mentioned, the greatest cellular changes due to environmental enrichment had been demonstrated.

As anticipated, the control animals, benefiting continuously from the 17% protein diet, were significantly heavier than the protein-rehabilitated animals, which in turn were significantly heavier than those retained on a 6% protein diet. Differential rearing did not significantly affect any of the body weights. But the cerebral cortices of the animals in the 6 groups did show differences, quite marked at times. In the frontal cortex, the standard colony controls were thinner than the environmentally enriched controls by 4%, the standard colony protein-rehabilitated animals were thinner than the enriched protein-rehabilitated by 6%, and the low-protein animals always had the lowest values in cortical thickness. The environmentally enriched animals also had significantly thicker somatosensory and occipital cortices than the standard animals. For example, in the occipital cortex, this difference amounted to 3% between the standard colony 17% protein group and the enriched-condition 17% protein group. As much as a 9% cortical thickness difference was seen between the standard colony rehabilitated and the enriched rehabilitated animals.

The dendritic branching patterns also showed some differences among the groups. The enriched-condition rehabilitated animals had significantly more high-order dendrites than those animals in the standard colony 17% protein group or the standard colony 6% protein group. When comparing the animals rehabilitated with the 17% protein diet, those in the enriched cages had 17% more dendrites than those in the standard colony cages. In fact, the protein-rehabilitated animals in the enriched condition had a greater number of dendrites than the standard colony controls, whose mothers, as well as they, had always had access to the 17% protein diet. The protein-rehabilitated animals in the enriched condition had only a slightly smaller number of dendrites than the enriched control. No cell counts were made in these studies, but dendritic branching was greater in the protein-rich environmentally enriched group than in the protein-rich standard colony group. In fact, in all areas of the cerebral cortex measured, it was the enriched environment plus the 17% protein diet which created the largest changes in thickness.

These experiments dealing with different types of protein deficiencies with both dietary and environmental rehabilitation clearly indicated that the type of environment in which the protein-deprived animal lives is very important in determining the development of cortical structure. The data clearly show that a protein-rich diet is beneficial for the healthy development of the cerebral cortex, but if for some reason this is not possible, then an enriched diet plus an enriched experiential environment will improve cortical development if provided during the early postnatal period. Postnatal environmental enrichment does play an important role in overcoming certain cortical structural deficiencies caused by dietary inadequacies during pregnancy and lactation.

Having dealt with the importance of protein in the diet and experien-

tial environments to enhance cerebral cortical development, we can turn
to another dietary factor significant to brain function, namely glucose.
Whereas other tissues such as muscles can rely on alternate fuels like fatty
acids, the brain depends almost exclusively on glucose for its energy. The
brain has a critical need for energy and oxygen to maintain its high
metabolic rate necessary to form and propagate substances for synaptic
transmission and to maintain proper ionic gradients. Synapses use a great
deal of energy, and glucose supplies this energy.

Different parts of the brain use glucose at different rates. In order to
learn what parts of the brain were most active in our enriched living
conditions, we studied glucose uptake (3, 4). We hypothesized that the
enriched animals would have a more active glucose uptake than the standard colony animals, because the enriched brains have larger neurons
with a greater dendritic surface for interaction with other neurons.
Therefore, one would anticipate greater metabolic activity in the enriched
brains compared to the standard.

For this study, 24 male Long-Evans rats were separated at 57 days of
age so that half entered the enriched condition and the other half, the
standard colony condition. After 30 days in these respective environments, a pulse of radioactive deoxyglucose was administered intrave-
nously, and concentrations of radioactive deoxyglucose and glucose in
the arterial plasma were monitored for a preset time between 30 and 45
minutes. At a prescribed time the brain was removed and prepared for
autoradiography to measure the localization of glucose utilization in 30
brain regions. Eventually, we had to consider this only a pilot study,
because final data were available on only four enriched and six nonenriched rats.

The 30 areas (including both right and left hemispheres) which were
compared were as follows: prefrontal cortex, frontal cortex, anterior cin-
gulate cortex, nucleus accumbens, septal nuclei, caudata putamen, diago-
nal band of Broca, parietal cortex, corpus callosum, globus pallidus,
lateral thalamus, ventral thalamus, medial habenula, lateral habenula,
hippocampal fimbria, CA_1 hippocampus, CA_1 hippocampus anterior,
dentate gyrus, amygdala, occipital cortex, medial geniculate, lateral geniculate, entorhinal cortex, superior colliculi, inferior colliculi, reticular
formation, auditory cortex, substantia nigra (two separate samples), and
area 17 of the visual cortex.

The results were the exact opposite from our prediction. Examination
of all of these regions revealed that only the frontal and parietal (somatosensory) cortex were significantly different ($p < 0.05$) between the en-

riched and standard control rats. In both the frontal and parietal cortices, rates of glucose utilization were 13% lower in the enriched rats than in the standard controls. Whether or not these effects were random events or were actually due to the experimental conditions can only be determined by a second series of experiments with larger samples of rats. These statistically significant glucose uptake changes did occur in parts of the cerebral cortex where thickness changes due to our environmental conditions had been found previously. One might suppose that the differences were related to the number and size of blood vessels in the frontal and parietal cortices. Other regions of the brain reportedly have richer blood supplies than the cortex, so vascular distribution is not the only factor to account for these uptake differences. However, both the frontal and parietal cortices have more blood vessels than the occipital region, for example, which did not show a significantly decreased uptake in the enriched animals. Yet, the occipital cortex possesses larger blood vessels in the enriched than in the nonenriched. Therefore, we do not believe that the vascular supply alone is the major factor involved in these glucose uptake differences.

Though we did not obtain the results we were expecting, i.e., an increased glucose uptake in the most active regions of the enriched animals' brains, we did learn that it was the cerebral cortex which was the most involved part of the brain in the enriched and nonenriched animals under these experimental conditions. In an earlier study we dissected the brains of the enriched and impoverished animals into 15 different areas, and only the cerebral cortex showed significant wet-weight differences. Therefore, whether one studies the brains by measuring wet weight or by utilizing radioactive glucose, the areas showing the greatest changes between the experimental environmental groups are in the cerebral cortex.

The fact that the enriched animals had decreased rather than increased rates of glucose utilization was unexpected. In every region measured, with but one single exception, the nonenriched rats had a greater glucose uptake than the enriched. The exception was the corpus callosum, where the values were equal. It is conceivable that the differences in ''adaptability'' between the enriched and nonenriched animals to the experimental procedures contributed to these surprising results. In order to inject the radioactive glucose to measure glucose uptake, it was essential to immobilize the rat. If this type of experimental procedure produced stress for the animal, then the meaning of our results could be that it was the enriched rat that could withstand the stressful situation more than the nonenriched. The enriched animal might be more "adaptable" to the confined condition; the nonenriched animals would then be using the additional glucose to combat the effects of stress on their metabolism.

In order to test whether stress is part of the explanation for the results of these deoxyglucose uptake studies, a future experiment might purposely restrain the rats by putting them in a confined enclosure after they had experienced the enriched or nonenriched conditions. Then the corticosteroids, the hormones produced by the adrenal cortex in response to stress, could be quantified to determine the degree of stress. If the nonenriched animals did show the higher concentrations of the steroids, then our interpretation of the deoxyglucose studies would be reasonable.

To continue with this line of reasoning, if immobilization was a stressful experience for the rats in these glucose uptake studies, then the immune system may be playing some role in the circle of events which follow stress, beginning with the adrenal cortex and its hormonal action on lymphocytes. We know that stress affects the immune system by decreasing the number of white blood cells which defend the body through acquired immune responses. It will be seen shortly that in our experiments with the nude mouse, an animal deficient in white blood cells called thymic T cells, it was the frontal and lateral regions of the parietal cortex which showed a decrease in cortical thickness measurements in comparison with a "normal" mouse used as a control. These were the very areas which showed the only significant changes in the glucose uptake studies in the nonenriched rats. This similarity in regions for these two quite different types of experiments may be only coincidental, but these findings should be mentioned in the event that such information may be useful as we learn more about the interaction among the cerebral cortex, stress, and the immune system.

The field which integrates these subjects called psychoneuroimmunology is yet in its infancy. But the correlation between the well being of the psyche (cerebral function) and the well-being of the body has been recognized since the time of Hippocrates. The hypothesis that regions of the cerebral cortex that are partially under the influence of voluntary control interact with the immune system is only now gaining acceptance. The results to be presented next suggest that specific areas of the cerebral cortex are associated with immune functions, which in turn can be affected by stress.

Renoux et al. (5), Bardos et al. (6), and Renoux (7) studied the effects of lesions in both the right or left cerebral cortices on the activity of the natural killer white blood cells. Their results suggest that the natural killer responses of mouse spleen T-cells are controlled primarily by the left neocortex with a modifying influence by the right neocortex. We were interested in refining the experiments of Renoux et al. and Bardos et al., who produced quite extensive cortical lesions in the dorsal and lateral parts of the frontal, parietal, and occipital cortex without penetrating the corpus callosum. Their later lesions destroyed only the frontal and parietal cortex.

We wondered if one cortical region more than another was responsible for the reported immune deficiencies in the lesioned animals. For about one year, we attempted to correlate various cortical lesions with T cell activity and mammary tumor growth (8). Having no success with such approaches, we decided to attack the problem from another direction and examine histologically the cerebral cortex of an immune-deficient animal: the nude mouse, a mouse with a greatly reduced functional thymus gland.

Our experiment was designed to explore differences in cortical morphology between the nude mouse of the BALB/c strain and the normal BALB/c mouse. We already knew that the nude mouse has endocrine problems such as a deficiency in gonadal hormones (9, 10), as well as some neurological problems, such as a reduction in cerebellar size (11). Yet, in spite of its known deficiencies, we learned that many cerebral cortical areas in the nude mouse did not differ significantly from those in the normal mouse.

Not only were we interested in identifying the areas of the cortex which might be deficient in the nude mouse, but we were also interested in any differences in cortical cell populations between the two groups of mice. Since antigen markers have been localized on glial cells, we wished to learn about glial cell populations in the cortices of these thymus-deficient mice. Some investigators had found glial cell differences in the nervous system of nude mice. For example, Kerns and Frank (12) made cell counts in the lumbar ventral gray matter of the spinal cord in homozygous and heterozygous nude mice. They reported a 29% decrease in oligodendrocytes and a 52% increase in astrocytes in homozygous mice compared with heterozygous mice. Another link between the immune system and glial cells has been shown more recently by Merrill et al. (13). They proposed that the T cells participating in inflammatory reactions catalyzed a process that induced proliferation and maturation of astrocytes and oligodendrocytes. In addition, Belokrylov (14) from the Soviet Union homogenized cerebral cortical tissue and found that it contained components which reconstituted the T cell population in the spleen of thymectomized animals, whereas white matter was less active and muscle tissue showed no activity at all. (Belokrylov did not specify whether the tissue samples were from the right or left cortex or from a particular cortical area.)

In light of these observations indicating that the cells in the central nervous system were related to immune function, we decided to compare the cortical thickness and differential cell counts in the immune deficient nude mouse with a control. First, thickness measurements of the frontal, parietal, and occipital cortex were made on transverse histological sections from female nude BALB/c mice and normal BALB/c mice. Second, neurons and glial cells were counted in the left area 18 (medial occipital cortex) in both groups of animals. Since the left area 18 cortex was statistically significantly thinner than the right in the nude mouse, this area was chosen for the cell counts in both the nude mice and the control mice.

The results from the BALB/c normal mouse disclosed that the right cortex was thicker than the left in 4 out of 9 cortical areas measured and so there was no distinct trend in asymmetry. However, in the female nude mouse, the right cortex was thicker than the left in 7 areas out of 9, with area 18 reaching a statistically significant difference. Thus, in general, the female nude mouse did have a thinner left cortex than right.

The cell counts in the left area 18 indicated that the nude BALB/c mouse had fewer neurons and glial cells per microscopic field than did the normal BALB/c mouse. However, the differences become statistically significant only in the oligodendrocyte counts, where the nude mouse had 25% ($p < 0.02$) fewer oligodendrocytes per field than did the normal BALB/c animal.

In these experiments, only the lateral frontal and lateral somatosensory cortex were significantly smaller in the female nude mouse than in the normal female BALB/c mouse (see Figure 34). At first glance these results appeared unusual, because when body size is examined, the normal mouse is considerably larger than the nude mouse. But, on the other hand, we had mentioned previously that in the enriched and impoverished rats, there was often a negative correlation between cerebral cortical dimensions and body weight, and so the fact that the nude had a smaller body weight than the control, yet had only two cortical regions which were significantly smaller, was not too surprising. In the investigations of Bardos et al. (6), lesions in the dorsal and lateral left cortex resulted in a 50% reduction in the number of splenic T cells and a severe depression of T cell–mediated responses. Our results suggest that the lateral frontal lobe might have a role in modifying immune deficiencies, since it is so much smaller in the nude mouse than in the normal.

In our experiment, however, it is both the right and left frontal lobes

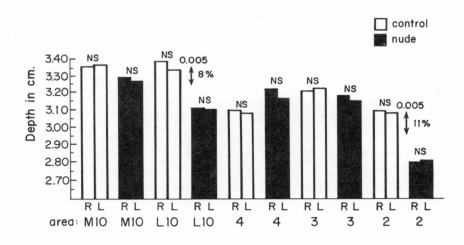

Cortical area and condition

FIGURE 34. Right-left cortical (frontal and parietal or somatosensory) thickness differences between BALB/c mothered and BALB/c nude mice.

which are deficient in the nude mouse. In their earlier work, Renoux et al. did not show a reduction in T cells with a right hemispherectomy, but their more recent reports indicate that the right hemisphere as well as the left play a role in immune function. Renoux (7) stated that partial ablation of the left neocortex did indeed inhibit T cell–mediated responses and natural killer cell activity and that a similar lesion in the right hemisphere caused a small but reproducible increase in these activities. Thus, there appears to be some interaction between both hemispheres in these immune responses. That the left hemisphere of the nude mouse had fewer oligodendrocytes than the normal BALB/c mouse supports the data of Kerns and Frank (12), who reported a decrease in oligodendrocytes in the central nervous system of the nude mouse. We have not counted oligodendrocytes in the right cortex in these mice.

The smaller size of the lateral somatosensory cortex could signify one of at least two things or possibly both. Since the nude mouse has no body hair, it could result from smaller amounts of sensory input from the body surface in this mouse. Or it may be that the lateral somatosensory area is another cortical region involved in the control of the immune system. Only further experiments in this field will help to clarify these results.

If the frontal cortex does closely monitor the immune system, then one might predict that people given frontal lobotomies would demonstrate immune deficiences. There are only two, not well-controlled clinical cases reported in the literature that bear on this prediction. First, in 1939, Messimy (15) reported that monkeys subjected to bilateral prefrontal lobectomy developed an unusual enlargement of the thymus and of the lymphatic system. This work has not been repeated, and the result may have been due to an undetected infection, since the responses to surgery affected lymphoid tissue other than that within the thymus gland. Second, in 1961, Ascengi (16) presented an unusual case of a nineteen-year-old male in whom enlargement of the thymus was noted three months following frontal lobe severance due to a self-inflicted gunshot wound. The thymus actually had an appearance similar to that of an infant. All other tissues were apparently normal. These are not well-defined cases, but they do suggest frontal lobe–thymus relationships.

Now how does this knowledge that the frontal lobe and the oligodendrocytes are reduced in the nude mouse, which is known to possess a deficient immune system, become important to us as we study the effects of experiential environments? We wish to learn whether we can produce measurable changes in the immune system as a consequence of our enriched and impoverished environmental conditions. We have demonstrated that both the right and left frontal lobes are altered when rats are placed in these conditions. Also, we have found that animals in the enriched condition have more oligodendrocytes than do those in the impoverished condition. Thus, differential environments can alter the number of oligodendrocytes and the frontal cortical thickness. In the future we will take the next step of investigating whether we can produce measurable changes in the immune system as a consequence of our environmental conditions. Why is it important to identify more precisely the mechanisms responsible for cerebral-cortical control over the immune system? At least one advantage is obvious. If the cortex does have mechanisms that regulate antibody-antigen activities in response to environmental input, then self-regulation of one's health becomes a responsibility. Evidence of cortical responsivity to environmental input would provide substantial support for the use of such cortical control processes as meditation and biofeedback.

In continuing our attempt to understand the relationships between the structure of the cerebral cortex and possible stressful situations, we investigated the effects of crowding on rats. Crowding is considered stressful under conditions where competition for space or food is likely. The usual number of rats which were housed together in our enriched conditions was 12. We hypothesized that by increasing this number we would be creating an overcrowded condition which might have deleterious or stressful effects on cortical development. Over the years we have purposely kept the same basic enrichment paradigm, with 12 animals past the age of weaning, to allow for as much consistency as possible in the amount of sensory input. If one of the main objectives of our investigation was to study the effects of enriched environments throughout the lifetime of the animals, then similar conditions had to be maintained for the entire period of study.

But the idea to change the number of animals in the enriched cage surfaced when my husband and I were invited to give lectures in China in the fall of 1985. Before going, I wanted to plan an experiment that might prove of interest to our hosts. The Chinese were already feeding 1 billion people. Nutrition would still be of interest as a subject for investigation, but I thought that the Chinese might now be more interested in the problems created by their crowded living conditions. We did not know the effect of overcrowding on brain development. Here was an appropriate moment to attempt an experiment by placing a larger number of animals together in the enriched cage than the usual 12 animals.

Overcrowding, defined as increasing the number of individuals in a confined space, has been considered both detrimental and beneficial. Deleterious effects, caused by too many rodents in a confined space, have been reported where competition for food and mates exists. Calhoun (17), working with mice, noted increased hostility, destructive behavior of adults toward the young, emotional instability, space enroachment, retardation of sexual maturity, and increased infant mortality. However, certain aspects of Calhoun's experimental conditions may have been more responsible for these outcomes than crowding per se. The cages in which the mice were confined were cleaned only every two weeks, and the dead mice were not removed daily. Anyone who has worked with mice knows how important it is to keep the cages clean because of the overpowering odors from urine, to say nothing of dead mice.

In contrast to the detrimental effects reported by Calhoun from his studies on mice, Ross (18) reported that crowding by itself did not seem a sufficient cause of aberrations in human behavior, noting that some communities thrive in close quarters. Needless to say, the factors affecting responses to crowding are complex, and we sought to illuminate at least some of them by examining the effects of crowding on brain development in our enriched rats.

For the initial experiment, we wished to place 60-day-old male rats in three conditions: (1) 12 rats separated into 3 per cage (32 × 20 × 20 cm), a standard colony condition with 213 cm² per rat; (2) 12 rats altogether in a large enrichment cage (70 × 70 × 45 cm with "toys," the usual enriched condition, with 408 cm² per rat; and (3) a "crowded" enriched condition. But we were not certain what would constitute "crowding." At first, we placed 24 rats into the enrichment cage, but the rats did not "look" crowded. Even when we increased the number to 30, we agreed that no obvious crowding existed, but by the time 36 rats were placed in the cage, there was a consensus that this condition was now considerably more crowded (even though the space per rat was well within the required limits stated by the Berkeley Office of Laboratory Animal Care). So 36 rats in a large enrichment cage with toys constituted the crowded enriched condition, 136 cm² per rat. The toys were matched in the second and third conditions in the cages and were changed from a common pool of clean toys two times each week during cage cleaning. The animals remained in their conditions for a 30-day period, because we had previously learned that most of the cortex responds to the experimental conditions during the age span from 60 days to 90 days.

The results indicated that whether there were 12 or 36 rats in the enrichment cage, the thickness of the medial occipital cortex increased significantly by 4 to 6% compared with the standard colony rats (see Figures 35 and 36). In addition, the crowded enriched group showed a significant 4% increase in area 39 that was not so clearly demonstrated in the enriched rats in the uncrowded condition. Since this region is one where multisensory integration takes place, it is possible that the additional crowding constituted a more stimulating sensory environment.

The environmentalist, Calhoun, offered some ideas that might be important in interpreting the results of our experiment (17). He postulated that escape factors allow human beings to tolerate, or to adapt to, high population densities, even under conditions where there is an overload of stimuli. Strain may occur early only in the subordinates in a group with no escape factors; with time, however, the effects of overcrowding may become manifest throughout the whole group. We hypothesized that interaction with the toys might be diverting the rats' attention or entertaining them sufficiently to mitigate the stress of the crowded condition.

Contrary to other reports on the effects of crowding, we observed no fighting among the 36 males in the enrichment cage. In fact, they seemed to be living in harmony for the duration of the experiment, to be finding sufficient space to be comfortable, and to be interacting well

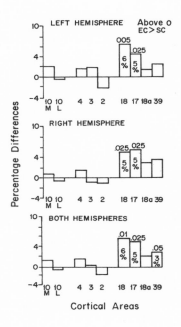

FIGURE 35. Percentage differences in cortical thickness between standard colony (12) and enriched condition (11) male Long-Evans rats.

with the toys. There was no apparent stress in this type of living arrangement.

It would be interesting to see whether males living in the same crowded situation would fight one another if females were introduced into their midst. In the experiment described in Chapter 6 in which six males and six females were housed in the enriched cage, no obvious fighting took place. If a female or group of females lived in a cage near the crowded cage or if a single female or several were introduced briefly into the crowded cage, I wonder if we would have made a similar observation.

In summary, the results in this section have shown that environmental enrichment can mitigate the impact of a range of deprivations and stressful situations. The enriched condition in conjunction with an enriched diet enhanced cortical development in animals subjected to early dietary insufficiency. The enriched environment appeared to have a beneficial effect on rats experiencing restraint during glucose administration.

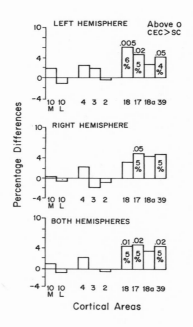

FIGURE 36. Percentage differences in cortical thickness between crowded enriched (16) and standard colony (12) male Long-Evans rats.

The enriched condition increased the cortical dimensions by a similar or even slightly larger amount whether 12 or 36 animals lived in an enrichment cage. Thus, the beneficial effects of enriched living conditions are found using many experimental variables. Evidence exists showing that the effects of stress and the immune system are related to the cerebral cortex. The lateral frontal and parietal cortices are suggested areas for further study in attempts to gain further knowledge on how the cortex can regulate immune functions.

8

THE IMPACT
OF AIR IONS

The possibility that physical environmental stimuli, such as electromagnetic waves, may have effects on the brain has already received some attention by other investigators. That the balance of positive and negative ions in the atmosphere may be another such stimulus is suggested by the early work of Sulman et al. (1). These investigators studied the responses of groups of "weather-sensitive" individuals to changes in the ionization of air. Though the relationship between air ions and weather-sensitive people is not well established, scientists are attempting to gain a better understanding of human sensitivity to weather and of the biological effects of atmospheric ions in general. According to Sulman, only about 30% of the population is weather-sensitive.

Being one of these weather-sensitive people, I found this developing field to be of great interest. As a girl, walking 2 miles home from school uphill through the sagebrush, I could always predict an oncoming thunderstorm by the presence of painful headaches. How could the weather cause my head to hurt? How could something in the atmosphere alter something within the skull? I like the passage in *Notes from the Underground* in which Dostoevsky carries out a discussion with his readers on whether "science itself will teach man that he never had any will of his own, . . . that everything he does is not done by his willing it, but is done by itself, by the laws of nature" (2). The laws of nature do sometimes act in unexpected ways, as we shall learn in this chapter by studying the responses of the cerebral cortex to the levels of air ions.

The word "ion" was coined by Michael Faraday because ions migrate. Ionization occurs in the air from collisions between particles. Air ions form when energy from radioactive compounds in the soil or from cosmic rays acts upon a gas molecule and causes it to eject an electron.

The molecule stripped of its electron becomes a positive ion, and the displaced electron then attaches to a neighboring molecule, which becomes a negative ion. Each molecular ion immediately attracts nonionized molecules to form a cluster of 8 to 12 molecules—an air ion. Negative ions can be produced naturally around falling fresh water, e.g., waterfalls or showers. In normal, clean air over land there are about 1500 to 4000 ions per cubic centimeter, but in polluted air in cities or in stale air in buildings, the ion content can be considerably lower. The ion content in the building where I work, the Life Sciences Building, was measured to have fewer than 100 positive ions per cubic centimeter.

In 1960 Krueger and Smith suggested that the known physiological and biochemical effects of air ions may be due to their ability to alter the metabolism of biogenic amines, of which the neurotransmitter serotonin is one (3). There is evidence that the cyclic nucleotides participate in some of the metabolic events underlying synaptic transmission within the brain and that changes in the brain content of compounds such as adenosine 3',5'-monophosphate (cyclic AMP) and guanosine 3',5'-monophosphate (cyclic GMP) may reflect interactions between some neurotransmitters and their synaptic receptors. We wondered whether air ions could influence serotonin, cyclic AMP, as well as cyclic GMP in our rat brains and, if so, were these changes related to behavior?

The neurotransmitter serotonin has been implicated in changes in mood. A well-controlled study correlating air ions, serotonin concentration in the urine, and mood was performed by Sigel at the University of California in San Francisco (4). She asked each of 33 men to spend 2 hours in a small room containing high levels of either positive or negative ions; later, each man spent 2 hours in a room with the other kind of ion. Sigel found that both types of ions reduced serotonin and made the men feel good. The results indicated that ions clearly influence behavior, but in a complex way that can only be understood one step at a time.

We decided to take one such step in our laboratory. Since no single investigator was adequately prepared to produce and monitor the ions, to design the behavioral paradigm, and to quantify the chemical changes, we formed a team of scientists: Elaine Orenberg, Ph.D., a neurochemist at Stanford University; Michael Yost, a graduate student in public health at Berkeley; Professor Albert Krueger, our specialist in the field of air ions; James R. Connor, a graduate student in the physiology and anatomy department at Berkeley; Michael Bissell, M.D., a neuropathologist at the Veterans Administration hospital in Martinez, California; and myself.

Our experiments were divided into three groups. The first study, which used pups as subjects, was undertaken to investigate whether the effects of negative air ions depended on whether the animals lived in enriched or impoverished environments; serotonin and cerebral cortical weight were measured.

In the first experiment (5), groups of male Long-Evans rats were housed in enriched or impoverished environments, with and without increased levels of negative air ions. Nine littermate pairs of 6-day-old pups were distributed among six mothers into two experimental environments: a multifamily enriched condition and a unifamily impoverished condition. (These behavioral conditions were similar to those reported in Chapter 5 in connection with our study of the effects of differential environments on the developing brain in animals not yet weaned.) In the multifamily enriched condition, three mothers, each with three pups, were housed in one large cage filled with toys. In the unifamily condition, one mother was housed with her three pups in a standard colony sized cage with no toys. There were three cages housing the unifamily rats.

To serve as controls animals lived in atmospheric conditions, i.e., received air delivered by the building ventilation system and contained fewer than 100 positive ions per cubic centimeter of air. These animals were grouped in a similar fashion and were housed in either a wire-mesh enrichment cage or standard laboratory cages (18 pups in the atmospheric-condition groups), but in a separate room. All pups lived in their respective housing from the age of 6 days to the age of 26 days.

Both the enriched and the nonenriched animals exposed to negative air ions lived in Lucite cages, with Lucite toys in the enrichment cage. A grounded wire-mesh floor was suspended over the sawdust waste collection tray at the cage bottom. A fan supplied continually moving air to each cage, and a filter was used to free the air of particulates.

An air ion density of 1×10^5 negative ions per cubic centimeter was maintained in both the large and small cages. Negative air ions were generated by corona discharge from Amcor Modulion power supplies and regulated in each cage by adjusting the ionization potential with separate variable transformers on the ac lines of each generator. The ion density of the air in each cage was measured with the aid of a Royco volumetric counter and was correlated with the flow of current from the wire-mesh floor to an earth ground. Daily checks of the current flow to ground were made to ensure proper operation of the ionization equipment.

Before brain samples were dissected for chemical and wet weight measures, all animals were coded to prevent experimental bias. Uniform samples of somatosensory and occipital cortices were surgically removed from both hemispheres, weighed, and frozen. All procedures were accomplished within 4 minutes.

The results of these experiments were most revealing, informing us of the many ways the ion content of the air can affect the cerebral cortex. First, in both the initial and the replication experiments the wet weights obtained before the chemical assays from the samples of the somatosensory and occipital cortices were heavier in rats receiving negative ions than in those living in atmospheric conditions. Here was evidence that exposure of rats to high levels of negative ions increased the weight of the outer layers of the brain.

The chemical changes were equally consistent. We learned that the enriched rats living in a negative ion atmosphere had significantly less serotonin (61%, $p < 0.01$) and cyclic AMP (45%, $p < 0.05$) in the somatosensory cortex than the enriched rats living in atmospheric conditions. Cyclic AMP is a second messenger; i.e., it translates extracellular messages into an intracellular response. Serotonin and cyclic AMP concentrations in the occipital cortex were also significantly less (45%, $p < 0.05$, and 35%, $p < 0.05$, respectively) in the enriched rats receiving negative ions than in the enriched rats living in atmospheric conditions. It appears that in the enriched condition, but not in the impoverished condition, negative ions prevent the increases in serotonin and cyclic AMP concentrations that occur in atmospheric conditions. The cyclic GMP levels increased slightly, though not significantly, in the somatosensory cortex and in the occipital cortex of both the enriched and impoverished rats receiving negative ions in comparison with their counterparts living in atmospheric conditions.

Our data on serotonin are consistent with other reports showing that negative air ions decrease brain serotonin. Gilbert (6) used negative ions to reduce emotionality caused by isolation; the reduction in emotionality paralleled a decrease in serotonin. Olivereau (7) found that brief exposure of rats to 1.5×10^5 negative ions per cubic centimeter of air modified their ability to adapt to a stressful situation. He considered the effect to be due to a reduction in serotonin caused by the action of air ions.

In most instances, the pattern of change in the content of cyclic AMP was in the same direction as the change in serotonin. If changes in cyclic AMP are serotonin-dependent, cyclic AMP might reflect the metabolic alteration in serotonin resulting from negative air ions, as well as from the living situation.

The content of cyclic GMP was relatively unchanged by either the atmospheric or the environmental state. This may indicate that the neuronal cells selectively control steady-state tissue levels of the two cyclic nucleotides by independent regulatory mechanisms.

We chose 6-day-old rats as experimental animals in this study in order to identify potential effects of air ions on neural development. There appears to be a serotonin-dependent adenylate cyclase system which participates in some of the metabolic events underlying synaptic transmission in very young animals, and which decreases in sensitivity with age. Our results showing that serotonin and cyclic AMP are similar in their response patterns to our environmental conditions may be due to this coupling. It is conceivable, however, that negative air ions could have shifted the apparent developmental stage of the rats in this study by changing the concentration of some hormones, such as prolactin, sex hormones, or serotonin-derived melatonin. A direct effect of air ions on prolactin levels was proposed by Olivereau in his study of the effects of air ions on the spontaneous movements of amphibian larvae. A direct hormonal effect of this kind in our system may have caused the increased cortical weights and decreased cortical levels of serotonin and the second messenger cyclic AMP reported here. A further study comparing the effects of negative and positive ions and different environments on various neurotransmitters would help clarify how the responses change the developmental stage of the animal brain. Undoubtedly, the direction of change of one transmitter does not indicate how other transmitters are altered.

Having shown these effects of negative ions on weight and neurotransmitter concentration in the young, developing cortex, we turn to our second study, one measuring the effects of elevated levels of negative ions in older brains. For this experiment we were interested in learning whether brains from animals living for an extended period of time in conditions with high levels of negative ions aged more rapidly than those from animals in atmospheric conditions. It seemed of importance to understand the effects of long-term exposure to these ions because of evidence which suggests that negative ions increase metabolic activity. For example, it has been shown that negative ions increase ciliary motility in the respiratory tract. In addition, as was found in the first experiment described in this chapter, the weight of the developing cerebral cortex increases with high levels of negative ions. With these two pieces of information, it appeared to us that negative ions might have the effect of accelerating maturation and aging by somehow increasing metabolic processes. If this were the case, could the ions affect the aging process of nerve cells? In order to answer this question, we planned an experiment with Professor George Ellman in the psychiatry department at the

University of California in San Francisco to learn whether the aging pigment called lipofuscin, found in nerve and glial cells and thought to be a metabolic biproduct, could be measurably altered with prolonged use of negative ions.

For this experiment, female Long-Evans rats, 7 months of age, were separated into one of four environmental conditions: (1) an enriched condition with the addition of 1×10^5 negative air ions per cubic centimeter (8 rats in a large cage, with the toys changed every other day excluding weekends); (2) a nonenriched condition with 1×10^5 negative air ions per cubic centimeter (2 rats per small cage, providing a total of 6 rats in 3 small cages); (3) an enriched condition with atmospheric air with the rats caged as in the first group; and (4) a nonenriched condition with atmospheric air, with the rats caged as in the second group. At 14 months of age, 7 months later, the somatosensory and occipital cortices of the left hemisphere were removed, weighed, and frozen in order to assay for the lipofuscin (8).

Since the results were statistically nonsignificant, they are mentioned only to show trends. Quite unexpectedly we learned that the lipofuscin concentration was less in the enriched animals than in the nonenriched, whether the animals were exposed to excess ions or not. The percentage differences in lipofuscin concentration between the enriched and nonenriched were quite large. With the negative ions, the differences were 16%, and in atmospheric conditions, 9%. The standard errors of the mean were much larger than those seen in the wet weights of the same tissues, for example. These data indicate that there is great variability in lipofuscin accumulation in individual rats during aging. They also suggest that animals living in an enriched condition do not accumulate lipofuscin at the same rate as animals living in a nonenriched condition. As has been mentioned previously, enriched rats have more large capillaries in their cortices than nonenriched rats. It is possible that the more efficient vascular system transports precursors of lipofuscin away from the cell. If so, then we still do not know the answer to our original question, Does lipofuscin accumulate faster in enriched or in nonenriched brains? Whichever way the process does work, the data suggest there is less of the pigment in the more active enriched brains when the animals have lived in their respective conditions for as long as 7 months during early adulthood. Since it is thought that an accumulation of lipofuscin in the cytoplasm of the cell can hinder its function, less pigment in the enriched cells could be interpreted as beneficial.

Though our primary interest in air ions was their effect on the brain, it was relatively easy to take blood samples and examine the effects of high negative ion concentrations on white blood cell counts, as well as on brain sections taken from the same animals. If we could find changes in the white blood cells, some of which are related to antibody-antigen responses, then we would be encouraged to utilize the brain slices to make the more tedious counts of glial cells, which also have antigen markers. In an experiment using mice in three separate age groups, we found that white blood cell counts were altered with high levels of negative ions. The design of this third experiment was as follows. One-month-old mice lived in standard colony mouse cages with 25 mice per cage. One cage, placed on an electrically grounded floor, was supplied with negative ions (2×10^3 ions per cubic centimeter), and the other cage had no electric field. The animals were exposed to these conditions for different time periods: 3 weeks, 2 months, and 3½ months. For the two groups of mice and for the three different age groups, the lymphocyte counts were greater by 11% ($p < 0.01$) to 18% ($p < 0.05$) in the ion-rich condition than in the animals living in the grounded cages. The neutrophil count was in the opposite direction: 25% ($p < 0.01$) to 36% ($p < 0.05$) lower in the ion-rich atmosphere than in the other group. These results clearly indicate that the number of white blood cells can be changed with high levels of negative ions. With these results we will some day return to our slides of brain sections to examine the ion effect on glial cell populations.

These experiments have informed us how sensitive nerve and blood cells are to different levels of atmospheric ions. In the brain cells, the strength of the effects depends on whether the animals are living in enriched or impoverished conditions. The high levels of negative ions decreased both serotonin and cyclic AMP in the enriched but not in the impoverished animals' brains. The ion studies have been used primarily to indicate how subtle changes in the ion content of the air can alter brain structure and chemistry, not to endorse or discriminate against the use of ions. Undoubtedly, further research will demonstrate that many other structures are equally sensitive to the ion content in the air.

9
LEARNING
AND BEHAVIOR

The anatomical changes documented in the preceding chapters are important in themselves as indicators of the brain's plasticity, but their broader significance lies in their implications for learning and behavior. Many behavioral studies have evolved out of Hebb's original hypothesis (1) that enriching experiences early in life lead to permanent brain changes that enhance problem-solving capabilities.

Psychologists have known for a long time that early experience influences the adult performance of an animal. In early experiments in the 1950s (2–6), investigators were interested in such matters as how much experience in complex environments was necessary to produce a highly intelligent adult animal and when, specifically, during early life this experience had to occur.

Forgays and Reid (7) investigated the second of these questions and attempted to learn when during the short maturation period a limited amount of exposure to the complex environment had to occur in order to effect superior problem-solving ability in the adult animal. Their animals lived in a large box (124 × 71 × 28 cm) with "playthings" and were compared with animals living in regular laboratory cages. Five groups were given the enriched experience, each during a different age period—0 to 21 days, 22 to 43 days, 44 to 65 days, 66 to 87 days, and 88 to 109 days—and a sixth group had no enriched experience. There were differences in error scores in the Hebb-Williams maze test among the six groups in this study when they were tested two weeks after their enrichment experience. For example, the findings from four groups are mentioned. The group exposed for 3 weeks immediately after weaning, from day 22 to day 43, made the fewest errors compared with those exposed during the first 3 weeks of life (0 to 21 days) and with those exposed at about the time of maturity (88 to 109 days). As anticipated, the nonenriched animals made the most errors; all of the enriched animals were better problem solvers than those with no enrichment. There did not appear to be a critical period for learning which would designate that only at one time can a specific influence be effective. The results from this experiment of Forgays and Reid are consistent with the evidence from our anatomical measures showing that the cerebral cortex can be altered in structure as a consequence of enrichment at any age, but at some ages more than at others.

Later, in 1968, Denenberg et al. (8) noted that virtually all of the studies that had tested Hebb's original theory found that exposure to an enriched condition soon after weaning enhanced problem-solving and perceptual abilities. But they pointed out that the experimenters had been testing the animals soon after removing them from the different environmental conditions and consequently they were not really testing Hebb's hypothesis that the induced changes were relatively permanent. The data from Forgays and Reid's experiment (7), in which the animals were tested about 2 weeks after experiencing enrichment, did support Hebb's theory. Denenberg et al. (1968), however, allowed an extensive period to intervene, about 1 year, between termination of the environmental conditions and testing. Between birth and 21 days of age, 38 rats were raised in maternity cages or in enriched free environments (one square meter of floor space with toys). At 21 to 50 days of age, the animals were placed either in laboratory cages or in free environments. Then all rats were kept in laboratory cages until testing at 371 days of age. They found that either preweaning enrichment (from birth to 21 days) or postweaning enrichment (21 to 50 days) had a significant effect on performance.

The smallest error scores on the Hebb-Williams testing maze were found in those animals that had received the free-environment experience both before and after weaning, when compared with the animals which had free-environment experience only before weaning. Though different error scores were obtained for the different groups, the data allowed the investigators to conclude that early enrichment brought about permanent brain changes as measured by enhanced learning experience after a period of one year.

These types of behavioral tests are continuing in the 1980s. Ivinskis and Homewood (9) studied the effects of preweaning environmental enrichment on later problem-solving behavior in rats. In essence the results they found through behavioral studies supported the findings from our own anatomical work, reported in 1971, that enrichment during preweaning significantly increased cortical thickness, whether or not the enrichment had taken place before the eyes first opened (10). Ivinskis and Homewood found that exposure to the enriched environment for a period of 7 days before the eyes opened improved rats' later problem-solving behavior above that of the controls, and even raised it to the level of rats that had received such experience after the eyes had opened. These investigators suggested that the presence of the mother in the enriched condition might result in additional stimulation to the pups during the preweaning period.

Warren et al. (11) chose to study middle-aged (600- to 750-day-old) enriched mice with matched controls on four learning problems and an activity test. This was fortunate because we had anatomical data on rats within this age group. Warren et al. found that the enriched mice were significantly superior on incidental learning and on a food-seeking task, but did not differ significantly from the controls on a brightness discrimination task, on the Lashley III maze, or on an activity test. The enriched mice also had more cerebrocortical cells with very high levels of RNA, leading the authors to conclude that the mammalian brain appears to have the capacity to remain responsive to environmental enrichment well into advanced age. These results support our morphological findings for this middle-aged group very nicely, but we still do not have any behavioral data from others to compare with our anatomical data in our very old (904-day-old) enriched rats.

Most investigators studying correlations among behavior, enrichment, and anatomy examine the difference between the means of their results. Watson and Livesey (1982) introduced an important consideration regarding the evaluation of data by pointing out that scientists should examine the variability of the experimental animals (12). These investigators found in comparing enriched and isolated rats which had lived in their experimental conditions for periods ranging from 10 to 51 days (in four experiments) that the enriched groups were more similar in their maze performance than were the isolated animals. These results suggest that enriched group living provides an environment for some biological processes to become more synchronized. This has been shown to be true in certain human living situations; for example, females living together have been known to develop synchronized menstrual cycles. The isolated rats appear to develop their own idiosyncratic behavior, as demonstrated by their more varied maze performance.

These examples of behavioral data, collected from the early 1950s to the 1980s, indicate that environmental enrichment facilitates learning, memory, and problem solving as tested by maze performance. However, one is still faced with the question whether the greater learning ability results because an enriched condition promotes better encoding or faster encoding or the encoding of more information, or whether a larger nerve cell caused by enrichment can just process information more efficiently. Any of these possibilities either singly or in combination may be partially responsible for the enriched rat's ability to perform better in a maze than the nonenriched rat.

In order to tease apart what cortical areas and neural structures are involved in enabling the enriched rat to be a better maze runner than the nonenriched animal, Rosalie Greer decided to study an abnormal rat, one with marked learning deficiencies. Its cortex could be compared with that of an animal without such deficiencies, a similar approach to that employed in the experiments examining the cerebral cortex of the immune-deficient nude mouse. She studied the cortex of the Brattleboro rat, which not only shows abnormalities in learning and memory but also possesses a defect in the synthesis and release of the hormone vasopressin, sometimes called the antidiuretic hormone. The question then surfaced whether an animal without vasopressin and with difficulties in learning and memory would develop changes in the cerebral cortex in response to stimulating environments. To answer this question, two types of rats were raised: (1) a heterozygous Brattleboro rat with an abnormal vasopressin concentration in certain brain regions and (2) a homozygous Brattleboro rat with a total absence of vasopressin. Greer compared the cortical thickness and dendritic patterns of these two types of Brattleboro rats (13–15).

In order to carry out this series of experiments, these special rats had to be ordered from the National Institute of Health and then bred in the Berkeley laboratories. The offspring from the animals were housed singly in standard cages for 48 hours at some time between 33 and 40 days of age to diagnose the level of the antidiuretic hormone by volume of water intake, in other words, to determine which were homozygous and which heterozygous. In our laboratories, enough animals were produced to form three groups of male homozygous and heterozygous rats. In the first group, 5 homozygous 60-day-old rats and 9 heterozygous 60-day-old rats living in standard colony conditions were sacrificed to serve as a baseline. In the second group, 5 homozygous 90-day-old rats and 5 heterozygous 90-day-old rats living in standard colony conditions were sacrificed. In the third group, 12 homozygous and 12 heterozygous rats which had lived since 60 days of age in enriched conditions were sacrificed at 90 days of age.

The brains from these rats were processed to reveal the effects of age and enrichment on the dendrites of pyramidal neurons in layers II and III in the occipital cortex, as well as on the cortical thickness. Cortical thickness increases in response to enrichment in both types of Brattleboro rat were greater and more widespread than in normal Long-Evans rats. Whereas the maximum cortical thickness response in normal rats has been in the medial occipital cortex, area 18, the maximum response in both types of Brattleboro rats was in the sample of the lateral posterior cortical sample, area 39. The location of the dendritic response within the occipital cortex was different for the homozygous and the heterozygous animals, with the homozygous responding more in the lateral cortex. In addition, in the Brattleboro strains many subcortical regions, such as the hippocampus and the region containing the thalamus and hypothalamus, showed increases in response to enrichment, something not seen in the other strains studied.

These results shed additional light on the response of the brain to enrichment, suggesting a two-component response: first, a generalized reaction consistent with the arousal hypothesis offered by Walsh and Cummins (16), i.e., the animal is actively alert in the enriched environment, and second, a more specific, localized response in regions of greater neuron impulse traffic, as suggested by Szeligo and LeBlond (17). In the normal rat, greater neuron impulse traffic plays a larger role as indicated by the localized changes. Whereas, in the Brattleboro rat, the generalized reaction predominates. In both types of Brattleboro rats, a predominance of the generalized reaction is suggested by the widespread increases in both cortical and subcortical brain dimensions and is consistent with their prolonged arousal (18). The increases seen in cortical thickness and dendritic branching may result from excessive arousal, and any associated memory storage is probably maladaptive.

In normal rats there is evidence that vasopressin is released into certain limbic regions which include the hippocampus. In these regions vasopressin activates the neurotransmitter epinephrine and enhances consolidation of emotionally significant information. Evidence suggests that the hippocampus might be activated to facilitate the consolidation process and to impose a temporal limitation on this process via habituation.

Abnormally persistent memory in the homozygous rats, those completely lacking in vasopressin, was demonstrated by Celestian et al. (19). It is possible that the homozygous Brattleboro rat, lacking vasopressin, cannot normally facilitate norepinephrine release in critical limbic regions during emotional stress; thus, both consolidation and habituation are impaired. However, in situations involving chronic stimulation, such as the enriched environmental conditions or classical conditioning, consolidation can occur. But if hippocampal function is abnormal, then habituation is defective, arousal is prolonged, and consolidation is excessive. Thus, learning and memory in the homozygous rat may be either absent or abnormally persistent.

In summary, the dendritic branching and cortical thickening response to enrichment in the homozygous Brattleboro rat may be a correlate of maladaptive consolidation. Behavioral testing after environmental enrichment is needed in this strain with increased cortical dimensions to shed more light on their learning and memory abilities.

As we pursue our search to understand the effects of enrichment and the resulting brain changes on the ability of rats to learn mazes, it is important to compare these results with brain changes due to learning alone. For, we wish to know whether maze training will change the brain in a manner similar to the alterations induced by an enriched environment.

To answer this question we examined cortical responses to the specific learning conditions established by Kay Kerker in the late 1960s (20). She started an experiment with a very simple maze pattern in the Hebb-Williams maze and gradually increased the complexity of the learning conditions. Ten pairs of female Long-Evans rats at 71 days of age were used for this experiment. One rat from each littermate pair was given formal maze training while the remaining littermate was placed in an identical maze for the same length of time, with an unchanged simple barrier pattern and without food reward. The initial simple pattern for both animals consisted of one barrier between the start and the goal at the opposite corner of the box.

The maze training consisted of two parts: 10 days of pretraining and 22 days of formal training. For the first four days of pretraining, each maze animal was fed wet mash in the goal box and allowed to explore the empty maze for 30 minutes each day. For the next six days of pretraining, each experimental animal was put in the start box and required to find the goal box through a very simple barrier pattern for 30 minutes each day. The complexity of the patterns and the number of trials increased from day 5 to day 10. During the 22 days of formal testing, a series of barrier patterns, progressively increasing in complexity, were given, one each day. The first 12 patterns were those used in formal Hebb-Williams maze training, and the last 7 were more complex patterns (for the most complex, see Figure 37). On the last 3 patterns a second trial was given to check retention on the following day.

For Kerker's experiments, the original Hebb-Williams maze running experimental design was somewhat modified, ranging from 45 to 50

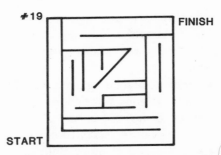

FIGURE 37. A floor plan of the most complicated maze, maze 19, used for testing brain changes with learning.

minutes in the maze, originally to 15 to 20 minutes, and in the goal box, from 20 seconds originally down to 10 seconds in the final patterns.

The running times and errors did not show a significant decrease with increasing trials for the first 12 barrier patterns, the Hebb-Williams training patterns. This was undoubtedly because they were so simple that the rats had no difficulty running the maze without errors on the first trial. Barrier patterns 13 to 19 were purposely made more difficult than the original Hebb-Williams patterns so that the rats could not solve them without errors on the first trial; also the feeding time was shortened.

In examining the cortical thickness differences between the brains of the maze-trained rats and those of the untrained littermates, Kerker found that only the lateral region of the posterior cortical section, area 39, showed a significant difference, 6% ($p < 0.025$). In addition to the cortical thickness in area 39 being greater in the trained animals, the neuronal nuclear diameter and nuclear area were 8% ($p < 0.05$) and 17% ($p < 0.03$) greater, respectively, in this region in the trained than in the nontrained.

No significant changes were found in the medial occipital cortex, the region which is usually modified in the normal enriched animals, or in the somatosensory regions. The responsive region was very localized in area 39, where multisensory integration is thought to take place.

To my knowledge, this preliminary investigation was the first to observe a morphological response of the cerebral cortex to problem solving in a maze. Over 10 years later, Greenough et al. (21) published their results showing the effects of formal training on dendritic branching in the occipital cortex. Adult rats were trained in two different types of procedures—a two-way alternative visual discrimination task and a Hebb-Williams maze. The experimenters found that neither procedure comparing the trained with untrained, induced the large increases in dendritic branchings from stellate neurons or in basilar dendritic branching from the pyramidal cells that were seen to result from comparing animals from enriched and impoverished conditions. Instead, the oblique or terminal branches from the apical shafts of pyramidal cells in layers IV or V were longer in the trained animals compared to the untrained.

We did not continue to measure apical or oblique branches in our enriched-impoverished experiments after we learned that it was primarily the basal dendrites which responded to this kind of input. Greenough et al. supported our initial, unpublished findings of measurable cortical morphological changes in response to formal learning in contrast to those found as a consequence of the enriched living arrangement. However, they did not specify which region of their occipital cortical sample showed the changes—whether medial or lateral. If lateral, then our results and theirs do support each other very nicely.

Now, we can return to compare the results showing brain changes due to learning with those due to enriched environmental conditions. In order to compare these findings it is necessary to use experimental conditions that are as similar as possible. The trained animals were 71 days of age at the beginning of the experiment and were trained for 32 days (10 days of pretraining and 22 days of formal training). The closest enrichment experiment that we have is one where the animals were 60 days of age at the start of the experiment and received 30 days of enrichment. With maze learning, only area 39 in the cortex showed significant increases; with enrichment, areas medial 10, 4, 18, 17 and 18a developed significant increases (Figure 29). The results bear out what one might anticipate. Since enrichment provides a general multisensory input, more of the cortex changes. Whereas, learning to run a maze requires the animal's focused attention, and consequently, only one area showed measurable alterations. Since enrichment most consistently alters the neuronal structure in area 18, and now we have the information that learning to solve a maze modifies the structure of area 39, we can now focus our attention on these two areas. More refined chemical and molecular studies of these regions may provide a fuller understanding of learning and memory processing in the cerebral cortex.

10

THE SIGNIFICANCE
OF ENRICHMENT

How much more do we know about how the brain works than we knew before we conducted our enriched and impoverished studies? We have learned a great deal about the interaction of the external and internal environment with the structure of the brain. We have learned that different regions of the cortex increase in size as the duration of exposure to the stimulating conditions is extended. We have learned that every layer of cortical neurons in area 18, the area responsible for visual integration, responds to our experiential environment, with the outer layers, II and III, showing the greatest changes. The neurons in the cerebral cortex exhibit an impressive amount of plasticity. We have learned that every part of the nerve cell from soma to synapse alters its dimensions in response to the environment.

The enlarged nerve cells with their more numerous glial support cells are apparently utilized by the rat to solve maze problems more effectively than rats without such modified cells. The mechanism by which the enlarged nerve cells improve learning ability is not yet known, but these findings clearly demonstrate brain enlargement as a result of brain use.

One often wonders how we can hold a train of thought for hours or record a memory for an extended period of 90 years or more if the flexibility of the cortical structures is so great. Obviously, some molecular configurations must remain stable at the same time that others exhibit change.

Just as the cortical neurons become larger in a stimulating environment, they decrease in size when there is less input from the millions of sensory receptors reporting from the body surface and the internal organs. It is just as important to stress the fact that decreased stimulation will diminish a nerve cell's dendrites as it is to stress that increased stimulation will enlarge the dendritic tree. We have seen how readily the cortical thickness diminishes with an impoverished environment, and at times, the effects of impoverishment are greater than those brought about by a comparable period of enrichment.

These cellular changes that we have measured in the brain provide us with a better understanding of how the environment interacting with an hereditary base possibly influenced the brains of higher organisms, including the human brain. Those members of species which happened— by genetic happenstance—to have free extremities, a tendency to explore, and/or bigger brains, were better able to survive and pass on those genes. The upright human, with free upper extremities, continuously sought new challenges, new enriched conditions, and in turn could alter the dimensions of his brain. It is the interaction of the environment with heredity which has changed the brain over millions of years.

Perhaps the single most valuable piece of information learned from all our studies is that structural differences can be detected in the cerebral cortices of animals exposed at any age to different levels of stimulation in the environment. First, we found that young animals placed in enriched environments just after weaning developed measurable changes in cortical morphology. Then, we worked backward in age to the animals not yet weaned and found such changes, and we even found measurable effects of prenatal enrichment. Later, we moved forward in age to learn that the enriched young adult demonstrated an increase in dendritic growth, not only above that found in his impoverished mates, but even above the level of the standard colony animal. In the very old animal, with the cortex following its normal decline with aging, we again found the enriched cortex significantly thicker than the nonenriched. In fact at every age studied, we have shown anatomical effects due to enrichment or impoverishment. The results from enriched animals provide a degree of optimism about the potential of the brain in elderly human beings, just as the effects of impoverishment warn us of the deleterious consequences of inactivity.

Our ultimate goal in studying the aging animal brain is to bring as much dignity as possible to the aging human being, to indicate the potential of aging cerebral cortical cells, and to challenge the myths regarding the aging brain by critically evaluating them. For example, one of the most prevalent popular beliefs is that once we reach adulthood our brain cells are dying by the hundreds each day and therefore our mental capacities must be diminishing as well. The belief received support in 1958, when Benedict Burns (1) calculated from Brody's data (2) and Leboucq's data (3) that during every day of our adult life more than 100,000 neurons die. These depressing data were derived in the following manner. Brody's estimation of neuron loss in the human cortex between 20 and 80 years of age was 30%, and Leboucq found a decrease in surface area of the brain between the ages of 20 and 76 years amounting to some 10%. Burns's estimated daily cell loss has been frequently quoted. More recently, however, Brody noted the prominence of this information in the lay literature and rejected it as scientifically inaccurate. The original studies included too few samples, and inadequate information was available about the living conditions of the brain donors prior to autopsy. Furthermore, Brody has since reported that some areas of the brain do not lose cells at all with aging, a finding similar to our own (4). Apparently, the loss of cells varies from region to region. For example, the locus ceruleus in the hindbrain and the nucleus of Meynert in the forebrain do lose nerve cells with aging; whereas, several of the cranial nerve nuclei and a nucleus in the hindbrain called the inferior olivary nucleus do not lose nerve cells throughout the lifetime of the individual.

There is some evidence that the decrease in brain weight and the degree of cortical atrophy in healthy old subjects who have no brain pathology is relatively slight. The brains of such individuals are within normal weight ranges for young adults and have cerebral hemispheres exhibiting no apparent cortical atrophy. Evidence does indicate that the number and size of the spines on cerebral cortical nerve cells are reduced in old individuals. But even spines can still be present in active old nerve cells; at least they are clearly present in animals two-thirds of the way through a lifespan. In studying the brains of old human beings it is important to be aware of the lifestyle prior to death, something scientists have been taking more seriously in recent studies. With such considerations, some medical texts now state that in many respects the healthy old brain is similar to the healthy young brain. The experiential environment is a major factor in maintaining the healthy old brain. A few of the myths about the deterioration of functioning during aging are slowly being replaced as scientific knowledge is beginning to offer some contrary evidence.

Such information stimulates us to adopt new attitudes toward aging and encourages us to plan for an active life in old age. Of course, many bright, energetic individuals have always done this; the knowledge of the potential of the brain was not a necessary inducement. Many people have looked to their grandparents who lived a long full life and concluded that they too could follow a similar path. There is no doubt that one's genetic background is important, but our studies suggest that the use of our nerve cells is critical to their continued health. Interviews with some active elderly supported this view. For example, the 89 year old California wine taster still had his acute taste buds as well as a keen olfactory sense for sniffing good wines. The perspective developed in this book suggests that his continuous attention to his senses of taste and smell enabled them to remain acute during aging. The university chemist active at 98, was still publishing and reading without his glasses. His alert 92 year old wife continued to read out loud to him. We all know older people like these whose lives illustrate what we have learned about the potential of the cortical nerve cells to respond to the information coming in from the environment.

But what about the millions of human beings who are discouraged and do not continue to stimulate their brains? Many people attend school for a dozen or so years and then find a job only to provide an income until retirement. Their living pattern usually moves toward slowing down until they finally fade away. The generally accepted knowledge about the brain is that it starts "going downhill" fairly early in life (which is true) and that after that, there is little one can do about changing this pattern (which is not true). As mentioned in Chapter 2, recent studies on the developing human brain have shown that the size of the cerebral cortex is already decreasing after the age of ten. In fact, the patterns of an increasing and subsequently decreasing curve were very similar for rats and humans during the early postnatal period. If we take advantage of our more recent knowledge regarding the plasticity of a lower mammalian cortex at any age, then we can offer encouragement to counteract the downhill slope in human beings. A different outlook emerges toward lifestyle, as a whole, and toward learning, in particular.

Opportunities for learning should be encouraged from shortly after conception and continued until death. The data from a Japanese laboratory and from ours showed the beneficial effects of stimulating environments during intrauterine life: improved maze behavior and increases in cortical structure in the animals after birth. Though the western world is only recently becoming aware of such a practice, for centuries Asian people have encouraged the pregnant mother to enrich her developing fetus by having pleasant thoughts and avoiding angry, disturbing behavior. At the same time, one is made aware of other beneficial factors in aiding the development of the fetus such as good diets and plenty of exercise after which the dendritic trees in cortical nerve cells are richly developed.

On the other hand, mothers need to be alerted to the negative effects on fetal development of such substances as alcohol. Alcohol administered to pregnant rats (5% alcohol in a protein-rich diet throughout gestation from day 2) has been reported to cause a decrease in the body size of cortical pyramidal cells and in their number of dendrites in the brains of the offspring. Other results have shown that the nerve cells adjacent to the ventricles in the brain are also defective in rats exposed to alcohol before birth. Thus, the prenatal brain has been shown to be sensitive to negative influences like alcohol and malnutrition as well as to the positive influence of enrichment.

We still do not know whether an enriched condition during pregnancy can prevent some of the massive nerve cell loss, as much as 50% to 65% of the total population of cells, which occurs during the development of the fetus. It is apparent that overproduction of neurons occurs in the fetus because most neurons do not reproduce themselves after being formed: an excess number is needed as a safety factor. Therefore, those that are not involved in the early neuronal processing are "weeded out." At the present time it is believed that the limits of cell number are set by the genetic constitution. As mentioned in Chapter 1, investigators found the same number of cells in a single column of cortical cells, in rats, cats, dogs, monkeys and human beings (5). The genetic regulation of these cells appears to transcend species. Understanding the causes of this constancy in number is a complex process, for even fluctuations in body temperature can influence brain cell number. The body temperature of the pregnant female has a marked influence on the number of neurons that survive in the fetus. If the temperature is increased in the female guinea pig by 3 to 4°C for 1 hour in the latter part of gestation, the fetal brain weight is reduced by 10 percent. This reduction in brain weight is due to a loss of brain cells. Hyperthermia has not yet been established as a cause of human fetal brain damage and mental retardation, but we should be alerted to this possibility whether studying animals or man.

Though enriched experiential environments have not been shown to alter the number of nerve cells, our results have indicated that variation in the experiential environment can readily alter the size of the preexisting nerve cells in the cerebral cortex, whether in the cell body or in its rich membrane extensions, the dendrites, or in synapses. The importance of stimulation for the well-being of the nerve cells has been demonstrated in many species. But of equally weighty significance is the possible detrimental effect of too much stimulation. The eternal question arises, When is enough enough or too much too much? The reputed pediatrician, T. Berry Brazelton, points out that infants exposed to too much stimulation respond either by crying, by extending their periods of sleep, or by developing colic or withdrawing from any new approaches. In providing increased stimulation for the young, the adult, or the old, one always has to keep in mind the need for adequate time at each phase of information processing: input, assimilation, and output. The integration of the input is essential before we can anticipate a meaningful output. As adults, we frequently say, "Let me think things over." It is essential to give the infant the same opportunity.

We have learned from our results that the nervous system possesses not just a "morning" of plasticity, but an "afternoon" and an "evening" as well. It is essential not to force a continuous stream of information into the developing brain but to allow for periods of consolidation and assimilation in between. I often tell the overworked student to go out and just lie on the lawn and watch the clouds drift slowly by.

We do not yet know the true capacity or potential of the brain. Our data at present suggest that nerve cells benefit from "moderate" sources of stimulation, allowing for new connections to be formed, and thus providing the substrate for more options. We have yet to try too much stimulation. Will the stimulated brain continue to increase or will its reticular formation sift out the excess stimulation?

To date we do not know whether there is a "ceiling" effect on brain growth beyond which no further expansion will occur. In our rats in the preweaning stage, one area (area 39) differed as much as 16% between the brains from the enriched rats and those from the nonenriched. A Swiss group (6), using super-enriched conditions, including additional space and toys, were also able to produce 16% differences in rats past the age of weaning. Does this mean that 16% cortical thickness differences represent the maximum change we can induce with environmental enrichment? I hesitate to accept such a premise at this time. Undoubtedly, with more imaginative experimental designs, utilizing additional creativity, we will find greater responses in the future. Of course, quantity of brain tissue is not our only goal. Quality is the ultimate objective. So far it has been shown that the thicker cortex is positively correlated with a better maze performance. Only further studies will provide information on the actual potential of the cerebral cortex to alter its structure with increased stimulation.

I recently uncovered a small book published in 1901 by the Macmillan Company called The Education of the Nervous System by Reuben Halleck (7). In essence, its message was that the best education we can provide the developing nervous system is one of stimulating all the five known senses. Halleck wrote that a person who has only one or even two senses properly trained is at best a pitiful fraction of a human being. He points out that recalled images of sensations we receive from the world around us are powerful and necessary aids in further modifying and developing the sensory cells; not images of sight alone, but of every sense. What does lilac smell like? How do the tastes of cinammon and nutmeg differ? It is possible for us to conscientiously train our senses, all of them, at any time in our lives. If we fine-tune the primary sensory areas early, the association cortices might then respond to more subtle differences in a greater variety of ways. Creative ideas could arise from a broader experiential base. The finding of more widespread changes in the brains of enriched rats than in those of rats trained to learn a specific task supports the claims of numerous educators, from Dewey on (8), that providing a wide variety of experiences to the growing child enhances intellectual development.

While all sensory input facilitates learning, the visual association cortex was the first to be responsive to enrichment in our experiments. This may be related to the fact that cortical association areas are the last areas to develop embryologically and the most recent phylogenetically. Thus, it is reasonable for the visual association area to show morphological changes in response to stimulation in a learning circuit. As far back as 1901, Fleschig (9) proposed that learning took place by impulses first entering a primary sensory cortical area, then going to the secondary or association cortex, and then into the limbic system. For visual input in Fleschig's model, the primary sensory cortex would be area 17 and the secondary or association cortex would be area 18, and then continuing to the limbic system. Within this pathway we might anticipate area 18 to be the region most likely to show change. And we find that it does respond in the shortest period of time to our experimental conditions. With a longer duration of exposure to the environmental conditions, area 17, the primary visual cortex, also demonstrates cellular changes. On the other hand, one part of the limbic system we have measured, the male hippocampus, has not demonstrated the same degree of plasticity as has the occipital cortex. However, some investigators have shown small amounts of hippocampal increases with enriched environments using female rats. Our findings offer support to our hypothesis that neural activity within the visual cortex is important for the initial information processing that facilitates learning. Our results indicate that it is the posterior part of the cortex rather than the frontal cortex which possesses the most plasticity. Future studies on the biochemistry of learning and memory in the mammalian cortex might therefore be most appropriately focused on this posterior region.

Though we have demonstrated the plasticity of the cerebral cortex, we are very much aware that the brain does not work by itself. Healthy support systems, i.e., the cardiovascular, respiratory, urinary, and digestive systems, are essential for the maintenance of the healthy brain. The heart and its accompanying blood vessels need to be maintained through balanced diet and exercise. With exercise, the connective tissue surrounding the skeletal muscles and blood vessels can remain strong and aid with efficient circulation of the blood. The lungs should be free of disease, such as enphysema which can be caused by smoking or breathing air contaminated with pollutants. The body needs to take in adequate fluids to keep the kidneys working efficiently; these, in turn, keep the blood free of concentrated waste products. The digestive system needs to benefit from strong teeth that can break down food for efficient digestion, and from a fibrous diet to maintain the well-being of the large intestine. All of this is nothing new. It was Plato who said, back in 400 B.C., that a healthy body promotes a healthy brain and a healthy brain, a healthy body.

Not only is the brain dependent upon other systems, but each part of the brain interacts with another. The cortex, with its more refined intellectual functions, attempts to coordinate with the limbic system, with its more emotional functions. One without the other is only half an experience. In Nathaniel Hawthorne's story *Ethan Brand* (10), his main character is searching for the unpardonable sin. He concentrates to such an extent on his intellectual pursuit that he becomes emotionally starved. He eventually becomes dismayed and throws himself into his fiery kiln. When others discover the remains, all that is left is his charred rib cage enclosing a cold marble heart. He had discovered the unpardonable sin by neglecting to integrate the warm, emotional heart, in a metaphorical sense, with his intellectual pursuit.

Satisfying emotional needs is essential at any age. As we learned from our studies on aging rats, by giving our old rats a little tender loving care, we were able to increase their lifespan; those rats that received additional attention lived longer than those that did not. These results imply that the two regions of the brain, the limbic system and the cortex, need to work together efficiently for the well-being of the whole individual. Thus, it is important to stimulate the portion of the brain that initiates emotional expression, which encompasses the connections between the cerebral cortex and the limbic system, including the hippocampus, amygdala and hypothalamus. In our studies it was the cortex which responded more readily to the environmental conditions and not those parts of the limbic system which we measured, such as the hippocampus and amygdala. The fact that these structures are less adaptable to a varied environment implies that they are more basic to the survival of the individual, suggesting that emotional well-being may be more essential for survival than intellectual. Other kinds of stimulation besides mental challenges, e.g., considerable personal attention and other forms of emotional involvement, may be essential to create changes in limbic structures. If this is so, how much more effort should we be making toward giving attention and care to each other? And how important it is for the intellectual components of the brain to be taught ways to guide the emotional ones.

Several of our measurements have indicated that even the deprived brain can adapt by changing in structure as a result of enriched living conditions. Such changes were discovered in both prenatally and postnatally deprived animals. If mother rats were protein-deprived during pregnancy and lactation and their newborn pups were given both protein-rich diets and enriched living conditions after birth, the pups' brains grew more than those of standard colony rats that were only nutritionally rehabilitated (11). In the experiment dealing with postnatal deprivation, the cerebral cortices were lesioned or damaged during infancy, and then the animals were placed in enriched living conditions (12). Upon measuring the length of these animals' cortices after enrichment, the investigators found that the length had increased to compensate for the previous damage. Thus, we must not give up on people who begin life under unfavorable conditions. Environmental enrichment has the potential to enhance their brain development too, depending upon the degree of severity of the insult.

In this limitless field of possibilities for future study, a few specific research avenues beckon most immediately. We wish to gain a better understanding about what elements are responsible for the growth of the cerebral cortex. In Chapter 1 the normal cortical growth pattern was presented, but we do not know what causes the rapidly growing cortex to reverse its direction shortly after birth. At present we are studying the role of opioid blockers, substances which block the endogenous or natural opiates (opioids) in the brain, because some investigators have demonstrated that various regions of the brain increase in size and cellular content when opioid receptors are blocked. Our initial results support these findings. In addition we wish to learn more about nerve growth factor and its role in cortical development. For years, nerve growth factor was thought to be confined to specific regions such as the sympathetic ganglia, but more recently it has been found in the hippocampus and cerebral cortex. We are particularly interested in its role and when it is active in the cerebral cortex. In light of the large number of people who are taking drugs for therapeutic reasons for long periods of time, it is important to learn more about how the cerebral cortex responds under such medication. Thus, one specific question I would like to pursue now is whether the enriched condition favorably alters the brains of animals on antiepileptic drugs. For example, it is possible to obtain a type of rodent, a gerbil, which has spontaneous seizures. If this animal is given a seizure-reducing drug, will the enriched environment still increase the cortical dimension?

In addition, we wish to pursue a study to determine what agents play a role in creating the enlarged cortex in the offspring, the F^1 and F^2 generations, from the enriched parents. The high level of progesterone during pregnancy was suggested as one possible responsible factor. This suggestion has to be tested as well as others.

The ultimate goal of all of our studies has been to gain a better understanding of human behavior by examining its source, the brain. The simple enriched environmental paradigm allowing rats to interact with toys in their cages produced anatomical changes in the cerebral cortex. Now how do we apply this knowledge for the benefit of people? Since no two human brains are exactly alike, no enriched environment will completely satisfy any two individuals for an extended period of time. The range of enriched environments for human beings is endless. For some, interacting with objects is gratifying; for others, obtaining information is rewarding; and for still others, working with creative ideas is most enjoyable. But no matter what form enrichment takes, it is the challenge to the nerve cells which is important. In one experiment where the rats could watch other rats "play" with their toys but could not play themselves, the brains of the observer rats did not show measurable changes. These data indicate that passive observation is not enough; one must interact with the environment. One way to be certain of continued enrichment is to maintain curiosity throughout a lifetime. Always asking questions of yourself or others and in turn seeking out the answers provides continual challenge to nerve cells.

Finally, now that we have begun to appreciate the plasticity of our cerebral cortex, the seat of the intellectual functioning that distinguishes us as human beings, we must learn to use this knowledge. It must stimulate and guide our efforts to work toward enriching heredity through enriching the environment . . . for everyone . . . at any age.

REFERENCES

1 Can We Change Our Brains?

1. Rockel, A. J., R. W. Hiorns, and T. P. S. Powell: The basic uniformity in structure of the neocortex, *Brain,* 103:221–244 (1980).
2. Malacarne, G.: *Memorie storiche intorno alla vita ed alle opere di Michele Vincenzo Giacinto Malacarne.* Padova Tipografia del Seminario, (1819), p. 88.
3. Ramón y Cajal, S.: *Histologie du système nerveux de l'homme et des vertébrés* Reprinted by Consejo Superior de Investigaciones Cientificas, Madrid (1952).
4. Tryon, R. C.: Genetic differences in maze learning in rats. *Nat. Soc. Stu. Educ. Yearbk.,* Public School Publishing Co., Bloomington, Ill. (1940).
5. Tryon, R.: The genetics of learning ability in rats. *Univ. Calif. Publ. Psychol.,* 4:71–89 (1929).
6. Rosenzweig, M. R., D. Krech, and E. L. Bennett: Brain enzymes and adaptive behaviour. In G. E. Wolstenholme and C. M. O'Connor (eds.): *Neurological Basis of Behaviour.* CIBA Foundation Symposium, Churchill, London (1958), pp. 337–355.
7. Hebb, D.: *The Organization of Behavior.* Wiley, New York (1949)
8. Krech, D., M. R. Rosenzweig, and E. L. Bennett: Effects of environmental complexity and training on brain chemistry. *J. Comp. Physiol. Psychol.,* 53:509–519 (1960).

2 Normal Forebrain Development and Aging

1. Diamond, M. C., D. Krech, and M. R. Rosenzweig: The effects of an enriched environment on the histology of the rat cerebral cortex. *J. Comp. Neurol.,* 123:111–120 (1964).
2. Krieg, W. J. S.: Connections of the cerebral cortex. *J. Comp. Neurol.,* 84:221–275 (1946).
3. Diamond, M. C.: Sex differences in the structure of the rat forebrain. *Brain Res. Rev.,* 12:235–240 (1987).
4. Yanaid, J.: Delayed maturation of the male cerebral cortex in rats. *Acta Anat.,* 104:335–339 (1979).
5. Winick, M.: *Malnutrition and Brain Development.* Oxford University Press, New York (1976).

6. Dobbing, J., and J. Sands: Quantitative growth and development of the human brain. *Arch. Disease Child,* 48:757–767 (1973).

7. Chugani, H. T., M. E. Phelps, and J. C. Mazziotta: Human brain functional development. *Ann. Neurol.* 22:487–497 (1987).

8. One important fact to be considered in analyzing the data from these brains is that two-thirds of the subjects included in the study were taking anticonvulsants daily. Although sedative effects were not seen, it is important to point out that in PET studies of adults taking multiple anticonvulsants, the deoxyglucose uptake in the cerebral cortex is increased by a mean of 37% after withdrawal of some anticonvulsants, indicating there has to be some effect of the anticonvulsants on brain function. Therefore, we have some problems in fully accepting these newer human studies, but they are among the best available at the present time. Nonetheless, these preliminary results on the human brain cortical development are intriguing, especially since the pattern follows closely that of the developing rat cortex.

9. Diamond, M. C., R. E. Johnson, and C. A. Ingham: Morphological changes in the young, adult and aging rat cerebral cortex, hippocampus and diencephalon. *Behav. Biol.,* 14:163–174 (1975).

10. Diamond, M. C.: Rat forebrain morphology: Right-left; male-female; young-old; enriched-impoverished. In S. D. Glick (ed.), *Cerebral Lateralization in Nonhuman Species.* Academic Press, N.Y. (1985), pp. 73–86.

11. Lewis, David: Unpublished (1987).

12. Gutmann, D.: *Reclaimed Powers.* Basic Books, New York (1987).

13. Sherman, G. F., J. A. Garbanati, G. D. Rosen, D. A. Yutzey, and V. H. Denenberg: Brain and behavior asymmetries for spatial preference in rats. *Brain Res.,* 192:61–67 (1980).

14. Stokes, K. A., and D. C. McIntyre: Lateralized asymmetrical state-dependent learning produced by kindled convulsions from rat hippocampus. *Physiol. Behav.,* 26:163–169 (1981).

15. Murphy, G.: An evolutionary perspective on hemispheric asymmetry: The human striatic cortex. Ph.D. Thesis, University of California, Berkeley (1984).

16. De Lacoste-Utamsing, C., and R. L. Holloway: Sexual dimorphism in the human corpus callosum. *Science,* 216:1431–1432 (1982).

17. De Lacoste, M. C., J. B. Kirkpatrick, and E. D. Ross: Topography of the human corpus callosum. *J. Neuropathol. Exper. Neurol.,* 44:578–591 (1985).

18. De Lacoste, M. C., R. L. Holloway, and D. J. Woodward: Sex differences in the fetal human corpus callosum. *Hum. Neurobiol.,* 5:93–96 (1986).

19. Allen, L. S., and R. A. Gorski: Sexual dimorphism of the human anterior commissure. *Anat. Rec.,* 214:3A (1986).

20. Bleier, R.: Can the corpus callosum predict gender, age, handedness or cognitive differences? *Trends in Neurosci.,* 9:391–394 (1986).

21. Barley, J. M., M. Ginsburg, B. Greenstein, N. J. Maclusky, and P. J. Thomas: A receptor mediating sexual differentiation? *Nature,* 258:259–260 (1974).

22. MacLusky, N. J., I. Lieberger, and B. S. McEwen: The development of estrogen receptor systems in the rat brain: Perinatal development. *Brain Res.,* 178:129–142 (1979).

23. MacLusky, N. J., C. Ch..ptal, and B. S. McEwen: The development of estrogen receptor systems in the rat brain: Postnatal development. *Brain Res.,* 178:143–160 (1979).

24. Sandhu, S., P. Cook, and M. C. Diamond: Rat cerebral cortical estrogen receptors: Male-female, right-left. *Exp. Neurol.,* 92:186–196 (1986).

25. Pappas, C. T. E., M. C. Diamond, and R. E. Johnson: Morphological changes in the cerebral cortex of rats with altered levels of ovarian hormones. *Behav. Neurol. Biol.* 26:298–310 (1979).

26. Leslie, M.: Estrogen receptors in the cerebral cortex of neonatal rats. Senior Honor Thesis. University of California, Berkeley (1987).

27. Diamond, M. C., G. M. Murphy, Jr., K. Akiyama, and R. E. Johnson: Morphologic hippocampal asymmetry in male and female rats. *Exp. Neurol.*, 76:553–566 (1982).

28. O'Keefe, J., and L. Nagel: *The Hippocampus as a Cognitive Map.* Oxford University Press, New York (1978).

29. Melone, J. H., S. A. Teitelbaum, R. E. Johnson, and M. C. Diamond: The rat amygdaloid nucleus: A morphometric right-left study. *Exp. Neurol.*, 86:293–302 (1984).

30. Braitenberg, V., and M. Kemali: Exceptions to bilateral symmetry in the epithalamus. *J. Comp. Neurol.*, 138:137–146 (1976).

31. Webster, W. G., and I. H. Webster: Anatomical asymmetry of the cerebral hemispheres of the cat brain. *Physiol. Behav.*, 14:867–869 (1975).

32. LeMay, M., and N. Geschwind: Hemispheric differences in the brains of great apes. *Brain Behav. Evol.*, 11:48–52 (1975).

33. Litteria, M., and M. W. Thorner: Inhibitory action of neonatal estrogenization on the incorporation of [^{3}H] lysine into cortical neuroproteins. *Brain Res.*, 103:584–587 (1976).

34. Litteria, M., and M. W. Thorner: Inhibition in the incorporation of [H^3] lysine into proteins of specific hypothalamic nuclei of the adult female rat after neonatal estrogenization. *Exp. Neurol.*, 49:592–595 (1975).

35. Garcia, E. P., J. H. Denari, and J. M. Rosner: Uptake and metabolic effects of estradiol in the guinea pig cerebral cortex. *Steroids Lipids Res.*, 4:248–256 (1973).

36. Wade, G. N., and H. H. Feder: Stimulation of [^{3}H] leucine incorporation into protein by estradiol-17B or progesterone in brain tissues of ovariectomized guinea pigs. *Brain Res.*, 73:545–549 (1974).

37. Diamond, M. C., R. E. Johnson, and C. Ingham: Brain plasticity induced by environment and pregnancy. *Int. J. Neurosci.*, 2:171–178 (1971).

38. Presl, J., J. Pospíšil, and J. Horský: Autoradiographic localization of radioactivity in female rat neocortex after injection of tritiated estradiol. *Experientia,* 27:465 (1971).

39. Kato, J., N. Sugimara, and T. Kobayashi: Changing pattern of the uptake of estradiol by the anterior hypothalamus, the median eminence and the hypophysis in the developing female rat. In M. Hamburgh and E. J. W. Barrington: *Hormones in Development,* Appleton-Century-Crofts, New York (1971), pp. 689–703.

40. Pappas, C. T. E., M. C. Diamond, and R. E. Johnson: Effects of ovariectomy and differential experience on rat cerebral cortical morphology. *Brain Res.*, 154:53–60 (1978).

41. Sheridan, P. J., M. Sar, and W. E. Stumpf: Autoradiographic localization of ^{3}H-estradiol or its metabolites in the central nervous system of the developing rat. *Endocrinology,* 94:1386–1390 (1974).

42. Pfenninger, K. H., and R. P. Rees: From the growth cone to the synapse: Properties of membranes in synapse formation. In S. H. Barondes (ed.), *Neuronal Recognition,* Plenum, New York (1976), pp. 131–178.

43. Peters, A., and I. R. Kaiserman-Abramof: The small pyramidal neuron of rat cere-

bral cortex: The synapses upon dendritic spines. *Z. Zellforsch. Mikrosk. Anat.,* 100:487–506 (1969).

44. Dyson, S. E., and D. G. Jones: Quantitation of terminal parameters and their interrelationships in maturing central synapses: A perspective for experimental studies. *Brain Res.,* 183:43–59 (1980).

45. Greenough, W. T. R., W. West, and J. T. Devoogd: Subsynaptic plate perforations: Changes with age and experience in the rat. *Science,* 202:1096–1098 (1978).

46. Medosch, C. M., and M. C. Diamond: Rat occipital cortical synapses after ovariectomy. *Exp. Neurol.,* 75:120–133 (1982).

47. Pappas, C. T. E., M. C. Diamond, and R. E. Johnson: Morphological changes in the cerebral cortex of rats with altered levels of ovarian hormones. *Behav. Neural Biol.,* 26:298–310 (1979).

48. Diamond, M. C.: Aging and environmental influences on the rat forebrain. In A. B. Scheibel and A. F. Wechsler (eds.): *The Biological Substrates of Alzheimer's Disease.* Academic Press, New York (1986), pp. 55–64.

49. For the statistical analysis of the data, the Student's t test was used in the early studies on cortical thickness, cell counts, and blood vessel dimensions. For the later dendritic measures the data were analyzed using analysis of variance (ANOVA) and Scheffe tests. Student's t test was used to determine statistical differences between types of spines from animals within the same age group. For some of the left-right comparisons, computations were carried out with the BMDP2V program. Effects were judged statistically significant when $p < 0.05$. However, we felt it important to note that a large number of statistical tests were carried out. According to the Bonferroni inequality, if nine tests were made (one for each cortical region), then the overall error rate did not exceed 0.05 when the p for an individual test was $0.05/9 = 0.0056$. We considered tests achieving this level of significance most reliable. For several comparisons, as with the crowded experiments, the data were analyzed with a two-way (mixed) analysis of variance for the factors "condition" (standard, enriched, crowded enriched) and "hemisphere" (right-left repeated measures) to assess main effects and interactions. Where appropriate, this was followed by one-way analysis of variance and Student's t tests on conditions, and a paired Student's t test comparing right and left hemispheres. Differences were considered significant at $p < 0.05$ by a one-tailed test (standard vs. enriched) and a two-tailed test (standard vs. crowded enriched and right vs. left hemispheres).

3 Development and Aging of Cortical Nerve Cells and Glial Cells

1. Diamond, M. C., F. Law, H. Rhodes, B. Lindner, M. R. Rosenzweig, D. Krech, and E. L. Bennett: Increases in cortical depth and glia numbers in rats subjected to enriched environment. *J. Comp. Neurol.,* 128:117–126 (1966).

2. Diamond, M. C., R. E. Johnson, and M. W. Gold: Changes in neuron and glia number in the young, adult, and aging rat occipital cortex. *Behav. Biol.* 20:409–418 (1977).

3. Diamond, M. C., R. E. Johnson, A. M. Protti, C. Ott, and L. Kajisa: Plasticity in the 904-day-old rat. *Exp. Neurol.,* 87:309–317 (1985).

4. Brizzee, K. R., N. Sherwood, and P. S. Timiras: A comparison of various depth levels in cerebral cortex of young adults and aged Long-Evans rats. *J. Gerontol.,* 23:289–297 (1968).

5. Vaughn, D., and A. Peters: Neuroglia cells in the cerebral cortex of rats from young adulthood to old age: An electron microscope study. *J. Neurocytol.,* 3:405–429 (1974).

6. Smart, I., and C. P. Leblond: Evidence for division and transformation of neuroglia cells in mouse brain, as derived from radioautography after injection of thymidine-H³ *J. Comp. Neurol.,* 116:349–367 (1961).

7. Diamond, M. C., A. B. Scheibel, G. M. Murphy, Jr., and T. Harvey: On the brain of a scientist: Albert Einstein. *Exp. Neurol.,* 88:198–204 (1985).

8. McShane, S., L. Glaser, E. R. Greer, J. Houtz, M. F. Tong, and M. C. Diamond: Cortical asymmetry—neurons-glia, female-male: A preliminary study. *Exp. Neurol.* 99:353–361 (1988).

4   The Effects of Enrichment and Impoverishment

1. Gomori, G.: *Microscopic Histochemistry.* University of Chicago Press, Chicago (1952).

2. Diamond, M. C., R. M. Diamond, E. L. Bennett, D. Krech, and M. R. Rosenzweig: Distribution of acetylcholinesterase in cerebral cortical tissue slices from maze bright and maze dull strains. *Anat. Rec.,* 139:221 (1961).

3. Krech, D., M. R. Rosenzweig, and E. L. Bennett: Effects of environmental complexity and training on brain chemistry. *J. Comp. Physiol. Psychol.,* 53:509–519 (1960).

4. Rosenzweig, M. R., D. Krech, E. L. Bennett, and M. C. Diamond: Effects of environmental complexity and training on brain chemistry and anatomy. *J. Comp. Physiol. Psychol.,* 55:429–437 (1962).

5. Ferchmin, P. A., V. Eterovic, and R. Caputto: Studies of brain weight and RNA content after short periods of exposure to environmental complexity. *Brain Res.,* 20:49–57 (1970).

6. Walsh, R. N., R. A. Cummins, and O. Budtz-Olsen: The time course of environmentally induced changes in brain and body weight. *Selec. Doc. Psychol.* 5:283–288 (1974).

7. Floeter, M. K., and W. T. Greenough: Cerebellar plasticity: Modification of Purkinje cell structure by differential rearing in monkeys. *Abstr. Soc. Neurosci.,* 4:471 (1978).

8. Rosenzweig, M. R., E. L. Bennett, and M. C. Diamond: Chemical and anatomical plasticity of brain: Replications and extensions. In J. Gaito (ed.): *Macromolecules and Behavior,* 2nd ed. Appleton-Century-Crofts, New York (1971), pp. 205–278.

9. Geller, E., A. Yuwiler, and J. Zolman: Effects of environmental complexity on constituents of brain and liver. *J. Neurochem.,* 12:949–955 (1965).

10. Bennett, E. L., M. R. Rosenzweig, and M. C. Diamond: Rat brain: Effects of environmental enrichment on wet and dry weights. *Science,* 163:825–826 (1969).

11. Bennett, E. L., and M. R. Rosenzweig: Brain chemistry and anatomy: Implications for theories of learning and memory. In C. Rupp (ed.): *Mind as a Tissue.* Hoeber Medical Div., Harper & Row, New York (1968), pp. 63–86.

12. Altman, J., R. Wallace, W. Anderson, and G. Das: Behaviorally induced changes in length of cerebrum in rats. *Dev. Psychobiol.,* 1:111–117 (1968).

13. Walsh, R. N., O. E. Budtz-Olsen, A. Torok, and R. A. Cummins: Environmentally-induced changes in the dimensions of the rat cerebrum. *Dev. Psychobiol.,* 4:115–122 (1971).

14. Rosenzweig, M. R., and E. L. Bennett: Effects of differential environments on brain weights and enzyme activities in gerbils, rats and mice. *Dev. Psychobiol.,* 2:87–95 (1969).

15. Walsh, R. N., R. A. Cummins, and O. E. Budtz-Olsen: Environmentally induced changes in the dimensions of the rat cerebrum: A replication and extension. *Dev. Psychobiol.,* 6:3–8 (1973).

16. Cummins, R. A., R. N. Walsh, O. E. Budtz-Olsen, T. Konstantinas, and C. R. Horsfall: Environmentally-induced brain changes in elderly rats. *Nature,* 243:516–518 (1973).

17. Cummins, R. A., P. J. Livesay, and R. N. Walsh: A developmental theory of environmental enrichment. *Science,* 197:692–694 (1977).

18. Cummins, R., and P. Livesay: Environmental enrichment, cortex length and rank order effect. *Brain Res.,* 178:89–98 (1979).

19. Kuenzle, C. C., and A. Knusel: Mass training of rats in a superenriched environment. *Physiol. and Behav.,* 13:205–210 (1974).

20. Diamond, M. C., D. Krech, and M. R. Rosenzweig: The effects of an enriched environment on the histology of the rat cerebral cortex. *J. Comp. Neurol.,* 123:111–120 (1964).

21. Eayrs, J. T., and B. Goodhead: Postnatal development of the cerebral cortex in the rat. *J. Anat.,* 93:385–402 (1959).

22. Glendinnen, B. G., and J. T. Eayrs: The anatomical and physiological effects of prenatally administered somatotrophin on cerebral development in rats. *J. Endocrinol.,* 22:183–194 (1961).

23. Altman, J.: *Organic Foundations of Animal Behavior.* Holt, Rinehart & Winston, New York (1966).

24. Altman, J., and G. D. Das: Autoradiographic examination of the effects of enriched environment on the rate of glial multiplication in the adult rat brain. *Nature,* 204:1161–1163 (1964).

25. York, A.: Personal communication (1987).

26. Szeligo, F., and C. P. Leblond: Response of the three main types of glial cells of cortex and corpus callosum in rats handled during suckling or exposed to enriched, control, and impoverished environments during weaning. *J. Comp. Neurol.,* 172:247–264 (1977).

27. Cummins, R. A., and R. N. Walsh: Unpublished data.

28. Craigie, E. H.: Vascularity of the cerebral cortex of the albino rat. *J. Comp. Neurol.,* 33:193–212 (1921).

29. Dunning, H. S., and H. G. Wolff: The relative vascularity of various parts of the central and peripheral nervous system of the cat and its relation to function. *J. Comp. Neurol.,* 67:433–450 (1937).

30. Holloway, R. L.: Dendritic branching: some preliminary results of training and complexity in rat visual cortex. *Brain Res.,* 2:393–396 (1966).

31. Greenough, W. T., F. Volkman, and J. M. Juraska: Effects of rearing complexity on dendritic branching in frontolateral and temporal cortex of the rat. *Exp. Neurol.,* 41:371–378 (1973).

32. Walsh, R. N.: Effects of environmental complexity and deprivation on brain anatomy and histology: A review. *Int. J. Neurosci.,* 12:33–51 (1981).

33. Uylings, H. B. M., K. Kuypers, M. C. Diamond, and W. A. M. Veltman: The effects of differential environments on plasticity of cortical pyramidal neurons in adult rats. *Exp. Neurol.,* 62:658–677 (1978).

34. Connor, J. R., Jr., M. C. Diamond, and R. E. Johnson: Occipital cortical morphology of the rat. Alterations with age and environment. *Exp. Neurol.,* 68:158–170 (1980).

35. Connor, J. R., J. H. Melone, A. R. Yuen, and M. C. Diamond: Dendritic length in aged rats' occipital cortex: An environmentally-induced response. *Exp. Neurol.*, 73:827–830 (1981).

36. Lindsay, R. D., and A. B. Scheibel: Quantitative analysis of the dendritic branching pattern of small pyramidal cells from adult rat somesthetic and visual cortex. *Exp. Neurol.*, 45:424–434 (1974).

37. Floeter, M. K., and W. T. Greenough: Cerebellar plasticity: Modification of Purkinje cell structure by differential rearing in monkeys. *Abstr. Soc. Neurosci.*, 4:471 (1978).

38. Ramón y Cajal, S.: *Histologie du système nerveux de l'homme et des vertébrés*. Reprinted by Consejo Superior de Investigaciones Cientificas, Madrid (1952).

39. Jacobsen, S.: Dimensions of the dendritic spine in the sensorimotor cortex of rat, cat, squirrel monkey, and man. *J. Comp. Neurol.*, 129:49–58 (1967).

40. Peters, A., and M. L. Feldman: The projection of the lateral geniculate to area 17 of the rat cerebral cortex. I. General description. *J. Neurocytol.*, 5:63–85 (1976).

41. Farien, A., and F. Valverde: Specific thalamo-cortical afferents and their presumptive targets in the visual cortex. A Golgi study. *Prog. Brain Res.*, 51:419–438 (1979).

42. Brizzee, K. R., J. M. Ordy, M. B. Kaach, and T. Beavers: Effects of prenatal ionizing radiation on the visual cortex and hippocampus of newborn squirrel monkeys. *J. Neuropathol. Exp. Neurol.*, 39:523–540 (1980).

43. Salas, M.: Effects of early undernutrition on dendritic spines of cortical pyramidal cells in the rat. *Dev. Neurosci.*, 3:109–117 (1980).

44. Globus, A., and A. B. Scheibel: Synaptic loci on visual cortical neurons of the rabbit: The specific afferent radiation. *Exp. Neurol.*, 18:116–131 (1967).

45. Globus, A., and A. B., Scheibel: The effects of visual deprivation on cortical neurons. A Golgi study. *Exp. Neurol.*, 19:331–345 (1967).

46. Valverde, F.: Apical dendritic spines of the visual cortex and light deprivation in the mouse. *Exp. Brain Res.*, 3:337–352 (1967).

47. Rothblat, L. A., and M. L. Schwartz: The effect of monocular deprivation on dendritic spines in visual cortex of young and adult albino rats: Evidence for a sensitive period. *Brain Res.*, 161:156–161 (1979).

48. Parnavelas, J. G., A. Globus, and P. Kaups: Continuous illumination from birth affects spine density of neurons in the visual cortex of the rat. *Exp. Neurol.*, 40:742–747 (1973).

49. Globus, A., M. Rosenzweig, E. L. Bennett, and M. C. Diamond: Effects of differential experience on dendritic spine counts in rat cerebral cortex. *J. Comp. Physiol. Psychol.*, 82:175–181 (1973).

50. Coss, R. G., and A. Globus: Social experience affects the development of dendritic spines and branches on tectal interneurons in the jewel fish. *Dev. Psychobiol.*, 12:347–358 (1979).

51. Burgess, J. W., and R. G. Coss: Crowded jewel fish show changes in dendritic spine density and spine morphology. *Neurosci. Lett.*, 17:277–281 (1980).

52. Feldman, M. L., and C. Dowd: Loss of dendritic spines in aging cerebral cortex. *Anat. Embryol.*, 148:279–301 (1975).

53. Connor, J. R., M. C. Diamond, and R. E. Johnson: Aging and environmental influences on two types of dendritic spines in the rat occipital cortex. *Exp. Neurol.*, 70:371–379 (1980).

54. Mervis, R.: Structural alterations in neurons of aged canine neocortex: Golgi study. *Exp. Neurol.*, 62:417–432 (1978).

55. Chang, H. T.: Cortical neurons with particular reference to the apical dendrites. N.Y. *Symp. Quant. Biol.*, 17:189–202 (1952).

56. Diamond, J., E. G. Gray, and G. M. Yasargil: The function of dendritic spines: An hypothesis. *J. Physiol.*, 202:116 (1969).

57. Connor, J. R.: A dichotomous response by two populations of layer V pyramidal cells in the old adult rat visual cortex to differential housing conditions. *Brain Res.*, 243:153–154 (1982).

58. Lorente de No, R.: Cerebral Cortex: Architecture, intracortical connections, motor projections. In J. Fulton (ed.): *Physiology of the Nervous System*. Oxford University Press, New York (1949), pp. 291–339.

59. Van Harreveld, A., and E. Fifkova: Rapid freezing of deep cerebral structures for electron microscopy. *Anat. Rec.*, 183:377–386 (1975).

60. Kandel, E. R., and W. A. Spencer: Cellular neurophysiological approaches in the study of learning. *Physiol. Rev.*, 48:65–134 (1968).

61. Møllgaard, K., M. C. Diamond, E. L. Bennett, M. R. Rosenzweig, and B. Lindner: Quantitative synaptic changes with differential experience in rat brain. *Int. J. Neurosci.*, 2:113–128 (1971).

62. Colonnier, M.: Synaptic patterns on different cell types in the different laminae of the cat visual cortex. An electron microscope study. *Brain Res.*, 9:268–287 (1968).

63. Peters, A., and I. R. Kaiserman-Abramof: The small pyramidal neuron of the rat cerebral cortex.The synapses upon dendritic spines. *Z. Zellforsch. Mikrosk. Anat.*, 100:487–506 (1969).

64. Greenough, W. T., R. W. West, and J. T. Devoogd: Subsynaptic plate perforations: Changes with age and experience in the rat. *Science*, 202:1096–1098 (1978).

65. Medosch, C. M., and M. C. Diamond: Rat occipital cortical synapses after ovariectomy. *Exp. Neurol.*, 75:120–133 (1982).

66. Tanzi, E.: I fatti e le induzioni nell'odierna istologia del sistema nervoso. *Riv. Sperim. de Fren. e de Med. Leg.*, XIX:419–472 (1893).

67. Ramón y Cajal, S.: *Textura del sistema nervioso del hombre y de los vertebrados*. Nicolas Moya, Madrid (1904).

68. Hebb, D.: *The Organization of Behavior*. Wiley, New York (1949).

69. Ramón y Cajal, S.: *Étude sur la neurogenèse de quelques vertébrés* (1929); L. Guth (trans.): *Studies on Vertebrate Neurogenesis*. Charles C. Thomas, Springfield, Ill. (1960).

70. Dawkins, R.: Selective neuron death as a possible memory mechanism. *Nature*, 229:118–119 (1971).

71. Eccles, J. C.: Possible ways in which synaptic mechanisms participate in learning, remembering and forgetting. In D. P. Kimble (ed.): *The Anatomy of Memory*, Science and Behavior Books, Palo Alto, Calif. (1965).

72. Sperry, R. W.: Embryogenesis of behavioral nerve nets. In R. L. DeHaan and H. Ursprung (eds.): *Organogenesis*. Holt, Rinehart & Winston, New York (1965).

73. Katz, B.: *Nerve, Muscle and Synapse*, McGraw-Hill, New York (1966).

74. Diamond, M. C., B. Lindner, R. Johnson, and E. L. Bennett: Differences in occipital cortical synapses from environmentally-enriched, impoverished and standard colony rats. *J. Neurosci. Res.*, 1:109–119 (1975).

75. West, R., and W. Greenough: Effect of environmental complexity on cortical synapses in rats: Preliminary results. *Behav. Biol.*, 7:279–284 (1972).

76. Cummins, R. A., and R. N. Walsh: Synaptic changes in differentially reared mice. *Australian Psych.,* 11:229 (1976).

77. Dorosz, L.: Electrically induced transcallosal response in enriched and impoverished rats. University of California, Berkeley (1970).

78. Walsh, R. N., R. A. Cummins, O. E. Budtz-Olsen, and A. Torok: Effects of environmental enrichment and deprivation on rat frontal cortex. *Int. J. Neurosci.,* 4:239–242 (1972).

79. Juraska, J. M., J. M. Fitch, C. Henderson, and N. Rivers: Sex differences in the dendritic branching of dentate granule cells following differential experience. *Brain Res.,* 333:73–80 (1985).

80. Scoville, W. B., and B. Milner: Loss of recent memory after bilateral hippocampal lesions. *J. Neurol. Neurosurg. Psychiat.,* 20:1121 (1957).

81. Stepien, L. S., J. P. Cordeau, and T. Rasmussen: The effect of temporal lobe and hippocampal lesions on auditory and visual memory in monkeys. *Brain,* 83:470–489 (1960).

82. Drachman, D. A., and A. K. Ommaya: Memory and the hippocampal complex. *Arch. Neurol.,* 10:411–425 (1966).

83. McLardy, T.: Unpublished.

84. Kaada, B. R., E. W. Rasmussen, and O. Kveim: Effects of hippocampal lesions on maze learning and retention in rats. *Exp. Neurol.,* 3:333–355 (1961).

85. Melone, J. H., S. A. Teitelbaum, R. E. Johnson, and M. C. Diamond: The rat amygdaloid nucleus: A morphometric right-left study. *Exp. Neurol.,* 86:293–302 (1984).

86. Sherman, G. F., J. A. Garbanati, G. D. Rosen, D. A. Yutzey, and V. H. Denenberg: Brain and behavioral asymmetries for spatial preference in rats. *Brain Res.,* 192:61–67 (1980).

87. Webster, W. G.: Territoriality and the evolution of brain asymmetry. *Ann. N.Y. Acad. Sci.,* 299:213–221 (1977).

88. Malkasian, D.: The morphological effects of environmental manipulation and litter size on the neonate rat brain. Ph.D. Thesis, University of California, Berkeley (1969).

89. Walsh, R. N.: Effects of environmental complexity and deprivation on brain anatomy and histology: A review. *Int. J. Neurosci.,* 12:33–51 (1981).

90. Dru, D., J. P. Walker, and J. B. Walker: Self-produced locomotion restores visual capacity after striate lesions. *Science,* 187:265–266 (1975).

91. Malkasian, D., and M. C. Diamond: The effect of environmental manipulation on the morphology of the neonatal rat brain. *J. Neurosci.,* 2:161–170 (1971).

92. Ferchim, P. A., E. L. Bennett, and M. R. Rosenzweig: Direct contact with enriched environment is required to alter cerebral weights in rats. *J. Comp. Physiol. Psychol.,* 88:360–367 (1975).

93. Rosenzweig, M. R., E. L. Bennett, and M. C. Diamond: Chemical and anatomical plasticity of brain: Replications and extensions. In J. Gaito (ed.): *Macromolecules and Behavior,* 2nd ed. Appleton-Century-Crofts, New York (1971), pp. 205–278.

94. Diamond, M. C., D. Krech, and M. R. Rosenzweig: The effects of an enriched environment on the histology of the rat cerebral cortex. *J. Comp. Neurol.,* 123:111–120 (1964).

95. Krieg, W. J. S.: Connections of the cerebral cortex. *J. Comp. Neurol.,* 84:221–275 (1946).

96. Paxinos, G. (ed.): *The Rat Nervous System*. Vol. 1: *Forebrain and Midbrain*. Academic press, Sydney, Australia (1985).

97. Denenberg, V. H., J. Garbanati, G. Sherman, D. A. Yutzey, and R. Kaplan: Infantile stimulation induces brain lateralization in rats. *Science*, 201:1150–1152 (1978).

98. Diamond, M. C., M. R. Rosenzweig, and D. Krech: Relationships between body weight and skull development in rats raised in enriched and impoverished conditions. *J. Exp. Zool.*, 160:29–36 (1965).

99. Asling, C. W., and H. R. Frank: Roentgen cephalometric studies on skull development in rats. 1. Normal and hypophysectomized females. *Am. J. Phys. Anthropol.*, 21:527–544 (1963).

100. Uylings, H. B. M., K. Kuypers, M. C. Diamond, and W. A. M. Veltman: The effects of differential environments on plasticity of cortical pyramidal neurons in adult rats. *Exp. Neurol.*, 62:658–677 (1978).

101. Massler, M., and I. Schour: Growth patterns of the cranial vault in the albino rat. *Anat. Rec.*, 110:83–101 (1951).

102. Weidenreich, F.: The brain and its role in the phylogenetic transformation of the human skull. *Trans. Am. Philos. Soc.*, 31:321–442 (1941).

103. Mayer, J., N. B. Marshall, J. J. Vitale, J. H. Christensen, M. B. Mashayekhi, and F. J. Store: Exercise, food intake and body weight in normal rats and genetically obese adult mice. *Amer. J. Physiol.*, 177:544–548 (1954).

104. Donaldson, H. H.: *The Rat*. Wistar Institute of Anatomy and Biology, Philadelphia (1924).

5   Enrichment and Impoverishment over the Lifespan

1. Nakae, K.: A historical study of the thought of "Taikyo." *Jpn. J. Educat. Res.*, 50:343–352 (1983).

2. Diamond, M. C., R. E. Johnson, and C. Ingham: Brain plasticity induced by environment and pregnancy. *Int. J. Neurosci.*, 2:171–178 (1971).

3. Kiyono, S., M. L. Seo, M. Shibagaki, and M. Inouye: Facilitative effects of maternal environmental enrichment on maze learning in rat offspring. *Physiol. Behav.*, 34:431–435 (1985).

4. Ivinskis, A., and J. Homewood: Effects of preweaning environmental enrichment on later problem-solving behavior in rats. *Anim. Learn. Behav.*, 8:336–340 (1980).

5. Reppert, S. M. and W. J. Schwartz: Maternal coordination of the fetal biological clock in utero. *Science*, 220:969–971 (1983).

6. Malkasian, D., and M. C. Diamond: The effect of environmental manipulation on the morphology of the neonatal rat brain. *Int. J. Neurosci.*, 2:161–170 (1971).

7. Dobbing, J.: The influence of early nutrition on the development and myelination of the brain. *Proc. R. Soc. Brit.*, 159:503–509 (1964).

8. Irvine, G. L., and P. S. Timiras: Litter size and brain development in the rat. *Life Sciences*, 5:1577–1582 (1966).

9. Diamond, M. C.: Anatomical brain changes induced by environment. In J. McGaugh and L. Petrinovich (eds.): *Knowing, Thinking, and Believing*. Plenum, New York (1976), pp. 215–241.

10. Krech, D., M. R. Rosenzweig, and E. L. Bennett: Effects of complex environment and blindness on the rat brain. *Arch. Neurol.*, 8:403–412 (1963).

11. Rosenzweig, M. R., E. L. Bennett, M. C. Diamond, S. Y. Wu, R. Slagle, and E. Saffran: Influence of environmental complexity and visual stimulation on development of occipital cortex in the rat. *Brain Res.,* 14:427–445 (1969).

12. Lehmann, D., and G. Koukkou: Neuronale Effekte der Caudtumreizung im visuellen Cortex. *Pflügers Arch.,* 280:297–315 (1964).

13. Venegas, H., W. E. Foote, and J. P. Flynn: Hypothalamic influences upon activity of units of visual cortex. *Yale J. Biol. Med.,* 191–201 (1969–70).

14. MacLean, P. D., and G. Creswell: Anatomical connections of visual system with limbic cortex of monkey. *J. Comp. Neurol.,* 138:265–278 (1969).

15. Akimoto, H., and O. Creutzfeldt: Reaktionen von Neuronen des optischen Cortex nach elektrischer Reizung unspezifischer Thalamuskerne. *Arch. Psychiat. Nervenkr.,* 196:494–519 (1958).

16. Skrebitsky, V. G.: Nonspecific influences on neuronal firing in the central visual pathway. *Exp. Brain Res.,* 9:269–283 (1969).

17. Uylings, H. B. M., K. Kuypers, M. C. Diamond, and W. A. M. Veltman: The effects of differential environments on plasticity of cortical pyramidal neurons in adult rats. *Exp. Neurol.,* 62:658–677 (1978).

18. Connor, J. R., M. C. Diamond, and R. E. Johnson: Occipital cortical morphology of the rat: Alterations with age and environment. *Exp. Neurol.,* 68:158–170 (1980).

19. Diamond, M. C., R. E. Johnson, A. M. Protti, C. Ott, and L. Kajisa: Plasticity in the 904-day-old rat cerebral cortex. *Exp. Neurol.,* 87:309–317 (1985).

---

6   The Interaction between Sex Hormones and Environment

1. Malacarne, G.: *Memorie storiche intorno alla vita ed alle opere di Michele Vincenzo Giacinto Malacarne.* Tipografia del Seminario, Padova (1819), p. 88.

2. Gowers, W. R.: *Epilepsy and Other Chronic Convulsive Diseases.* William Wood and Co., New York (1885).

3. Diamond, M. C., R. E. Johnson, and C. Ingham: Brain plasticity induced by environment and pregnancy. *Int. J. Neurosci.,* 2:171–178 (1971).

4. Pappas, C. T. E., M. C. Diamond, and R. E. Johnson: Effects of ovariectomy and differential experience on rat cerebral cortical morphology. *Brain Res.,* 154:53–60 (1978).

5. Wade, G. N.: Some effects of ovarian hormones on food intake and body weight in female rats. *J. Comp. Physiol. Psychol.,* 88:183–193 (1975).

6. West, C. D., and T. L. Kemper: The effect of a low protein diet on the anatomical development of the rat brain. *Brain Res.,* 107:221–237 (1976).

7. Colmenares, A.: Effects of malnutrition on the development of the cerebral cortex of the rat. *Neurosci. Abstr.,* II(1):210 (1976).

8. Hoover, D., and M. C. Diamond: The effect of norethynodrel administration on the rat visual cortex exposed to differential environment: A preliminary study of electrolytes and water. *Brain Res.,* 103:139–142 (1976).

9. Beaconsfield, P. M., E. Abrams, J. Ginsburg, and R. Rainsbury: Oral contraceptives and the vital organs. *Lancet,* II:832–833 (1968).

10. Meyerson, B.: Relationship between the anesthetic and gestagenic action and estrous behavior-inducing activity of different progestins. *Endocrinology,* 81:369–372 (1967).

11. Bennett, E. L., M. R. Rosenzweig, and M. C. Diamond: Rat brain: Effects of environmental enrichment on wet and dry weights. *Science,* 163:825–826 (1969).

12. Dorosz, L.: Electrically induced transcallosum response in enriched and impoverished rats. Ph.D. Thesis, University of California, Berkeley (1970).

7 Overcoming Deprivation and Stress

1. Carughi, A.: The effect of environmental enrichment during nutritional rehabilitation on certain parameters of cortical development. Ph.D. Thesis, University of California, Berkeley (1987).

2. Winick, M., and A. Noble: Cellular response in rats during malnutrition at various ages. *J. Nutr.,* 89:300–306 (1966).

3. Our experiment was carried out in cooperation with Dr. Carolyn Smith, from the Laboratory of Cerebral Metabolism, National Institute of Mental Health, Bethesda, Md.

4. Sokoloff, L., M. Reivich, C. Kennedy, H. H. Des Rosiers, C. S. Patlak, K. D. Pettigrew, O. Sakurada, and M. Shinohara: The [^{14}C] deoxyglucose method for the measurement of local cerebral glucose utilization: Theory, procedure, and normal values in the conscious and anesthetized albino rat. *J. Neurochem.,* 28:897–916 (1977).

5. Renoux, G., K. Biziere, M. Renoux, and J. M. Guillaumin: The cerebral cortex regulates immune responses in the mouse. *C.R. Acad. Sci. D.* (Paris), 290:719–722 (1980).

6. Bardos, P., D. Degenne, Y. Lebranchu, K. Biziere, and G. Renoux: Neocortical lateralization of NK activity in mice. *Scand. J. Immunol.,* 13:609–611 (1981).

7. Renoux, G.: The mode of action of imuthiol (sodium diethyldithiocarbamate): A new role for the brain neocortex and the endocrine liver in the regulation of the T-cell lineage. In M. A. Chirigos (ed.): *Mechanisms of Immune Modulation,* Marcel Dekker, New York (1983), pp. 607–624.

8. In collaboration with C. Beeson, K. Mark, A. B. Scheibel, and P. Blair.

9. Jankovic, B. D., and K. Isakovic: Neuroendocrine correlates of immune response. *Int. Arch. Allergy,* 45:360–372 (1973).

10. Shire, J. G. M., and E. M. Pantelouris: Comparison of endocrine function in normal and genetically athymic mice. *Comp. Biochem. Physiol.,* 74A:993–1000 (1974).

11. Henderson, R., B. McEwen, and E. M. Pant: Pituitary and cerebellum of nude mice. *Thymus,* 3:359–368 (1981).

12. Kerns, J. M., and M. Frank: A quantitative study of lymphocytes and neuroglia in the nude mouse spinal cord. *Anat. Rec.,* 196:96A (1980).

13. Merrill, J. E., S. Kutsumai, C. Mohlstrom, F. Hofman, J. Groopman, and D. W. Golde: Human T-lymphocytes promoted proliferation and maturation of oligodendroglial and astroglial cells. *Science,* 224:1428–1430 (1984).

14. Belokrylov, G. A.: Cortical tissue from syngenous brain as a stimulator of immunogenesis in thymectomized mice. *Bull. Eksp. Biol. Med.,* 86:327–330 (1978).

15. Messimy, R.: Les effects, chez le singe, de l'ablation des lobes prefrontaux. *Rev. Neurol.,* 71:1–37 (1939).

16. Ascengi, A.: Relationship between prefrontal lobes and thymus. *J. Neuropathol. Exp. Neurol.,* 20:119–126 (1961).

17. Calhoun, J. B.: Death squared: The explosive growth and demise of a mouse population. *Proc. R. Soc. Med.,* 66:80–88 (1973).

18. Ross, G.: Population modeling: View toward the human. In J. B. Calhoun (ed.): *Environment and Population Problems of Adaptation.* (1983), pp. 74–76.

8   The Impact of Air Ions

1. Sulman, G. G., D. Levy, A. Levy, Y. Pfeifer, E. Superstine, E. Tal: Air ionometry of hot, dry desert winds (sharav) and treatment with air ions of weather sensitive subjects. *Int. J. Biometeorol.*, 18:313 (1974).

2. Dostoevsky, F. M.: *Notes from the Underground* (1864; R. E. Matlaw, trans.). Dutton, New York (1960).

3. Krueger, A. P., and R. J. Smith: The biological mechanisms of air ion action. Negative ion effects on the concentration and metabolism of 5-hydroxytryptamine in the mammalian respiratory tract. *J. Gen. Physiol.*, 43:533 (1960).

4. Reported at the VIIIth International Congress of Biometeorology, Shefayin, Israel.

5. Diamond, M. C., J. R. Connor, Jr., E. K. Orenberg, M. Bissell, M. Yost, and A. Krueger: Environmental influences on serotonin and cyclic nucleotides in rat cerebral cortex. *Science*, 210:652–654 (1980).

6. Gilbert, G. O.: Effect of negative air ions upon emotionality and brain serotonin levels in isolated rats. *Int. J. Biometeorol.*, 17:267 (1973).

7. Olivereau, J. M.: Influence des ions atmosphériques négatifs sur l'adaptation à une situation anxiogène chez le rat. *Int. J. Biometeorol.*, 17:277–284 (1973).

8. Diamond, M. C.: The aging rat forebrain: Male-female; left-right; environment and lipofuscin. In D. Samuel, S. Algeri, S. Gershen, V. E. Grimm, and G. Toffano (eds.): *Aging of the Brain*. Raven Press, New York (1983), pp. 93–98.

9   Learning and Behavior

1. Hebb, D.: *The Organization of Behavior*. Wiley, New York (1949).

2. Bingham, W. E., and W. J. Griffiths, Jr.: The effect of different environments during infancy on adult behavior in the rat. *J. Comp. Physiol. Psychol.*, 45:307–312 (1952).

3. Forgays, G., and J. Forgays: The nature of the effect of free environmental experience in the rat. *J. Comp. Physiol. Psychol.*, 45:322–328 (1952).

4. Hymovitch, B.: The effects of experimental variations on problem solving in the rat. *J. Comp. Physiol. Psychol.*, 45:313–321 (1952).

5. Beach, F. A., and J. Jaynes: Effects of early experience upon the behavior of animals. *Psychol. Bull.*, 51:239–262 (1954).

6. Forgus, R. H.: The effect of early perceptual learning on the behavioral organization of adult rats. *J. Comp. Physiol. Psychol.*, 47:331–336 (1954).

7. Forgays, D. G., and J. M. Reid: Crucial periods for free-environmental experience in the rat. *J. Comp. Physiol. Psychol.*, 55:816–818 (1962).

8. Denenberg, V. H., J. M. Woodcock, and K. M. Rosenberg: Long-term effects of preweaning and postweaning free-environment experience on rats' problem solving in the rat. *J. Comp. Physiol. Psychol.*, 66:533–535 (1968).

9. Ivinskis, A., and J. Homewood: Effects of preweaning environmental enrichment on later problem-solving behavior in rats. *Animal Learn. Behav.*, 8:336–340 (1980).

10. Malkasian, D., and M. C. Diamond: The effect of environmental manipulation on the morphology of the neonatal rat brain. *Int. J. Neurosci.*, 2:161–170 (1971).

11. Warren, J. M., C. Zerweck, and A. Anthony: Effects of environmental enrichment on old mice. *Dev. Psychobiol.*, 15:13–18 (1982).

12. Watson, J. S. and P. J. Livesey: Early rearing conditions and with-in group behavioral variability. *Behav. Neural. Biol.* 36:98–101 (1982).

13. Greer, E. R.: Environmental enrichment in rats with a memory deficit (Brattleboro strain). Ph.D. Thesis, University of California, Berkeley (1981).

14. Greer, E. R., M. C. Diamond, and G. Murphy, Jr.: Increased branching of basal dendrites on pyramidal neurons in the occipital cortex of homozygous Brattleboro rats in standard and enriched environmental conditions: A Golgi study. *Exp. Neurol.,* 76:254–262 (1982).

15. Greer, E. R., M. C. Diamond, and J. M. W. Tang: Environmental enrichment in Brattleboro rats: Brain morphology. *Proc. Int. Symp. Brattleboro Rat,* Dartmouth Medical School, September 1981. *Ann. N.Y. Acad. Sci.,* (1982).

16. Walsh, R. N., and R. A. Cummins: Mechanisms mediating the production of environmentally induced brain changes. *Psych. Bull.,* 82:986–1000 (1975).

17. Szeligo, F., and C. P. LeBlond: Response of the three main types of glial cells of cortex and corpus callosum in rats handled during suckling or exposed to enriched control and impoverished environments following weaning. *J. Comp. Neurol.,* 172:247–264 (1977).

18. Bohus, B., Tj. B. Van Wimersma Greidanus, and D. de Wied: Behavioral and endocrine responses of rats with hereditary hypothalamic diabetes insipidus (Brattleboro strain). *Physiol. Behav.* 14:609–615 (1975).

19. Celestian, J. F., R. J. Carey, and M. Miller: Unimpaired maintenance of a conditioned avoidance response in the rat with diabetes insipidus. *Physiol. Behav.,* 15:707–711 (1975).

20. Kerker, K.: The effect of Hebb-Williams maze training on the morphology of the adult female rat brain. Senior thesis. University of California, Berkeley (1968).

21. Greenough, W. T., J. Juraska, and F. Volkmar: Maze training effects on dendritic branching in occipital cortex of adult rats. *Behav. Neural Biol.* 26:287–297 (1979).

10   The Significance of Enrichment

1. Burns, B. D.: *The Mammalian Cerebral Cortex.* Arnold, London (1958).

2. Brody, H.: Organization of the cerebral cortex. III. A study of aging in the human cerebral cortex. *J. Comp. Neurol.,* 102:511–556 (1955).

3. Leboucq, G.: Le rapport entre lepoids et la surface de l'hémisphère cérébrale chez l'homme et les singes. *Mem. Acad. R. Med. Belg.,* 10:55 (1929).

4. Brody, H.: Cell counts in cerebral cortex and brainstem. In R. Katzman, R. D. Terry, and K. L. Bick (eds.): *Aging. Alzheimer's Disease: Senile Dementia and Related Disorders,* Vol. 7. Raven Press, New York (1978), pp. 345–351.

5. Rockel, A. J., R. W. Hiorus, and T. P. S. Powell: The basic uniformity in structure of the neocortex. *Brain,* 103:221–244 (1980).

6. Krienzle, C. C., and A. Knusel: Mass training of rats in a superenriched environment. *Physiol. and Behav.,* 13:205–210 (1974).

7. Halleck, R.: *The Education of the Nervous System,* Macmillan, New York (1901).

8. Dewey, John: *The Child and the Curriculum and the School and Society,* second edition, University of Chicago Press, Chicago (1956); *Democracy and Education,* The Free Press, New York (1966); *Experience and Education,* Macmillan, New York (1963).

9. Fleschig, P.: Developmental (myelogenetic) localization of the cerebral cortex in the human subject. *Lancet,* II:1027 (1901).

10. Hawthorne, N.: *Ethan Brand.* In *The Snow Image,* Riverside Press, Cambridge (1893).

11. Carughi, A.: The effect of environmental enrichment during nutritional rehabilitation on certain parameters of brain development. Ph.D. Thesis, University of California, Berkeley (1987).

12. Will, B., M. R. Rosenzweig, E. L. Bennett, M. Hebert, and H. Morimoto: Relatively brief environmental enrichment aids recovery of learning capacity and alters brain measures after post-weaning brain lesions in rats. *J. Comp. Physiol. Psychol.,* 91:33–50 (1977).

INDEX